LOOK TO THIS DAY!

LOOK TO THIS DAY!

*The Lively Education
of a Great Woman Doctor:
Connie Guion, M.D.*

by
NARDI REEDER CAMPION

with

ROSAMOND WILFLEY STANTON

Illustrated with Photographs

LITTLE, BROWN AND COMPANY

BOSTON   TORONTO

*Published simultaneously in Canada
by Little, Brown & Company (Canada) Limited*

PRINTED IN THE UNITED STATES OF AMERICA

For Doctor Connie Guion,
the warm and wise woman who lived this story.
Her sense of humor, sense of values,
and sense of direction
have shaped her life.
Her gift for laughter and colorful memory
have made the recapturing of that life
an adventure.

"Listen to the Exhortation of the Dawn!
Look to this Day!
For it is Life, the very Life of Life.
In its brief Course lie all the
Verities and Realities of your Existence:
The Bliss of Growth,
The Glory of Action,
The Splendour of Beauty;
For Yesterday is but a Dream
And Tomorrow is only a Vision;
But Today well lived makes
Every Yesterday a Dream of Happiness,
And every Tomorrow a Vision of Hope.
Look well therefore to this Day!
Such is the Salutation of the Dawn!"

A poem by an unknown author translated from the Sanskrit and used by William Osler in his book, A Way of Life, copyright 1937, Paul B. Hoeber, Inc.

* *

Authors' Note

* *

Dr. Guion has spent countless hours with the authors, sharing her memories of people and events. Many of her legion of friends and associates have also helped to insure the authenticity of scene and dialogue. We particularly want to thank Miss Esther Anderson, Miss Ferebe Babcock, Arthur Bingham, Dr. David P. Barr, Miss Elizabeth Beard, Mrs. James DeNyse, Dr. Edward Flood, Miss Elsie Goddard, Miss Ridie Guion, Dr. Joseph C. Hinsey, Director, the New York Hospital–Cornell Medical Center, Dr. Gustavus Humphreys, Mrs. O. E. Hunt, Dr. Hugh Luckey, Dr. A. Parks McCombs, Mrs. Robert Meriwether, Mrs. Henry B. Pennell, Dr. Merle M. Potter, Dr. George Reader, Mrs. Eugene Saxton, Miss Olive Smith, Miss Ruth Smith, and Miss Martha Von Briesen, Director of Public Relations, Sweet Briar College.

We also received valuable assistance from the diaries of Ione Morrison Overfield, Wellesley, 1906, from the New York Public Library, the Cornell Medical College Library and the alumnae offices of Northfield School, Wellesley College and Cornell University. The Oral History Department of Columbia University released to us a lengthy transcript of Dr. Guion's medical reminiscences which had been recorded for posterity, and this was most helpful.

NARDI REEDER CAMPION
ROSAMOND WILFLEY STANTON

Foreword

To WRITE a foreword about Dr. Connie Guion is indeed a privilege for one who has been an admiring friend as well as a patient of Dr. Guion's for almost thirty years. My natural impulse is to express personal feelings of gratitude, admiration, respect — and great affection — for Connie Guion. But there is much more that should be said about the career of this remarkable woman.

Dr. Guion has filled many roles with unique perception, ability and deep humanity. She has been teacher, guide, philosopher and friend, as well as physician. She personifies those qualities that give meaning and dignity to our lives as individuals and to the social structure of which we are a part. It is the spirit that guides all the devoted men and women who apply their talents and skills toward the advancement of human well-being.

Like many of her friends, I have come to think of Dr. Guion as the dean of women doctors in America. She was the first woman in this country to be made a professor of clinical medicine, and is now in her forty-fourth year of teaching at Cornell Medical College. She was also the first woman member of the Medical Board of The New York Hospital and the first to be made an honorary member of the Board of Governors of that hospital. The Doctor Connie Guion Building — which houses more than eighty outpatient clinics at The New York Hospital — is, I believe, the first hospital building in the world dedicated to a living woman doctor. This great building is actually an extension of the spirit of Doctor Guion — her concern for others, her professional competence and high standards, and above all, her warm capacity to share with and inspire both her patients and her students.

At The New York Hospital, Dr. Guion has been a leader in teaching and promoting the Comprehensive Care Program which coordinates all aspects of medical care for each individual outpatient. This program has had an effect not only on American hospitals, but on those in other countries as well, because it has been studied by visitors from all over the world who have emulated at home what they have found here. It has been a real pioneering project in which Connie Guion has been one of the important contributors.

In this day of specialties Dr. Guion remains truly a family physician, exemplar of the traditions of the great physicians of the past, in her knowledge of and skill with people. Partly because of her womanly qualities, but mainly because she is a great physician, she has fulfilled the role that society and medicine need and has stood as an inspirational example to her patients, her colleagues and her students.

There remains one facet of Connie Guion's humanity for which, in addition, we can be profoundly grateful. She has demonstrated convincingly that women — whatever their chosen career or role in life — have an ability and a responsibility to contribute to our society, the potential of which extends far beyond what most of us recognize today. Dr. Guion's social pioneering in this endeavor — the full utilization of all our human resources — may well prove as significant as her medical career.

At every turn in her life Connie Guion has risen to the challenge of responsibility. In meeting this challenge, she has become a great and beloved human being.

LAURANCE S. ROCKEFELLER

Contents

LOOK TO THIS DAY!

✳ 1 ✳

Why Call a Doctor?

"CONNIE, run tell Louis to fetch the doctor." Mrs. Guion spoke quietly but her voice was strained. She sank heavily into a chair and put her hand to her forehead.

"Baby comin', Mama?"

"Yes, Connie. Get Louis, quick."

Connie trotted out the door and disappeared into the September sunlight. Mrs. Guion knew she would find her brother, for this little girl of five was already a responsible person. In a family of ten children you learn quickly how important it is for people to know they can count on you.

Connie found Louis sorting tobacco leaves with the Negro field hands. Although the year was 1887 — just twenty-two years after the Civil War — and the place was North Carolina, white and black worked shoulder to shoulder on the Guion plantation.

"Louis! Mama's ready! She needs Dr. Lawing right now."

Louis dropped the tobacco leaves and ran toward the house. As Connie followed him, her bare feet sank into mud that oozed between her toes. Connie, who hated shoes, judged the weather by her feet. This gooey red mud could only mean the autumn freshets had come. Looking down toward the river, she saw the bottomlands were already covered with water.

Louis dashed into the house and out again, banging the

screen door behind him. A minute later he was astride a mule, his long legs flailing to urge it into a gallop.

"Watch out, Louis," yelled Connie, "river's risin'!"

"Don't worry 'bout me," Louis called over his shoulder. "Help Elsie take care of Mama till I bring Dr. Lawing."

Connie found her mother stretched out in the huge walnut bed, her long black hair almost covering the white pillow. Elsie, the former slave who had been with the Guions nearly all her life, hovered over her. Connie took up a position at the foot of the bed to watch the proceedings. She had seen all kinds of animals born on the plantation, but this promised to be the most exciting birth yet.

"Is it going to be a boy or a girl, Elsie?"

"Hush up, chile, or I'll chase you out of here."

I hope to goodness it's a girl, thought Connie. *Four brothers are enough. What I need around here is a baby sister. 'Course I got five sisters now, but they're all so old.*

Mrs. Guion moaned. Connie wished her father would come home. Benjamin Guion, who was the superintendent of the Raleigh and Gaston Railroad, always seemed to be away, especially during emergencies.

The door opened, and Oaf, one of the family helpers, stuck his head into the room.

"Miss Elsie," he said in a hoarse whisper, "the bridge washed out! Hope to God Mr. Louis doan wash out with it."

"Scat!" hissed Elsie, and Oaf scatted. "I don't need a doctor. Deliverin' babies is old Elsie's middle name."

If Elsie was unmindful of the danger to Louis, Connie was not. She knew her brother was in real peril. The Catawba River wound around three sides of the plantation, and there were only two ways to get into Lincolnton — across the rickety wooden bridge or through the ford, a rocky place where the water was shallow. Even little Connie knew that if the river

Catherine Caldwell Guion   Benjamin Simons Guion
(Connie's mother and father)

was high enough to wash out the bridge, it was too rough to ford. Louis suddenly became more important than the new baby.

Oh Lord, Connie prayed, *bring Louis back safe. We need Louis, Lord. Louis is my brother.*

Kate Caldwell Guion, in the throes of childbirth, prayed for Louis's safety too. No matter what her own needs were, she naturally thought of her family first.

At last Elsie held up the brand-new baby by the heels and spanked its small red bottom. "I tole you it'd be a girl, praise the Lord. Them males don't give you nothin' but trouble."

Connie, still standing at the foot of the bed, nodded her head dazedly. *Where, oh where, was Louis?* She kissed her mother's pale cheek and walked slowly out to the porch to wait for her brother. Sitting on the steps, she watched the

September sky change from blue to apricot. Soon a white star glittered on the horizon. A whippoorwill whistled mournfully in the distance and a chill breeze blew. Tears began to run down the little girl's cheeks. What good was a baby sister if you had to lose your big brother to get her? Connie buried her blond head on her knees and sobbed. Before long she had cried herself to sleep.

It was dark when she was awakened by the clop-clop of hooves and Louis's voice calling, "Here's Dr. Lawing. Are we in time? Bridge washed out, we had to ford the river. It was high as Rock's belly and —"

Elsie cut him off. "The baby's quite well grown up by now, thank you. Why, *good evenin'*, Dr. Lawing."

Connie Guion barely heard her. She was too busy hugging her big brother.

Not long after the new baby came, Connie was awakened in the middle of the night by her brothers and sisters shouting, "Papa's home! Get up, everybody! *Oysters!*"

Connie ran lightly downstairs in her skimpy flannel nightgown. Her father was sitting in a rocker beside her mother's bed, holding the tiny new baby.

"Hello, Con," he said. "Got a name for Number Eleven?"

She eyed her father suspiciously. Was he going to kiss her and rub his curly yellow beard against her cheek? How she hated that scratching. But no, he was too busy with the baby.

"Why don't you call her Little Dorrit, after the child in the story Mama's readin' us? Lord knows she's little."

Benjamin Guion looked across the children's heads to his wife's dark eyes. He was twenty years older than she, and a graduate of the University of North Carolina, but he often thought she was the better educated of the two.

"How do you find time to read Dickens to these children, Kate?"

"Cousin Alice and I read aloud every night when you're away, Mr. Guion. Even if our children can't go to school, they can learn to love books." Kate Guion was proud of the sets of classics she had inherited from her father, and she wanted her children to love them as much as she did.

"What about the oysters, Papa?" demanded Mary Wood.

"Aye, aye, Captain," said Mr. Guion. Handing the baby back to his wife, he stood up and saluted Mary Wood, the Captain of the Light Brigade. Although Mary Wood was only eleven, she was in charge of all the younger children — Ben, aged nine; Vivian, seven; Connie, five; and Alex, two.

Mr. Guion brought in the bucket of oysters and the Light Brigade cheered. He shucked them skillfully, for he had grown up on the coast in New Bern, North Carolina. Whenever his railroad took him into Tidewater, he brought seafood back to his upcountry family, and because there was no refrigeration at River Bend Plantation, he had to wake the children up to eat it at once.

The next morning Elsie drew Mr. Guion aside and whispered ominously, "I think we'd better Christianize this baby right off, Marse Ben. She looks mighty puny."

"All right, Elsie, I'll send Louis into town to ask Mr. Wetmore to come out and baptize her tomorrow."

Excitement ran high when the children heard there was to be a baptism in their own parlor. They usually drove to the little church in Lincolnton for their christenings.

"I wish Mr. Wetmore would do it in the river," said Connie, who loved the Negro baptisms that took place in the Catawba River during the August camp meetings. When the repentant sinners waded out into the current, with their white robes billowing around them, the evangelist would shout, "Jesus Christ is the Jay Gould and Vanderbilt of heaven!" Connie had no idea who Jay Gould and Vanderbilt were, but she felt sure they were important.

Connie sighed wistfully, "I wish we were Baptists."

"Don't be silly," said Mary Wood. "You should be proud we're Episcopalians. At christenings Episcopalians don't dunk, they just dribble."

When the children saw Mr. Wetmore driving down the Big Road in his Studebaker "carryall," they ran to meet him. Next to Dr. Lawing, Mr. Wetmore was the most important man in the community. "This is the eleventh Guion I've christened," the minister told Mrs. Guion, "and each time your children act like it's the first. You'd think they'd be used to new babies."

"The sun goes down every day, Mr. Wetmore, but we never get used to sunsets. Each one is different."

"And what are we going to call this little ray of sun?" asked Mr. Wetmore, looking at the baby in Elsie's arms.

"Maria Justice Guion, after my niece," announced Benjamin Guion.

"*Maria Justice?*" cried Connie. "A big old stiff name like that for a sweet little baby?"

"At least you can tell it's a *girl*," Vivian said feelingly. His name was not his greatest joy.

"Can we call her Ridie, Papa?" asked Connie. "That's what everyone calls Cousin Maria. Ridie's a whole lot better than Maria Justice."

"Ridie she'll be," said her father. "When she gets bigger we'll give her to you to bring up, Con."

The family and the servants gathered by the fireplace in the parlor for the ceremony. Elsie and Oaf had already laid out refreshments on the parlor table. A fire blazed in the hearth to take the September chill out of the room and the sweet smell of applewood filled the air.

Everyone was ready — but Mr. Wetmore turned to Connie and said, "Well, we can't have a baptism without water. Run get some, child."

Delighted to have a part in the occasion, Connie raced out to the pump. She was not a child who did things halfway. When she started pumping she kept at it until she got ice-cold water; then she picked up the earthenware jug and took it inside. The water in it was so cold her fingers felt numb.

"Dearly beloved —" began Mr. Wetmore, reading in hollow tones from the Book of Common Prayer. The words had a grand roll to them, but Connie couldn't get the meaning. She heard Mr. Wetmore ask that this child "enjoy the everlasting benediction of thy heavenly washing" and she thought, *He could wash her a sight cleaner in the Catawba.*

Taking the baby in his arms, the minister said, "Name this child." He thrust his fingers into the jug of water, then gasped aloud. "Excuse me," he mumbled, blushing to the roots of his white hair. He turned to Connie. "What are you trying to do, freeze your baby sister to death?"

Connie opened her mouth, but no words came out.

"I can't put ice water on a brand-new baby, and a frail one at that." The minister thumped Connie on the side of the head, hard. "Take this water to the kitchen and heat it."

To Connie his voice sounded colder than the water. Her gray eyes filled with tears. It wasn't just that her head hurt. How could anyone think that she wanted to freeze her baby sister?

Maria Justice Guion was finally christened, and at the end Connie heard Mr. Wetmore say, "Grant you to be strengthened with might by his Spirit in the inner man." She liked the sound of that.

After the ceremony Elsie served cider and ginger cookies and everybody said how good Ridie was, and wasn't it funny about Connie bringing in ice water.

Connie followed Elsie out to the kitchen. She wanted to get away from the others. "Elsie, what's the inner man?"

"Lord, chile, I don't know. I reckon it's something to do with Jesus."

"Elsie, don't you think the baptizings you all have during camp meeting are better'n this one?"

"This did seem mighty dry-like to me."

"Same here. If only we'd sung 'Roll, Jordan, Roll' and done some shouting. Then my sister Ridie would *really* be strong in the spirit."

"Don't you worry about that, Con." Elsie gave the little girl a hug. "One thing you Guions got is strength in the spirit — and Con, honey, you got enough of it to last you all your life, and then some."

Mud Pie Doctor

"Wake up, Connie." Laura pulled gently on her sister's curls. "You told me to call you so you could watch me milk Old Red. Hurry, it's after five." Connie's eyes flew open. The crystal light of an early June morning filtered through the window behind Laura, making her golden hair glow. *She looks like a princess,* thought Connie. Hopping out of bed, Connie pulled on her "underbody" and gingham coverall and slipped quietly out of the room, hoping not to awaken the younger children. Just this once she wanted to be alone with Laura and Old Red.

Laura strode swiftly toward the barn and Connie danced along behind her, the wet grass tickling her bare feet. From the horizon, rays of light shot upward and bird songs floated on the summer air. Connie's heart sang. She loved the farm and she loved to go milking with Laura.

There were twelve Guion children now, and each one except baby Jo had essential chores to do on the five-thousand-acre plantation. The older boys plowed the fields and hoed the corn and the older girls milked and churned and made clothes. The younger girls took care of the little ones, and even the little ones pulled weeds and picked worms off the tobacco and tomato plants. Connie's current job was looking after Alex, Ridie, and Jo. She hated being a nursemaid and longed to labor in the fields with her older brothers, but she knew enough not to question her mother's instructions. Mrs. Guion expected, and got, obedience from her offspring.

"Yoo hoo, Con-nee, wait for us!" A small voice shattered Connie's peaceful mood. She did not have to turn around; she knew who "us" was. In a minute, Alex and Ridie padded up beside her. The two children had obviously dressed themselves; each one was missing some important item of clothing.

"Alex, where is your gingham coverall?" scolded Connie.

"I won't wear an apron," said Alex, planting his feet far apart. He looked as stubborn as a mule.

"Oh, well," Connie laughed, "come on, let's watch Laura milk Old Red."

Laura was seated on a stool, milking rapidly with both hands; the milk hit the wooden bucket in a hard stream. Suddenly she turned the cow's teat and shot warm milk into Connie's face. Connie spluttered and everyone laughed. The three children gathered around Laura and opened their mouths. One by one, she squirted the warm foamy milk into each small mouth, never missing her mark.

"Land," said Ridie. "That's 'licious."

"If you lived up North," Laura said, "you'd get your milk out of a bottle."

"Wouldn't that be awful?" said Connie. "I declare, bottled milk serves those damn Yankees right."

"Connie!" Laura stopped milking and looked at her little sister. "Don't ever swear like that."

"Papa does it. He told me damn Yankee is one word."

"Will you *stop* saying that?" exclaimed Laura. "Papa fought in the War between the States and I reckon he has a right to curse Yankees, but I want you to grow up to be a lady."

"What's a lady?" asked Alex.

Laura resumed her milking; she was silent for a minute,

thinking. Then she said slowly, "A lady is someone who acts *right,* no matter what happens. Like Cousin Alice. She's a real lady."

"Is Mama a lady?" asked Connie.

"She could be," said Laura, "if she wasn't so tied down running this fool plantation. Mama hasn't time to —"

"Well," interrupted Connie, "if Mama ain't then I ain't. I'm gonna be just like Mama and *do* things."

"Ain't — ain't! Will you children never learn? Somehow I've got to pull you off this farm and send you to school." Laura's large blue eyes filled with tears at the impossibility of the task. Suddenly, a whistle blew in the distance. "Time for breakfast," she said.

The Guion family lived by the whistle at Mr. Rhinehart's spindle factory, two miles up the river. When the factory whistle blew at six in the morning, breakfast was ready. The twelve-o'clock whistle was a signal for the farm hands to stop and eat, and the whistle at six meant work in the fields was over.

By six o'clock the Guions had already done what many people would consider a day's work. Breakfast was a man-sized meal. Along with eggs, there would be beefsteak or ham, and hominy or corn meal mush, with lots of gravy. They always had hot biscuits which they slathered with strawberry preserves made by Cousin Alice, their mother's cousin who lived with them. Coffee was unheard of; it was far too expensive. Like most Southerners in those days, the Guions drank tea.

One morning after breakfast, Connie's mother said to her, "Do you want to go with me to look after the sick?"

Connie jumped up. "Sick people or sick animals, Mama?"

"Both."

"Let's go."

Connie scrambled into the buggy beside her mother and they drove to a branch of the Catawba River, where Mrs. Guion pulled Old Jule to a halt. "What are we stopping here for, Mama?"

"Mud."

"*Mud?* I thought we were going to look after sick people."

"So we are. Hitch up your skirts, Connie. I want you to wade into the branch and fill my bucket with that white clay. I need it to treat the boil on Noie Brown's neck."

Connie never had to be told twice to go into the water. She grabbed the bucket and splashed in, hoisting her skirts as she went. The water rushing over the white clay was transparent and icy cold. Connie dug her toes into the mud and quickly filled the bucket, patting the wet clay as though she were making mud pies.

They found Noah Brown lying in bed, moaning with pain. Of the twenty families who lived and worked on the big plantation, Noie and his wife Frances were the only white couple. Noie looked scared, but Mrs. Guion sat down and talked to him, trying to divert him before applying the poultice of French clay to his boil.

"Noie," she said, "did you hear about the mother whose baby was crying? She said to her son, 'Willie, rock the baby,' and Willie said, 'I would, if I had a rock.' "

Noie's big body shook with laughter. Afterwards Connie said, "Mama, if you're so busy, how come you take time to tell jokes?"

"I'll tell you a secret about sick people, Connie. What goes on in their minds is just as important as what happens to their bodies. Sometimes a good laugh is worth a peck of medicine."

Mrs. Guion drove briskly to the barn. The next patient

was Laura's Old Red. Connie watched her mother skillfully pry open the cow's jaws and pour in a pint of castor oil. "Whew! I'm glad it's Old Red, not me."

"Con-*nee!* Con-*nee!*" Vivian came running toward them, waving his arms and shouting. "Come quick! Tom Wetmore's here to see Alice and he brought you a present!"

"What is it?"

"Can't tell. He made me promise not to. But wait till you see it! Wow!"

Connie took off with Vivian across the fields. He was two years older, but she kept right up with him. Tom Wetmore, the minister's son, sometimes brought her sister Alice a box of fudge or a bunch of violets, but he had never brought Connie anything. She wished it would be caramels. Or oranges. The Guion children seldom saw an orange, except at Christmas.

When Tom handed Connie a large brown basket, she peered into it and her heart sank. Peanuts. The basket didn't have anything in it except peanuts in the shell, which were common as dirt on the plantation. She tried to think of something to say. She did not want to be rude to Tom, since he was Alice's beau. But peanuts! And then the peanuts moved! A small black nose stuck through the shells. Connie squealed, "*A puppy!*"

She put her hand into the peanuts and drew out a small ball of reddish-brown fur. "Oh Lordy, it's the dearest thing I ever saw. Is he really mine?" She looked at Tom Wetmore. He nodded his head. "I'm going to name him Tom."

"You've overlooked one thing," said Tom. "He's a she."

"Good night, I must be excited. I hadn't even looked. What's your middle name, Tom?"

"Cardell."

"I hereby christen thee Cardell Guion. Tomorrow we'll

have a proper baptizin' in the Catawba, with singing and shouting and calling on the Lord. There ain't nothing in this world too good for my Cardell."

Each day Connie lived for the twelve-o'clock whistle. When it blew she liked to run out to the tobacco fields and ride home one of the mules which her brothers brought back to the barn to feed. But she was not allowed to leave the house unless she had first gotten the baby to sleep for her noon nap, a trying task.

One spring morning almost a year later Connie was having a particularly hard time getting Jo to close her eyes. It was a typical North Carolina April day. The air was sweet, the sun warm, and the blue sky was flecked with white clouds, but Connie was trapped until the baby went to sleep. First she sang, but she was not a musical child and her "lullaby" seemed to stir things up, not quiet them down. Then she lay flat on her back and started shoving the buggy to and fro above her.

The day was so fine that it was hard to concentrate on even so simple a task as rocking a buggy. Along the front fence, Cousin Alice's hyacinths were in bloom and the air was heavy with their fragrance. In the tulip tree near the porch, a mockingbird sang. Connie loved the noisy birds. This one seemed to be calling, "Come away, Con-nee, come away."

Back and forth the wicker carriage rolled on its large wheels. Back and forth. Connie squinted out at the sun, now almost overhead. Any minute the factory whistle would blow. She began to roll the buggy faster. The increased speed seemed to help. Jo grew quieter. Faster and faster Connie pushed the buggy. And then it happened.

Somehow Connie missed catching the hind end of the carriage as it rolled past her. Buggy, baby and all, sailed off the porch, hurtled into the air, and crashed upside down on the ground. Connie threw herself off the porch and raced to save the baby. Her mother and Elsie appeared from nowhere. The noon whistle blew, but for once Connie ignored it. In dumb horror she watched her mother and Elsie pick up the buggy. She felt sick all over; she was sure she had killed her baby sister. Suddenly she realized that the earsplitting noise she heard was not the noon whistle. It was Jo, screaming. *The dead don't scream,* thought Connie, *she must be alive after all.*

"Lucky thing this baby was strap' in, Miss Kate," said Elsie, "else you'd have one less daughter."

Mrs. Guion nodded silently. She was examining Jo with great care. "Jo's going to be all right. Take her inside, Elsie, and quiet her. I have something to attend to." Connie hung her head. She knew what was coming. Elsie went into the house, crooning softly to Jo, who nestled into her shoulder. Connie stood facing her mother, her hands behind her back.

"Connie," said Mrs. Guion severely, "in a large family the older children *must* take care of the younger ones. Do you think you acted responsibly today?"

"No, *ma'am.*"

"I know you will never be so careless again, but I shall give you a reminder anyway."

Connie was well acquainted with her mother's "reminders." Mrs. Guion pulled a penknife out of her pocket and tested the sharpness of the blade with her thumb; then she cut a slender switch off a peach tree. "Bend over, Connie," she commanded. Connie did not cry easily, but this time she sobbed. It was not the sting of the peach tree switch that hurt, it was the bitter gall of guilt.

That afternoon Connie retired to her apple tree. In a family of twelve, privacy is hard to come by, but when Connie climbed up in her apple tree everyone knew she wanted to be alone. She settled herself on a branch high in the old tree. The buds of the apple blossoms, still tightly closed, were a deep rich pink and an aura of faintly spiced sweetness hung in the air. Before long, the buds would open to hide Connie's secret place in a cloud of blossoms, but now she was clearly visible from the ground.

"My dear Connie, do come down. I wish to speak with you."

The soft voice floated up from below. Connie knew who was calling because Cousin Alice was the only person on the plantation who spoke in those gentle tones. Alice B. Owens, who was twenty years older than her first cousin Kate Guion, had lived with the Guions ever since the war. Her husband had been killed at Appomattox and her children had died of the "flux," but these tragedies had not diminished her unquenchable spirit.

To the Guion children Cousin Alice was a kind of fairy godmother. She was petite and pretty, with long corkscrew curls which she wrapped around bamboo sticks at night. She played the piano and sang and read poetry. "Mother is like a fresh loaf of homemade bread," said Laura, "but Cousin Alice is the icing on the cake."

Connie climbed down swiftly in answer to Cousin Alice's call. Almost no one else could have gotten her to budge. "Connie," said Cousin Alice, "I don't want you to brood. To-day you learned something which should be helpful to you always. You learned about the *quality of attention*. If you'd given attention to your job, Jo's buggy would not have crashed."

Connie nodded. She was impressed. Cousin Alice nodded, too. Then she turned and walked off toward the house, holding a sprig of apple blossom before her and reciting:

'Tis education forms the common mind:
Just as the twig is bent the tree's inclined.

Cousin Alice wasn't the only one who tried to bring cul-
ture to the young Guions. Kate Guion did her best to edu-
cate them. One night the children sprawled on the floor as
usual and listened to their mother read Dickens. Mrs. Guion
was coming to the end of *The Old Curiosity Shop*. An April
storm had cooled the air and a fire crackled in the big fireplace, making flickering shadows dance about the room.

The death of Little Nell was almost more than the children could bear. Tears ran down Mary Wood's cheeks and
Ben blew his nose repeatedly. " 'Little Nell never murmured
or complained,' " Mrs. Guion read softly, leaning toward the
kerosene lamp, " 'but, with a quiet mind, and manner quite
unaltered — save that she every day became more earnest
and more grateful to them — faded like the light upon a
summer's evening.' "

"Heaven's sake, why didn't they get a doctor?" demanded
Connie.

"They were too poor, stupid," said Viv. "Don't you remember, Nell's grandfather gambled all their money away."

"Doctors take care of poor people, too."

"Indeed they do," said Mrs. Guion. "My father had many
patients who could not pay him, and so did his five brothers
who were doctors."

"I'm going to be a doctor, too," Connie announced.

Ben let out a hoot. "A *woman* doctor? I bet your patients
will die faster than Little Nell."

"That's enough, Ben," said his mother firmly. "If Connie
decides to be a doctor, she will be a good one. Your great-
grandmother was a doctor long before the War between the
States."

"Did she go to medical school?"

"Heavens no. In those days in North Carolina, doctors learned medicine from other doctors."

"I'm going to medical school," said Connie.

"You'd better learn to read and write first," said Laura. "Mama, when is Connie going to school? She's almost eight and the only thing she can write is her name."

Mrs. Guion sighed. "School's out of the question as long as we live so far from town. She's learning other things, though, Laura, things that may be as important as reading and writing."

One of the things Connie learned was how to entertain younger brothers and sisters. "Come on," she would call to her charges, "let's watch Louis mate the bull with the cows." The only thing the Guion children enjoyed more than the breeding of animals was helping to deliver the baby calves, piglets, lambs, and puppies.

"When do you reckon Cardell will have her pups?" asked Alex one day.

"Any minute," said Connie. "She's swollen up like a watermelon. I wish Mama would let me keep Cardell in the house."

"No pets and no fights inside this house," said Alex, imitating their mother's voice. "If you want to scrap, go behind the barn and fight it out."

"Who is Cardell's puppies' papa?" asked Ridie, who had an abiding interest in cause and effect.

"Who cares?" said Connie. "All the dogs around here are setters, just like Cardell, and setters beget setters, as it says in the Bible."

"Where does it say that?" asked Alex.

"Oh, the Book of Genesis, probably. I'll ask Miss Azzie tomorrow at Sunday school."

"Me begat Sunday cool," said Jo, who now chimed in on every conversation.

The children passed the woodshed, where Ben and Viv were cutting wood. Connie stopped and leaned on the split rail fence to watch her brothers. Both of them were blond and strong, but Ben was thin and serious and Viv round and harum-scarum. Connie admired them both extravagantly.

The two boys worked well together. Viv would shove the wood out on the sawhorse for Ben to chop. "Why, I could do *that*," Connie muttered to herself. Ben's muscles flexed as he swung the axe and a crack rang out when he struck the wood. Swing-crack, swing-crack. The rhythm was hypnotic.

"*Yeooooooooooow!*" Viv let out a hideous scream.

"Father in heaven!" yelled Ben.

"What happened?" cried Connie.

"I cut off Viv's finger!" Ben was gasping for breath; he could hardly speak.

Horror flooded through Connie. Still screaming, Viv held up his hand. His first finger was hanging by a thread.

"Get Mama!" shouted Ben.

Connie felt as though she were in a nightmare; the faster she ran, the less distance she covered. She found her mother working in the plantation office.

"Mama! Come quick! Ben cut off Viv's finger!"

Without a word, Mrs. Guion rose and ran toward the shed. Except for the paleness of her face, she betrayed no alarm. It was impossible for Connie to imagine an emergency her mother could not cope with. "Get a clean sheet and scissors," Mrs. Guion called over her shoulder. "Tell Elsie to bring boiling water and iodine." Connie did as she was told. She felt sick at her stomach, but she hated to miss seeing her mother remove the finger from Viv's hand.

When Connie and Elsie reached the scene of the accident, Viv was stretched out on the ground and Mrs. Guion knelt beside him, bending over his hand. Ben was leaning over the fence, sobbing and vomiting. "Cut the sheet into strips," Mrs. Guion said without looking up. "About an inch wide. I'll try to bandage the finger back on. Stop blubbering, Ben. Everybody has an accident sometime. Fetch me a couple of sticks for splints." Ben jumped up, thankful for something to do. Viv moaned like a dying bull.

Skillfully, Mrs. Guion bandaged the finger back on to Viv's hand. She placed the swathed finger between two splints and bandaged again. "That will do till we get to Dr. Richardson's."

"Can I go with you?" begged Connie.

Mrs. Guion nodded. "Ben, you stay here and do your chores. No matter what happens, life goes on. You might as well learn that right now." Ben nodded his head dully. He seemed to have lost the power of speech.

Connie never forgot that visit to Dr. Richardson. It was the first time she ever saw a doctor handle an emergency. "You did a good job, Miss Kate," said the doctor. "You're practically an M.D."

"Can you save the finger, Dr. Rich?"

"Yes. Viv's finger will never be quite right again, but it'll be there."

Connie was lost in admiration as she watched Dr. Richardson stitch Viv's finger into place. *Dr. Rich is putting Viv back together again,* she thought. *All the king's horses and all the king's men couldn't do that, but Dr. Rich can. And someday I'm going to do it, too.*

✳ 3 ✳

Plain Mules and Fancy Mules

CONNIE'S DESIRE to be a doctor was treated with increasing respect by the family. Ridie and Jo could get her to play with them any time simply by announcing that one of their dolls was sick. "Dolly frow up," said baby Jo. "Con-Con fix." And Connie would.

By the time she was ten Connie was promoted from doctoring dolls to doctoring chickens. Some people might not consider this an advance, but to young Connie Guion it was significant. Her mother asked her to rub asafetida on the chickens who had the pip.

"I hate that stinking stuff, Mama. It smells like rotten garlic."

"If you're going to be a doctor, Con, you'll have to get used to bad smells."

Like many Southern women, Mrs. Guion had great faith in asafetida. She made anyone who went to Rhinehart's factory store tie a bag of it around his neck. Once inside the store, no one noticed the hideous odor of the asafetida, because everybody was wearing it, to prevent a mythical malady called "salta-heum."

Connie felt like a chemist as she shook the asafetida into a cup of axle grease and stirred the revolting mixture. Then she went around the chicken yard, searching for pippy chickens and smearing the medicine over the bumps on their heads.

That night she asked her mother, "What's that junk supposed to do for the Black Minorcas?"

"It stops their itching. Asafetida soothes the nerves."

"Chickens' nerves maybe. Not mine."

Connie's older sister Ferebe, known as Ef, looked up from her books. "What's asafetida made of, Mama?" Ef, who had been working since she was sixteen as a nurse at the State Hospital for the Insane in Raleigh, was home for Easter. She was a small, strong and determined young lady, whose ambition was to be the best nurse in North Carolina.

"I've no idea," said Mrs. Guion, examining her mending. "Good heavens, Connie, all my safety pins are in the hem of your dress. It's time you learned to sew, my girl."

"I think I'll look it up in the dictionary," said Ef.

"Safety pins?" asked Connie.

"No, goose, asafetida. A-s-a. Here it is, 'asafetida: a gum resin often used in medicine. It occurs in commerce in the form of tears and dark-colored masses.' "

" 'In the form of tears and dark-colored masses,' " murmured Cousin Alice. "That's almost a poem."

"Oh, Cousin Alice," said Mrs. Guion, "everything sounds like a poem to you. Life just isn't like that."

"It is to me," said Cousin Alice.

Isn't that wonderful? thought Connie. *Mama speaks of asafetida and thinks of pippy chickens. Cousin Alice speaks of asafetida and thinks of poetry.*

Connie's carefree days on the plantation were punctuated by holidays. Easter was, in some ways, a better day for the Guions than Christmas. It was a struggle to find enough Christmas presents for everyone at River Bend Plantation, but there was never a shortage of eggs. The Guion children made their own dyes and colored dozens on top of dozens of eggs. To get green they wrapped an egg in onion tops and boiled it. For red, they used beets; for yellow, old carrots; for purple, pokeberries. The Guions had a gift for improvising.

On Easter morning the family got up at four to go to the sunrise service at St. Luke's Church in Lincolnton. It was still dark when they piled in the wagon and headed the mule toward town. As they jogged along, Cousin Alice led them in "Christ the Lord is risen to-day." By the time they filed into the dark church they were glowing with Easter spirit.

Later, after a breakfast that was indistinguishable from Sunday dinner, the endless egg hunt began. In the afternoon all the children walked to Dr. and Mrs. Richardson's for the Sunday school celebration. The Richardsons lived two miles down the Big Road in Woodside, a handsome brick home surrounded by hedges. "Miss Azzie," as everyone called Mrs. Richardson, was the godmother of the countryside. She had built a small chapel where she held services each week for the children, black and white alike, who were too far from town to go to St. Luke's.

Miss Azzie's Easter service was simple but effective. A staunch Episcopalian, she adhered strictly to the Book of Common Prayer and the Episcopal hymnal. She gave each child one egg and one religious card and the children could not have been more delighted. They sang and prayed and recited their Easter pieces with gusto.

Walking home from the Richardsons' one Easter, Connie said, "Ben, how come Old Jule didn't take us to church this morning? Seemed funny to go behind Rock." To Connie, mules were as important as people.

"She stepped into a posthole, Con, but she'll be all right."

Cardell came bounding toward Connie, the late afternoon sun glinting on her reddish-brown coat. Connie hugged her dog. "Of all the animals on this farm, I love Cardell and Old Jule the best. 'Course Cardell's my own, and that makes her special."

A few days later Ben surprised Connie by saying, "Mama, will it be all right if Con goes with me and Viv on the mules this morning?"

Connie saw her mother raise her eyebrows. "All right, but do be careful. Be sure to send Connie back before —" Mrs. Guion stopped suddenly.

Connie climbed happily onto Old Jule, bunching up her skirts until her knee-length underpants showed. Mrs. Guion and all the girls rode sidesaddle, except Connie. Connie not only rode astride, she preferred to ride bareback. Ben mounted Rock, Viv climbed on Kit, and the three of them set out across the fields. Connie was so happy she burst into a little unmusical song. How she loved to go riding with her brothers!

The Guions did not own any horses; mules were better for heavy farm work. Before the War between the States, Mrs. Guion had had a beautiful horse named Colonel. When the Yankees came marching down the road she hid Colonel in the smokehouse, but a Union officer found him and galloped him away. Kate Guion never got over it.

Connie and Ben and Viv practically lived with the three mules, feeding, currying and exercising them. Connie always rode Old Jule, and despite the fact that she was the youngest rider and Jule was the oldest mule, they usually won the races. On this day, however, there was no question of racing. Old Jule was definitely limping. Connie patted the mule's neck and talked to her. Ben and Viv were oddly silent and Connie sensed something was the matter. They rode through meadows splashed with blue and white and yellow spring flowers.

Then, without a warning, the boys pulled their mules to a halt.

"Ben," cried Connie, "what is it?"

"You'd better get off and run home, Con." Ben was four years older than Connie and he tried to sound commanding.

"Connie," said Viv, "do what Ben says."

"If I leave Old Jule here, who'll fetch her back to the barn?"

"We'll take care of her," said Viv.

"Connie, go home now — or you'll be sorry." Something in the urgency of Ben's voice made Connie decide she had better leave. She slid off Old Jule, kissed her soft nose, and started toward home.

Connie walked slowly. When she came upon a bed of violets, she picked one that was as dark as a pansy and walked on toward the house, examining the flower. It had two petals of purple velvet and two of silk. Suddenly, a shot rang through the air. Connie ran home shouting, "Mama, Mama, what was that?" But she already knew in her heart what it was.

Mrs. Guion put her arms around Connie. "The boys had to shoot Old Jule, Con," she said gently.

"No, no, *no!* Not my Old Jule!"

"Connie, stop that shouting," said her mother. "It was the best thing. I talked it over with Dr. Rich. Old Jule had a compound fracture and nothing could be done."

Connie rubbed her finger under her nose and sucked in her breath. She hated to have anyone see her cry, even her mother.

"Death is part of life, Connie. We simply have to accept that fact and live with it. That's what those Easter hymns are all about."

Ben and Viv did their best to keep Connie from brooding about Old Jule. They knew she liked to fish in the Catawba, a dangerous sport forbidden by their father, and since he was away they invited her to go with them. Early in the morning, Connie and her two brothers tiptoed out of the house and ran toward the river. With their bare feet they felt the hard dirt of the Big Road, then the wet grass of the open field, the spongy needles in the pine grove, and finally the slippery clay of the steep riverbank. The Catawba, about two hundred feet wide at this point, was very swift and dangerous.

Connie looked around apprehensively. "Elsie told me never to come down here. She said hoop snakes would get me if I did. They put their tails in their mouths and roll down the bank and poison whatever child might be in their way."

"We'll roll 'em away from you, Con," laughed Viv.

Connie and her brothers sat under a willow and held their long bamboo poles out over the river. The sun broke through the trees, dappling the three blond heads. They sat motionless, suspended in space and blissfully happy. Occasionally, one of them would haul in a catfish or a pike and the others would offer congratulations. Otherwise they fished in silence. "Mama sure would whale us if she caught us," Viv said cheerfully.

"Since that last drowning, she dreads this river worse'n the devil does holy water," observed Ben.

As the sun rose the day grew hotter, and the boys decided to go swimming. "I'm going, too," said Connie.

"Oh, no, you're not," said Ben. "The river's too rough for a girl." He stripped down to his underwear and jumped in the swirling water. Viv splashed in after him.

Connie stood on the bank, glowering. "I'm good and sick of being a girl," she called.

"I don't blame you," shouted Viv. "It's hard luck."

It was breakfast time when the fishermen started home. They knew they'd be caught, which they were, and that their mother would whip them, which she did. They did not care. That was the price you paid for a morning on the river.

Mrs. Guion was a spirited woman who could ride and shoot like a man, but she was afraid of one thing — the river. Yet when an emergency arose, she did not hesitate to send one of her children down to the river to save a life. One hot summer night she was sitting on the front porch watching distant lightning when she heard fearful screams coming from the Catawba. "Help!" bellowed a voice. "I'm drowning!"

Mrs. Guion recognized that voice. She ran up to Louis's bedside and shook him. "Wake up, Louis. Old Jake Johnson is drowning."

Louis tried to shake the sleep out of his eyes. "That good-for-nothing old drunk?"

"Yes, Old Jake. And you have to save him."

"Aw, Maw!"

"*Get up,* Louis. Hurry."

Connie, who seldom missed a crisis, slipped out of bed and followed Louis and her mother. Judging by her mother's urgent tone, this emergency promised to be more exciting than most. It was an odd little procession that set off into the dark night. Mrs. Guion led, carrying a lantern and a heavy coil of rope. Louis followed, mumbling and grumbling, and far behind came Connie in her nightgown. Occasionally a flash of lightning showed them the way. Wind twisted the trees until they moaned, and rain splattered on the leaves.

It was easy to locate Old Jake by his bellowing. They found him sloshing around in shoulder-deep water at the river's edge. "I'm drowning, *drowning!*" he blubbered, flailing his arms violently. Apparently he had lost the ability to move his legs. Whether this was because of drink or being stuck in the mud, it was impossible to tell.

Mrs. Guion surveyed the scene with the keen eyes of a field marshal. It took her less than a minute to devise a plan. "Louis, climb out on the limb of that button tree. Tie one end of the rope around the limb, throw the other end down, and tow him to shore."

"Oh, Ma, do I have to? He ain't worth saving."

"Louis, *any* human being is worth saving."

Louis, who was nimble and strong, managed to haul the "drowning" man to dry land without being dragged into the river himself. Jake Johnson was a muddy, blubbering mess. "Lead him to the house, Louis," Mrs. Guion said briskly. "We'll scrub him and sober him up."

In a day when ladies blanched at the thought of encountering a drunken man, Mrs. Guion understood that alcoholism is a disease and alcoholics need care, not abuse. Years later, when Dr. Connie Guion was an intern at Bellevue Hospital, caring for some of New York's worst derelicts, she recalled her mother standing by the river, holding her lantern aloft and saying: "Louis, *any* human being is worth saving."

When Mr. Guion finally returned to the plantation, his wife had a lot to tell him. He frowned as she described the punishment of the three young fishermen and the rescue of Jake Johnson. He stroked his curly blond beard and said, "I don't like it, Kate. That river is no place for children."

"But what can we do, Mr. Guion? It draws them like a magnet."

Mr. Guion paced up and down the room. For a long time he did not say anything. Mrs. Guion sat quietly, her dark eyes following him. "I've got a plan," he said.

"What kind of plan?"

"Ah," he said, holding up his forefinger, "that would be telling."

The next day Mr. Guion began his project. With the help of Noah Brown and Oaf, he dammed up the rill streams that gushed down from the hills and created a pool about two hundred feet in diameter. He stocked the pond with pike, bass and catfish and built a flat-bottom boat for the children to row. He even made a little dock at one end of the pond. A thick hedge of osage orange was planted around the pond and eventually it grew tall and impenetrable. Here, in this private, secluded fishpond, fed by pure mountain water, the young Guions splashed away the summer days.

"Well, Mr. Guion," said his wife, "when you set out to do something, I must say you do it. Your fishpond is a raring-tearing success. It has even made the children forget the excitement of the Catawba."

"One only has to use one's imagination," said Mr. Guion.

As Captain of the Light Brigade, Mary Wood was, to a certain extent, in charge of excitement. One day she banged into the house yelling, "It's coming! It's coming, you all!"

"A lady never raises her voice, Mary Wood," said Cousin Alice.

"What's coming?" demanded the children.

"The circus! They're plastering posters on all the trees. It's coming on July twenty-third, Laura's birthday."

"Three cheers for Laura!" shouted Viv.

"Three cheers for the circus," said Laura.

"We don't have to go to a circus, we live in one," groaned Alice, who had just turned twenty-one and was very dignified. "Circuses cost money — I hope you children have some saved up."

Since the Guions made or grew everything they needed,

money was almost unknown on the plantation. The circus cost a quarter, which for a family of twelve was a lot, but no-body suggested they stay home. The Guions put first things first.

Just before Circus Day, Mrs. Guion asked Connie to drive a wagonload of peaches into town and sell them to get some cash. Connie was thrilled; until now she had been considered too young for such a task. Oaf hitched up Kit, the gentlest mule, and filled the Studebaker wagon with huge pink-cheeked peaches that still had dew on them. Connie, clad in a light calico dress, proudly climbed into the driver's seat and turned Kit towards Lincolnton.

"Don't try to go too fast, Con," said her mother.

"Don't worry, Mama, I'm a careful driver."

When she reached the bridge, Connie turned and waved. With a spyglass, Mrs. Guion watched her cross the river and start up the long hill toward town. She watched until the wagon was out of sight.

Connie relished her grown-up assignment. She breathed in the summer air and sang "Kitty, kitty, kitty, won't you climbeo?" almost in tune. When Kit reached the brow of the hill, Connie could see spread out in the valley the roofs of Lincolnton, shimmering in the July sunlight. She tried to halt the mule to admire the view. But Kit had other ideas; she kept going down the steep hill. Suddenly, Connie felt a spring snap and the wagon slipped forward against the mule's hind legs. Kit went faster and the wagon bumped harder. Kit broke into a dead run.

Connie grabbed the seat and held on. She knew she could not stop the mule, but she had to do something. Letting go of the seat, she clambered along the wagon shaft and climbed on Kit's back. She threw her arms around the mule's neck and hung on tight. Through the main street of Lincolnton they raced — mule, wagon, girl and peaches. People scurried out of their path and stood laughing by the side of the road. Boys ran after the wagon, picking up peaches.

Even though Connie was frightened, she was enjoying the wild ride. It wasn't every day that you could race a mule through town. Her only hope of stopping Kit was to head her up a hill. She tugged on the bridle and they swerved toward the schoolhouse hill. As they went up, the heavy body of the wagon slid backward and Kit slowed down. By the time they reached the top, Kit was meek and exhausted and Connie was again in control.

News of Connie Guion's riotous peach ride traveled quickly. When she got back to the grocer's, her mother was there to meet her. "Well, young lady, I thought you were a safe driver."

"Oaf didn't hitch this bloomin' wagon right and the spring busted. But we had a peachy run."

"Peachy is the word," said her mother. "Our peaches are scattered all over town."

Mr. Lander, the grocer, was weak from laughter. "Oh, Mrs. Guion," he said, "I've had enough fun to make up for any lack in the number of peaches."

Laura's nineteenth birthday, July 23, 1890, was warm, breezy and memorable. Each child made a present for her and wrapped it in brown paper and string; tissue paper and ribbon were unknown on the plantation. Laura, who was adored by everyone, was perhaps the prettiest Guion. She had blue eyes, sun-tanned creamy skin, and long blond hair that she brushed up into a pompadour.

That morning the plantation chores were done at top speed. Since daybreak people had been riding or walking past the house, going toward the circus grounds. Everyone in

Laura

Lincoln County who was not bedridden seemed to be heading in that direction. By noon the Guion plantation was deserted. Everybody had gone to the circus.

Connie's eyes sparkled when she saw the circus tent topped by flapping flags. The first thing the Guions did was visit the sideshows. Connie gasped at the glassblowers and bagpipers, the bearded ladies and tattooed men. But when they reached the menagerie, she stopped in her tracks. "What," she demanded, "is *that?*"

"A zebra, stupid," said Viv. "Didn't you ever see a picture of one?"

"Never. Oh, isn't he beautiful!" Connie walked up to the animal to inspect it more closely. Dark brown stripes ran all over his cream-colored body, up and down his face, and diagonally along the sides of his head. Even his long ears and short thick mane were striped. "A zebra?" she repeated. "Looks like a fancy mule to me."

"Don't get so close, Con," warned Louis. "Zebras can be dangerous."

"I'm not afraid of him," said Connie, stroking the zebra's neck with her open palm.

"You don't have to worry about Buzz-Fuzz," said the keeper. "We brought him up by hand. Only wild zebras are dangerous."

Connie's brothers pulled her away from the zebra, but she kept thinking about that fancy mule. She had never seen an animal she admired so much.

The circus was beyond words wonderful. There were bears in ruffs riding bicycles, girls in spangled dresses swinging on trapezes, and tigers performing at the crack of the ringmaster's whip. A smell of roasted peanuts, damp tanbark and exploding fireworks filled the air. And then, before anyone realized it, the show was almost over and it was time for the grand finale. Just before the parade was to start, Connie got up and left.

"Where are you going?" called her mother.

"Out. Back in a minute."

"Do be careful. The elephants are lining up already."

When it was time for the parade to begin, Connie had not returned. Mrs. Guion looked around anxiously. It was not like Connie to miss anything. Where in the world could she be?

The band, dressed in gaudy red uniforms, marched into the tent, tooting "There'll Be a Hot Time in the Old Town To-night." The elephants followed, each holding the tail of the one ahead. Next came the clowns, one with enormous feet and cardboard ears; another, wearing a mop for hair and balloons for bosoms, pushing a cigar-smoking baby in a buggy. Behind the clowns came the zebras.

"Ye gods!" yelled Viv. "Will you look at that?"

"*Connie!*" breathed Mrs. Guion.

"Well, I never!" said Cousin Alice.

At the head of the zebras pranced old Buzz-Fuzz, and perched up on top of Buzz-Fuzz sat little Connie Guion. All of the Guions stood up, waving and shouting. Connie waved back and blew them a kiss. Then she leaned over and hugged the zebra. "I declare," said Laura, wiping her eyes with a handkerchief, "what do you suppose will become of a child like that?"

The Hard-Headed Woman

THE GUIONS were courageous, but like all rural folk they were afraid of fire. All their water was pumped out of a well and there were no fire engines available. The risk of fire was great, too, as the house was lighted by kerosene lamps and heated by open fireplaces. One windy autumn day, fire came to River Bend Plantation and no one ever forgot it. Oddly enough, it was not accidental; it was deliberate.

Early that morning Mrs. Guion had her oft-repeated conversation with six-year-old Alex. "Mama, why do I have to wear an apron?"

"To keep your clothes clean. Poor old Elsie runs a full-time laundry as it is. She's out in the backyard right now boiling dirty clothes."

"This ding-dang apron makes me look like a girl."

"Nothing could make you look like a girl, Alex," said his mother, tying the coverall firmly. "You're too tough."

That morning everybody was hurrying to finish the daily chores in time to harvest the purple grapes in the arbor. Each fall the family made red wine from the arbor grapes and white wine from the scuppernongs that grew wild along the river. When company came Mrs. Guion took pride in bringing out cake and homemade wine.

After breakfast, Alex went out to feed the pigs and sweep the barn, sulking all the while. Nobody knew how he hated that apron. Nobody even cared. Suddenly he ran across the yard to Elsie, who was stirring the clothes around in a ten-gallon iron pot suspended over a blazing fire. "Look out Elsie! There's a hoop snake behind you." Elsie turned around and Alex untied his apron strings and shoved them in the fire. Instantly, the cotton material blazed up.

"There ain't no hoop snakes. You trickin' me, Smart Alex?" Then Elsie screamed, "Alex, you're on fire! Help! *Fire!*"

Alex dropped the flaming apron ties. They hit his bare legs and he jumped into the air. Screaming, he darted around the yard, leaving a trail of burning grass. *Fire! Fire!* The cry went up across the plantation. People came running from every direction. Ben and Viv and Connie chased Alex. The faster they ran, the faster he ran; sparks from the burning apron flew out behind him. He ran through the grape arbor littered with dry leaves. A moment later the arbor burst into flames. He streaked into the brown wheat field. In a few seconds the wheat field was on fire.

At last Ben and Viv caught him. They tore off the blazing apron and threw him down on the ground, rolling him over and over to put out the fire. Alex's body shook with dry sobs.

The plantation hands grabbed anything they could find to fight the fire. Some picked up tow sacks, others brooms or dead branches. As though trained, they made a circle around the fire and began beating it from the outer edges, closing in rapidly. It took less than twenty minutes to get it under control. Only the cool-headedness of the farm hands kept the whole place from going up in smoke, for the fire came perilously close to the big house itself.

As usual in any emergency, Mrs. Guion was the quiet one at the center of the storm. Carefully, she picked up her sooty son and started for the house. "You gonna punish him, Mama?" asked Connie.

"No, he's already been through fire and brimstone."

"What you goin' to do with him?"

"Take him upstairs and put a clean apron on him. Thank heaven he's not hurt."

Illness was surprisingly rare at River Bend Plantation. When someone asked Mrs. Guion why her family was so healthy she replied, "We haven't time to be sick." There were, however, a few memorable sieges of illness. One winter, when Connie was three years old, nine of the children came down with measles at the same time. During another bleak stretch, the mother herself was stricken with typhoid fever. Mr. Guion was away and the children would have gone adrift if it had not been for Mrs. Richardson. Each morning Mary Wood and the Light Brigade tramped to Woodside where they spent the day and often the night.

Mrs. Richardson was a delightful woman, as round and warm as a baked potato. When Dr. Richardson drove out on his calls, "Miss Azzie" went with him, weighing down her side of the black phaeton until it looked as though the springs had given way.

One night, Miss Azzie diverted the children by reading aloud from *St. Nicholas* magazine. She chose a story by a new Southern writer, Joel Chandler Harris, about a character named Uncle Remus. It was called "The Hard-Headed Woman." " 'Yasser,' " read Mrs. Richardson, imitating Uncle Remus's rich accent, " 'de doctor oughter come an' look at you — an' when I say doctor, I mean doctor, an' not one er deze kin' what goes roun' wid a whole passel er pills what ain't bigger dan a gnat's heart. What you want is a great big double-j'inted doctor wid a big black beard an' specks on, what'll fill you full er de rankes' kin'er physic.' "

"If you're going to be a doctor, Con," said Viv, "maybe you ought to grow a beard like that lady at the circus."

"Don't tease Con," said Mrs. Richardson. "There have been some great women doctors. Not many, but a few. Take Elizabeth Blackwell —"

"Who was she?" asked Connie.

"The first woman doctor in America. She and her sister started a medical college for women in New York."

"When I grow up, I want to be like Elizabeth Blackwell," observed Connie.

"Stop, Miss Azzie!" said Dr. Richardson, "I don't want our Connie Guion to turn into one of those female doctors. Talk about hard-headed women."

"Dr. Rich," said his wife, "women can do more than you men will admit. Someday they're even going to vote."

"Heaven forbid!" said Dr. Richardson.

Connie loved to go to the Richardsons' Sunday school, but she hated getting ready for it. One by one the Guion children were sent out to the spring house for an icy shower bath, a ritual which could be enjoyed only by a full-blooded Eskimo. Mr. Guion considered cold showers next to godliness, but when winter set in, he allowed the children to bathe in the shed off the kitchen. They sat in sawed-off barrels which had brought New Orleans molasses to the plantation, and sloshed themselves with warm water from the copper kettle.

Toilet facilities at River Bend were far more pleasant. At the end of the garden was a little frame house, with two doors, painted white and covered with orange-flowering trumpet vines and honeysuckle. Each side held a wooden "two-seater" toilet. The outhouse was kept spotlessly clean and it was, in a way, one of the nicest places on the plantation. When Connie encountered her first bathroom in Charlotte, she felt sorry for the city girls who had no cozy outhouses where one could chat with one's sister, while watching humming birds dart into the trumpet vine at the window.

The question of whether or not to go to Sunday school never arose with the Guions, who were deeply religious. Each evening they gathered around the fire and took turns reading the Bible. Whenever Mary Wood read "and it came to pass," she tossed the Bible to the person next to her.

"Mary Wood," scolded Mr. Guion, "why can't you be more serious like your sister Kate?" Kate, the eldest of the twelve Guion children, who was studying nursing at Massachusetts General Hospital in Boston, had none of Mary Wood's harum-scarumness.

Mrs. Guion picked up the Bible and said, "Mr. Guion, now it's my turn to read." Slowly, she read: " 'There is one glory of the sun and another glory of the moon, and another glory of the stars: for one star differeth from another in glory.' " She put down the Bible and added, "And one Guion differeth from another in glory."

Connie gasped. This was as close as her mother had ever come to correcting her father. All the children held their breath, waiting for their father's reaction. He looked at his wife a moment, then he walked over and kissed her. "I have a Bible verse for you, too," he said. " 'Her children shall rise up and call her blessed.' "

The Guions wore their best clothes to Sunday school, hand-me-downs sent by a friend of their mother's named Mrs. Picksickanny, but unless the weather was bitter cold they went barefoot. They hated to wear the high copper-toed boots made on the plantation.

Miss Azzie's sister, Miss Ida, conducted the service while Miss Azzie lined out hymns on a hand-pumped organ. Miss Ida also gave out the attendance tickets. They came in different colors with pictures on them and a religious verse. If you got fifty different tickets, you could turn them in for a picture of Jesus. The Guions treasured their Sunday school tickets almost as much as their birds' eggs collection. Connie also collected Octagon soap wrappers. If she ever got two hundred, she could send in for a watch. Right next to being a doctor, the thing Connie Guion wanted most was a watch. She had about given up on the zebra.

One day Connie was quietly waiting in line to get a yellow ticket with a picture of a lamb on it, when she got into trouble. It is not easy to get into trouble while waiting in line at Sunday school, but Connie managed it. In front of her stood a boy named, mysteriously, Charley Horse. She was staring at Charley's frayed collar and soiled neck when she saw something move. She looked closer, then shouted, *"Charley Horse has got a louse!"* Miss Azzie was pumping out "From Greenland's Icy Mountains." The organ wheezed to a stop and all eyes fastened on Charley Horse, who slapped both hands against his red neck. "Charley Horse has got a louse!" yelled Connie, circling the room like Paul Revere warning against the British.

Suddenly, Connie halted in her tracks. Before her stood a familiar figure. "That will do," said her mother. She took Connie by the arm and marched her out of the Sunday school and down the Big Road. Mrs. Guion did not have to explain to Connie that she had hurt a poor boy's feelings. Her silence spoke volumes. Even when they reached home, Mrs. Guion said only a few words: "Connie, you know right from wrong as well as I do. When you do something wrong, either I'll punish you — or life will. In this case, we haven't time to wait for life. Fetch the peach-tree switch." It was a bad whipping, almost as bad as never getting a yellow ticket with a lamb and shepherd on it.

The Big Road that wound past River Bend Plantation was

a source of mystery and excitement for the Guion children. Whatever life they knew outside of the family came down it. A red dirt road, fringed with Queen Anne's lace and shaded by maples, it was seldom the same. On rainy days, mules could scarcely pull their legs out of the sticky mud. In summer the sun baked it into a shiny trail, while in winter frost dusted the deep red ruts.

During Court Week the sleepy country road was filled with color and drama. It was then the country people traveled to Lincolnton for the autumn session of the circuit court, bringing their produce and animals to sell or swap in the courthouse square: mules, cows, pigs—everything. Connie and her brothers would sit in front of their house, greeting the travelers as they came by. They knew everybody.

Often during Court Week, an unsteady traveler would stop by Mrs. Guion's for a sobering cup of hot tea. Her kind heart won her the trust and affection of all who knew her, and drunks, especially, depended on her. One of these men told the Guion children a secret. He said if they could ever find a drunken man on a horse, they could buy the horse for a quarter. The boys hooted at this, but Connie was impressed.

It took her five weeks to earn a quarter. Eggs were her only source of income and they sold for ten cents a dozen, so progress was slow. No one in the family knew why she was saving her pennies, nor did they know how she longed to own a horse. Early in life Elsie taught Connie the security of silence. "Chile," she said, "if you really want something, don't put your mouth on it."

At long last October came, with a crisp rustle in the cornfield and a tang of windfall apples in the air. Once more the colorful Court Week crowd streamed down the Big Road. Connie sat on the horse block, biding her time. She not only had her quarter, she had even picked out her drunk. He was a preacher from Lincolnton named Wolfe who could always be counted on to drink too much during Court Week.

Finally Mr. Wolfe came cantering down the Big Road. It was evident from the wild angle of his hat and the looseness of his jaw that Connie had caught him at just the right time. Boldly, she stepped out and flagged him.

"Why, it's little Connie." He reined in his horse. "What you want, little Connie?"

"I want to buy your horse."

"Izzat so?"

"Yes, sir. I'll give you a quarter for him."

Mr. Wolfe scratched his head. Then, very seriously, he said, "Done." He dismounted, handed the reins to Connie, picked up the quarter, bit it, and put it in his pocket. He helped Connie mount and thumped the horse on his rump.

"Bye-bye, Spareribs," he said. "Be good to Miss Connie."

"I'm much obliged to you, Mr. Wolfe."

"My pleasure." The preacher made a sweeping bow, lost his balance and almost tumbled over.

Connie nudged Spareribs into a trot and rode off down the Big Road. A cardinal trilled in a loblolly pine nearby. Connie threw back her head and repeated his whistle. She turned the horse into the fields and cantered toward the barn. The sun had dropped now and swallows dipped in and out of the pink sky. Inside the barn, she slid off Spareribs and quickly removed his saddle and bridle. She wanted to curry her horse before she introduced him to the family. When she finished, his chestnut coat glistened.

Connie found her mother in the kitchen lighting kerosene lamps. The odor of kerosene was edged with the fragrance of freshly baked bread.

"Where's Mr. Wolfe?" asked Connie.

"I sent him upstairs. He was — ah — tired."

"Did he tell you the good news about my horse?"

"What on earth are you talking about?"

"I bought his horse, that's what. Spareribs is mine."

"You *bought* his horse?"

"Yes ma'am. Horse, saddle and bridle, all mine."

"May I ask what you bought them with?"

"The money I been saving up. My quarter."

"You gave Mr. Wolfe a *quarter* for his horse?"

"Yes ma'am."

"Connie, what ever made you think of such a thing?"

"A man told me if you can catch a drunk, he'll sell you his horse for a quarter."

Mrs. Guion put both hands on Connie's arms and looked into her eyes. "Do you mean to say you took *advantage* of a drunken man?"

Connie said nothing. She had not meant to take advantage of anyone.

"The idea of your thinking you could buy a horse for nothing! Go upstairs immediately and apologize to Mr. Wolfe. Tell him you'll bring his horse up from the stable whenever he wants it."

Connie was crushed. With a heart of lead, she returned Spareribs to Mr. Wolfe, who made a big speech, full of legal phrases, and gave her the quarter. Connie wanted to throw it in his face. Ben and Viv were doubled up with laughter, which did not help. As soon as she could, Connie went outside and climbed up in her apple tree. Its bare branches were heavy with red apples. She sat in the crotch of the tree, crunching an apple and thinking long, long thoughts.

When November came to River Bend the woods grew black and the winter grain glistened with hoar frost. Work in the fields was over until spring and at last Connie and her brothers had time for rabbit hunting. This was the time of year she loved. She and Ben and Viv set up their wooden traps in the fields of feathery brown broomsage, and every morning they put on their rabbit-skin jackets and caps and set out to collect their catch. Rabbits are great fighters and must be handled carefully. Connie and Viv held the tow sack, while Ben dumped the rabbit into the bag and smothered it. "Are you sure the rabbit don't suffer, Ben?" asked Connie.

" 'Course, that's why I do it so fast — same as you kill chickens." Connie was a master at killing chickens. She could swing a Black Minorca until its neck snapped and the body flew off, leaving the head in her hand.

One winter a new and different excitement struck River Bend Plantation, a project that eventually gave Alice a job. There were no telephones in Lincoln County; the only way to get news was to meet the morning train from Charlotte or wait for the *Charlotte Observer,* which came by slow mail. A group of imaginative young people, led by Alice and Laura Guion, decided to start a telegraph to dispense news. They established a central office in a house in Lincolnton and strung miles of lines to homes around the countryside.

The project turned out to be a howling success. The little box in the Guion hallway was forever going dit-dit-da. The girls would take down the message and then tap out an answer. Lots of news, good and bad, was relayed over those wires. All the Guions became Morse Code experts. "Now, Ben," Alice would say, "which letters are the dashes?"

"T — one dash, M — two dashes, O — three dashes."

"Which are the dots, Mary Wood?"

"E.I.S.H."

"What is S.O.S., Connie?"

"I can't remember that old code, Alice. I got more important things to think about, like Christmas."

As the days grew colder and shorter, all the Guions began chattering about Christmas. Christmas at River Bend was a simple affair, with no Christmas trees, no decorations, and few presents, but there was plenty of excitement. By five o'clock Christmas morning the children were outside shooting off fireworks. Then they ran to empty their stockings, which were filled with candies and nuts, and, miraculously, an orange.

On Christmas afternoon Mr. Guion gave out the presents. Each child received one gift. Handmade doll clothes for the little girls, homemade kites and tops for the boys; and beautiful, nearly new clothes for everyone from one of Mrs. Picksickanny's magic boxes.

One Christmas Connie's mother called her aside. "Con," she whispered, "I have something special for you this year. I suppose I should give it to one of the boys, but you've yearned for one for so long. Merry Christmas." She handed her a small package wrapped in white paper. It lay in the palm of Connie's hand, rather heavy and about three inches long.

Connie ripped open the paper, and there was a metal pocket knife! On it were printed the words *Thorn's O.H.M. Whisky*. Her mother had gotten it somewhere as an advertisement. All the children wanted a knife, but she had given it to Connie. Connie pressed it against her cheek. It was the best Christmas present she ever had received.

Mr. Guion always managed to get home for Christmas and his gaiety brightened up the holiday. But that Christmas night he seemed depressed. "Kate, there's something I have to talk to you about."

"Yes, Mr. Guion?"

"Money. We not only don't have any, we're in debt."

"What are we going to do? Tobacco prices are scraping bottom and I know the railroad won't pay you any more."

"It isn't just the railroad, Kate. Times are hard. If only we could get a Democrat in the White House. Ever since the war, it's been one Republican after another — Hayes, Garfield and, worst of all, Chester A. Arthur. We need someone who'll help the South, not knock it down. If only Mr. Grover Cleveland could be elected —"

"Ben Guion," interrupted his wife, "our help is not going to come from *Washington!*"

Mr. Guion looked puzzled at his wife's vehemence. "Where is it coming from, Kate?"

"Where help always comes from — your family."

"Family? How can we expect more from them? Kate's nursing at Massachusetts General and Effie's at St. Luke's. They send home all they can, but it's not a drop in the till. Who else is there? We have to keep Alice here to help you with the children and Louis has to study. I mean for him to go to the University of North Carolina, no matter what."

"Well, Laura will help," said Mrs. Guion. And sure enough, Laura did help.

It was not easy for a woman to find work in the 1890's, but through her mother's cousins, Laura was lucky enough to get a job in the post office in Charlotte.

"How much will they pay you to sell stamps, Laura?" asked Connie as she was helping her sister pack.

"I'm going to make seventy-five dollars a month, Con."

"Seventy-five dollars a month!" exclaimed Connie, dancing around the room. "We'll all be rich!" This was, in fact, a startling salary. The only other jobs open to women in Charlotte were teaching, or clerking in Mr. Baruch's Dry Goods Store, which paid a lot less.

There was great excitement over Laura's new venture, until the day came for her departure. Then gloom enveloped the family. After she drove off in the wagon, waving her handkerchief forlornly, Alice said, "It's just like a funeral."

"Worse," said Louis. "At least at a funeral you get some food to ease your grief."

The word grief was, to Connie, only a word — until a few months later. Then she met it for the first time, head on. Oddly enough, it was her own father who broke her heart. Mr. Guion had no idea what he was doing to Connie and her violent reaction baffled him.

On that fateful day Connie went to the Richardsons' to play with Miss Azzie's daughter, Julia, and her father took advantage of her absence.

"Oaf," he said, "that red setter of Con's is filling this place up with pups."

"Yassir. She gets a litter every six months."

"Well, today is the day I do something about it."

"What you goin' to do, Mr. Ben?"

"I'm going to have to shoot her."

"Shoot Miss Connie's dog?"

"Yes. Fetch Cardell for me, Oaf. We can't go on feeding setter pups forever."

"Mr. Ben, I don't think Miss Con's —"

"I didn't ask what you think. I know what has to be done. Go get the dog for me, Oaf. Now."

It was almost supper time when Connie returned from the Richardsons'. Her mother came out to meet her. The minute Connie saw her she knew something was wrong. "Mama, what's the matter?"

"Oh, Connie, something terrible has happened. I had no idea —"

"Mama, what *is* it? Tell me."

Mrs. Guion put her arms around her daughter's shoulder. "Con, dear, Cardell is dead."

"Dead? Not Cardell! No, *no!*"

"Yes, dear. I'm afraid so. If I'd known, I would have stopped it."

Connie's luminous gray eyes suddenly widened. "What do you mean, you would have stopped it? Stopped what? What happened?"

"I know Papa thought he was doing the best —"

"*Papa?*"

"Connie, dear, don't scream."

"What did he do to you, Cardell?" shouted Connie. "*Mama, what did he do?*"

"I can't bear to tell you, Con. The fact is he shot her."

The words seemed to explode Connie into the house. She was literally beside herself with rage. Her father was sitting before the fire, sipping his evening toddy and talking with Louis. Connie lunged at him. "Killer!" she yelled. "I'm going to beat you up."

Quickly Louis sprang to her side. "Connie, Connie, quiet down."

Mr. Guion looked utterly dismayed. It had never entered his head Connie would react this way. "Con," he said, "don't carry on so. I have one of Cardell's pups for you, a male pup. He'll be your very own dog."

"I don't want Cardell's pup, *I want my Cardell.*"

"Connie," said her mother, "that will — do."

Connie whirled around and ran sobbing out of the room. Her tears shocked the family more than her shouts, for she almost never cried. Upstairs, she threw herself on the bed, shaking with sobs. She did not know how long she lay there. Much later, she felt a hand on her shoulder. Her sister Alice was sitting beside her. "Connie, you ought to be ashamed of yourself." The older girls worshipped their father and Alice was deeply shocked by Connie's rampage.

"I don't see why *I* should be ashamed. I'm ashamed of *him.*"

"I think you'd better come down and talk to your father."

"You go talk to *your* father. I haven't got a father."

It was a long, long time before Connie recovered from her anger. For days she avoided her father; if she met him, she refused to speak. The poor man was stunned by the force of his daughter's fury.

One night about a month later, during Bible reading, Mr. Guion read, "For the trumpet shall sound, and the dead shall be raised."

"Papa," Alex piped up, "is the trumpet vine on the out-house gonna blow?"

In spite of herself, Connie looked toward her father and for the first time in weeks their eyes met. He laughed, then she laughed, then they both laughed together. And in their laughter, a truce was sealed. But deep in her heart Connie never got over the death of Cardell.

✳ 5 ✳

The Manure Pile

"Connie," said Louis, "don't you wish you could read? Most ten-year-old kids can."

"Oh, I'm in no hurry. It's more fun to be read to."

Connie and Louis were working in the apple shed, wrapping apples in paper and putting them in sand for storage. Since Cardell's death, Louis had gone out of his way to ask Connie to help him.

"You can learn a lot from books, Con. When I go to Chapel Hill, I'm going to study like sixty and make up for all I've missed."

The Guion children's education was indeed sporadic. The older boys and girls hiked three miles into Lincolnton to school, but this was too far for Connie to walk, and besides she was needed at home to take care of Ridie, Jo and Alex. The Lincolnton school was in session only from November first to March first, because the rest of the year the pupils had to help on the farm.

"I know a lot of things more important than reading, like how to find a field sparrow's nest, or how to cure a bloated mule of green colic, or how to spot long-toed possum tracks in the mud."

Louis laughed. "If you decide to keep possums for a living, you're all set." Connie laughed, too, never suspecting that one day she would keep possums for scientific reasons.

On their way back to the house, Connie and Louis stopped to talk with their father, who was getting his hair cut on the back porch. Mr. Guion's health had been poor, and he was spending more time at the plantation. Alice, who was the family barber, snipped his wavy hair with professional skill.

"You're next, Con," called Alice. "Your hair's almost over your ears."

"Shucks, Allo," said Louis. "Can't you let Con's hair grow? It's time she started looking like a girl."

"No girl in this family has long hair until she can take care of it herself," said Alice.

"Con doesn't want to look like a girl," chuckled their father. "I caught her ducking her head in the horse trough to soak the curl out."

"Sh-h-h-h," whispered Connie, pointing to a small black and white bird that nipped up one of Mr. Guion's curls and flew away with it. "The snowbirds are going to warm their nests with your hair, Papa."

"I'm glad to be of *some* use," said Mr. Guion, who was also glad to be addressed by Connie. He had not gotten over the weeks following Cardell's death when she refused to speak to him. "Mama has something important to tell you, Con. She got a letter from Laura today."

"Laura? *A letter!* Yippee!" Connie bounded up the stairs two at a time. The Guions got mail once a week when they went into Lincolnton to sell produce. Letters always caused excitement at River Bend and a letter from Laura was an event. But when Connie learned the contents of Laura's letter, her joy turned to woe.

Laura wrote that she was settled in her new job and had met a lot of people, because sooner or later everyone comes to the post office. She enclosed a money order to help the family budget — and then came the shock: "Mama, I know you and

Papa worry because Connie can't go to school. Thank goodness I can help now. Please let her come to Charlotte to live with me and go to the graded school. She ought to start soon. As it is, she'll be the only ten-year-old in the first grade."

"Oh, Mama, don't send me away," moaned Connie. "I love the plantation. I want to stay right here."

"Your father and I agree the time has come for you to go to school, Con. This is something we have dreamed about and we're lucky that Laura can make it possible. We're going to send Louis to the University, too. Thank heaven that's free."

"Alice and I will make you some pretty new clothes for the trip, Con," said Cousin Alice.

"I don't need new clothes. I want to stay here and wear my old ones. They suit me fine."

But Connie knew the jig was up, and when the sewing started she almost found it interesting. Alice unearthed some dark blue cotton to make her new dress. Connie had never had a new dress before and she was disappointed when there was not enough material to make a whole dress.

"Fiddle-faddle," said her mother. "I have some white pique. We'll piece it out by putting a white vest in front." This they did and Cousin Alice said that it made Connie look cunning, like a white-breasted nuthatch.

"White-bellied swallow is more like it," said Connie, who knew her birds. "But I *feel* like a black-hearted old crow," she added gloomily. Actually, the oddly constructed dress delighted her. Her mother had even added two huge pockets because she knew Connie needed plenty of storage space. With Alice's help, Mary Wood made underbodies for Connie out of flour sacking, with buttons at the waist for attaching petticoats and drawers. Across the chest of each underbody was printed

Hodges Pure Flour but fortunately, the letters were not visible through the white pique vest. A novice with the needle, Mary Wood had to rip out every seam at least once.

"As ye sew, so shall ye rip," observed Cousin Alice.

Everybody worked to get Connie ready for the big trip. Cousin Alice knit her long white stockings and Uncle Jigleg Jake, the cobbler, made her a new pair of copper-toed boots.

"In Charlotte you'll have to wear shoes every day, Con," said her mother.

"But Mama, I hate shoes. I feel like my feet are in jail."

Connie's misery reached its high-water mark in the coat-and-hat crisis. Her mother pulled out of Mrs. Picksickanny's box an astonishing plaid coat striped in red, blue, pink, orange and crimson. Connie thought the coat-of-many colors was beautiful, but the bonnet that went with it was an out-and-out horror made of red velvet with little white frills around the face. Her mother tied it under her chin and said, "There! Now you look like a little lady."

Connie peered into the looking glass. She had never worn a hat, except the simple caps made by her mother. "I look like a little jackass. Hee-haw, hee-haw!" She ripped off the bonnet and hurled it across the room.

"Connie," said her mother, "pick up that hat. You're about to set out on an adventure and you can't let a little thing like a bonnet upset you. What you wear simply isn't that important."

" 'Consider the lilies of the field,' " said Cousin Alice. " 'They toil not, neither do they spin, yet even Solomon in all his glory was not arrayed like one of these.' "

"Con's a lily of the field, all right," laughed her mother. "You can almost see the hayseed sticking out her ears."

In the end, of course, Connie wore the despised bonnet, but she could not summon up her mother's spirit of adventure. She looked a fright, and she knew it.

At last the day of departure arrived. Mrs. Guion was to take Connie to Charlotte, and Louis was going with them on his way to Chapel Hill. Louis was the first of the twelve Guion children to go to college and the whole family was proud of him.

"I hope you'll be able to play football, son," said his father. "When I was at the University in 1848, we didn't have football."

"I'm afraid I'm too small, Papa. I'm only five feet six."

"But you're still growing," said Mrs. Guion, eyeing his sleeves, which were well above the wrist, and his "high-water" trousers. With his homemade shirt and flat hat, Louis was quite a sight.

Everyone went to the train to see the travelers off. "Honey, don't let them city folks pester you," Elsie said to Connie. "If you don't get enough to eat, Elsie'll send you a fried chicken."

Connie gave her a big hug. "I reckon I'll miss you the most."

"Write us a letter, Con," called Mary Wood. "Soon as you learn how to write, that is."

Connie was just about to step up into the train when Viv slipped a small package into her hand. "Here's somethin' me and Ben made you, Con." She tried to thank him but the words would not come.

Mr. Guion turned to his wife. "I've arranged for the children to have a ride in the red caboose." He looked at Con's and Louis's long faces. "Maybe that will cheer them up."

"All-ll-ll aboard!" called the conductor. "We have to pull out now, Mr. Guion," he added apologetically. Black smoke belched out of the locomotive; the train gave a couple of violent jerks and chugged down the track.

"Good-by, Con!"

"Good-by, Louis!"

"Good-by!" everyone shouted.

Connie sat on the hard plush seat and pressed her forehead against the cold window glass. She looked down at the package in her hand and, for a moment, the lump in her throat dissolved. She tore off the newspaper wrapping and there lay a brand new top. She examined it carefully, then she laughed. Her brothers had driven a brass nail through the center so that in a top-spinning contest no one could split it open. Ben and Viv were sending their sister out into the world well armed.

Connie had been on trains before, because the Guions had a pass on the Seaboard Airline Railroad. Her mother had taken her to Charlotte a number of times to visit "Cousin" Connie Jones, Connie's godmother, for whom she was named. Those trips were fun, but this trip was different. It was wretched.

After the second stop, the conductor took Louis and Connie to ride in the caboose. Even that did not help. Connie felt cooped up in the jolting train and in her itchy city clothes. Wistfully, she looked out the window at the tiny cabins where hound dogs and happy children played together in broom-swept yards. Those children were free and she was not.

As they jiggled along the tracks Mrs. Guion chattered cheerfully. "Isn't North Carolina beautiful? Look at the red earth and the dark green pines. Your ancestors on both sides have been North Carolinians since the seventeenth century, and don't forget it."

Laura met the train in Charlotte. She looked so pretty and

gay, and seemed so glad to see them, that Connie almost did not mind saying good-by to Louis. But the minute they walked into Mrs. Miller's boarding house, her spirits plummeted. To a country girl, the once handsome mansion was cold and forbidding. An elaborate chandelier hung from the high ceiling and the room was filled with stiff, straight-backed leather chairs. A black horsehair sofa stretched across one wall and the whole place smelled faintly of pipe tobacco. Even the red carpet and the big fireplace did not warm up the parlor for Connie. She wished she were back in her own, book-filled living room in Lincolnton.

"And here is Laura's dear little sister," Mrs. Miller gushed.

"What is *that?*" gasped Connie, pointing to a gold-framed tinted photograph mounted on an easel beside the piano. It was a picture of a boy, dressed in a blue velvet Lord Fauntleroy suit, standing beside a billy goat. A full head of long yellow curls hung to the boy's shoulders.

"That is my son, Ambrose," said Mrs. Miller. "Ambrose," she called, "come meet Miss Laura's little sister."

Ambrose appeared in the doorway so quickly that Connie knew he had been hiding behind the green plush curtains. Far from being a baby, he was about a year older than Connie and several inches taller. His golden curls had, fortunately, been cut off, but there was still only one word to describe Ambrose Miller: prissy.

Connie stared and her mother nudged her. She knew she should try to be polite. "Hello," she said, smiling. "My brothers gave me a slick new top. Do you like to spin tops?"

"I prefer Parcheesi," Ambrose sniffed. "Tops are so common."

In that moment the battle line was drawn. Connie never felt sorry for Ambrose again. It was obvious that he was her natural enemy.

When Laura took her little sister upstairs to their room, Connie was surprised to find a tall, dark-haired woman sitting on one of the beds. "Con, this is Miss Laura Little, my roommate," said Laura. "She says she doesn't mind your moving in with us."

Connie looked around the chilly room. There were two cherry beds, two large bureaus and two wash stands with heavy white china bowls and pitchers; beneath each bed was a flowered china chamber pot. "Where do I sleep, Laura?"

"Mrs. Miller is going to put a cot in here for you."

"I trust you will be comfortable," said Miss Little.

I'd be more comfortable in a cow barn than in this stuffy old house, thought Connie.

Mrs. Guion left the next morning. "Work hard, girls," she said. "That's the only way to get where you want to go." Connie nodded. Their mother had shown them by example what she meant by hard work.

Laura took Connie to school the first day. The graded school was in a large red brick building that had once housed the Charlotte Military Academy. To Connie it looked like a prison. The principal told her she had to enter first grade. This hurt, because Connie was four years older than the other first-graders and they already had a head start on her. The teacher, Mrs. Josephine Durant, welcomed the oddly dressed girl with the boy's haircut, but the children snickered at her.

Mrs. Durant went to the blackboard and wrote *cat*. She turned around and said, "Connie Guion, will you tell me all the words you know ending in *at?*" Connie opened her mouth to answer.

"You must learn to stand up when you recite, Connie."

Connie jumped to her feet. Her desk seat banged up behind her and the children laughed. "That fat rat Pat sat at bat," said Connie, glaring. The children laughed again and Connie plopped down behind the little desk that was too small for her. She wished she could disappear.

At last recess came. Connie went out and stood in the schoolyard, first on one foot, then on the other, painfully aware of the way she looked. She wished her mother had not made her promise to wear the velvet bonnet with the silly ruching around her face. Two boys pointed to Connie's plaid coat and fussy bonnet and laughed. This was the last straw. In a flash, she jumped on one of them and knocked him down. Straddling his chest, she beat him with her fists. Mrs. Durant ran out and pulled Connie off the sobbing boy. "You must not do that," she scolded. "It's not nice to fight."

"Yes," said Connie, "and it's not nice to laugh at other people's clothes, either. These are the only clothes I've got and I mean to wear them." After that, no one laughed at Connie Guion.

For Connie, Charlotte was a new and depressing world. The citified boys and girls had no animals; they could not swim; they could not climb trees; they even turned up their noses at Connie's two talents, marble-shooting and top-spinning. They played Parcheesi, dominoes, and games that required quick arithmetic and a knowledge of reading and spelling. Once they discovered Connie's ignorance of these subjects they never missed a chance to embarrass her. Their teasing would have made most girls dissolve into tears. With grim determination Connie set about the task of mastering first grade.

School began each morning with a chapel service in the auditorium. The principal, Mr. Alex Graham, read from the Bible and the children sang Southern songs like "Swanee River," "My Old Kentucky Home," and "Carry Me Back to

Old Virginny." The service closed with a rousing rendition of "Dixie" and the pupils marched to their classrooms.

Connie found Mrs. Durant a strict teacher but a good one. A tiny woman who always dressed in black in memory of her dead husband, she reminded Connie of a blackbird as she darted about the room. Nothing escaped Mrs. Durant. She sensed at once Connie's eagerness to learn and gave her extra lessons. Connie worked with a will, and the harder she worked, the more she liked school.

It was the long afternoons that she dreaded. School was over at two o'clock and Mrs. Miller served dinner at two-thirty. All eleven boarders came home for dinner, so the meal was fairly lively, although Connie detested the boiled food the Millers ate. Connie, Laura and Miss Little were the only girls in the boarding house. The other eight boarders were young men, all of whom, Connie discovered, were in love with Laura. Connie received considerable attention from her sister's suitors and enjoyed the reflected glory.

As soon as dinner ended, everyone went back to work and Connie was left alone in that big parlor. She practiced her writing, studied her multiplication tables, read her dreary little primers, and wallowed in loneliness. She recalled hearing her mother ask an old man who lived alone in a cabin on the plantation, "Don't you get lonesome out here, Uncle Jimson?" And she remembered his answer:

"'Deed I do, Miss Kate, but I *likes* to be lonesome."

Connie was not like Uncle Jimson. She hated to be alone, at least she thought she did, until Mrs. Miller came in to keep her company. Mrs. Miller made loneliness seem attractive. "Did you enjoy living on a farm, Connie?" she would say.

"Yes ma'am."

"Do you miss it?"

"Some."

"What is life like out there?"

"Not bad."

Mrs. Miller eyed Connie's stockinged feet and the high boots beside them. "Why don't you like to wear shoes, Connie?"

"They smell."

"That doesn't sound very lady-like."

"I don't want to be a lady."

There was a short pause while Mrs. Miller regrouped her forces for another attack. "Why don't you play with my son Ambrose, Connie?"

Because you've made such a boob out of him, thought Connie, *fussing over him and feeding him special dishes while the rest of us eat cabbage.*

"I think I'll go see Mr. Fastnot," said Connie. "Maybe he'll let me do some sweeping."

"What do you do with the pennies you earn at Fastnot's Bakery? Save them?"

"Oh, no. I buy tops, lots of tops." This wasn't true. Connie was still using the top her brothers gave her, and none of the Guions ever bought anything they did not have to buy.

"It does seem strange for a girl to be so fond of marbles and tops," Mrs. Miller remarked as she left the room. Connie kicked her shoes across the rug. She wished Laura would come home.

In the evenings the boarding house, like Cinderella's pumpkin, changed miraculously from a dreary prison into a gay house party. The gas lights and the fireplaces burned brightly. The young men played cards and Miss Laura Little played the piano while Laura and her swains waltzed around the living room.

Of Laura's beaus, Connie's favorite was Mr. Carmichael because he liked her the best. He was superintendent of the ice factory and on Saturdays he took Connie to the plant and coached her in arithmetic, spelling and reading. She also learned how ice was made through the evaporation of ammonia gas, her first brush with the wonderful world of science.

Laura was partial to a young man from Columbia, South Carolina, named Alex Haskell, a serious fellow with a long nose and long teeth and a long face, who adored Laura's gaiety. Alex Haskell seemed a little shy to Connie, but she struck up a warm friendship with a handsome young man named Donald Newton. A graduate of the University of Tennessee, he was a great reader. Connie's knowledge of *Ivanhoe* and *David Copperfield* delighted him and the name of his home town delighted her.

"Tell me again where you were born, Mr. Newton."

"Ooltewah, Tennessee. Do you remember how to spell it?"

"O-o-l-t-e-w-a-h. Isn't it funny, I can spell Ooltewah, but I can't spell Charlotte."

"That's because you want to spell Ooltewah, but you don't like Charlotte. You've stumbled on one of the secrets of learning, Connie. 'For where your treasure is, there will your heart be also.' "

"You're quoting Saint Matthew, aren't you?"

"For a little girl who can't read, you do pretty well," laughed Donald Newton.

The men in the boarding house liked to see Connie get the best of the neighborhood boys. When they came home from work they would pool their nickels as a prize for the winner of the next marble game. Then they would stand on the sidelines and goad the big boys because they couldn't beat Con-

nie. With incredible precision she would knock the other marbles out of the ring, and after she won the money, she would
turn around and sell the losers' marbles back to them at a tidy
profit.

Sometimes the boarders would back Connie in top spinning
contests. The idea was to throw your top down onto your op-
ponent's top with one swing. If you hit the right place, you
could split his top wide open and win the game. Connie's
top with the brass nail in the center was unbeatable, and so was
Connie. Nail or no nail, the little girl could out-spin all the
boys on "C" Street, and the men loved to see her do it.

Poor Connie was not only homesick, she was animal-
sick. Mrs. Miller kept no pets, unless you counted her son
Ambrose, and Connie, the country girl, could scarcely endure
her animal-less existence. On Saturday afternoons she would
visit Wadsworth's Livery Stable just to inhale the strong odor
of horse. Once Mr. Wadsworth let her sit on the back of a
horse, which was bliss beyond belief.

One day a new misery descended upon the lonesome little
girl. Laura, whose ambitions for her younger sister were limit-
less, talked Miss Laura Little into giving her piano lessons.
Like her mother, Connie did not have a musical bone in her
body. The lessons were sheer anguish for Connie, who could
hear the boys outside spinning tops, and anguish, too, for Miss
Laura Little, who could hear all the sour notes. Since Miss
Little had no sense of humor, and Connie was usually on the
verge of exploding into laughter, they were seldom in tune,
but the lessons banged on, painful for everyone within earshot.

There were few girls around for Connie to play with, but
she preferred boys anyway. They liked her and she liked
them, all except Ambrose Miller. Walter and Julian Taliaferro,
Hamilton Jones and Willie Myers Jones became Connie's

constant companions. One windy March day they were climbing trees when Ambrose decided to join them. "Why don't you climb up the big oak?" he asked.

"The trunk's too long to shinney up," said Connie.

"*I* can climb that tree," said Ambrose.

"Like to see you do it," said Walter.

"Bet you a nickel you can't," said Connie.

"That's a bet." Ambrose disappeared into the woodshed and came out lugging a ladder.

"Oh, you can't use a ladder," laughed Julian Taliaferro. "Anybody can climb a tree with a *ladder*."

"I never said *how* I'd get up there," sneered Ambrose. "I just said I *could*." Obviously pleased with himself, he placed the ladder against the tree and climbed until he reached the bare branches. Connie and the boys watched, dumb-founded by such underhand play.

"Miss Smarty Guion," called Ambrose, "you owe me a nickel."

Connie's cheeks burned. To be outwitted by Ambrose Miller was unthinkable. Holding one finger against her lips, she pointed to the ladder. Julian winked and tiptoed to the tree. He hoisted the ladder on his shoulder and carted it silently away. The other boys, chuckling, seemed to melt in thin air. Connie headed for the house. In the dark hall she almost ran over Mrs. Miller.

"Connie, do you know where Ambrose is?"

Connie grinned. "Haven't a ghost of a notion."

She hurried to her room, and she had most of her homework finished by the time Ambrose's bellowing reached his mother's ears. Connie stood at the window and watched Mrs. Miller trying to help her son out of the tall tree. "Think I'll skip supper tonight," she said to Laura over her shoulder.

"Why?"

"Oh — I'm not very hungry. Give Ambrose this nickel for me, will you? Tell him I got my money's worth."

Thanks to Mr. Carmichael's tutoring, and Laura's help, Connie easily outstripped the other first-graders. On the last day of school Mrs. Durant announced, "Connie Guion has completed two years' work in one and is promoted to third grade." Connie's joy over her promotion was totally eclipsed, however, by the thought of returning to River Bend Plantation. She could hardly wait to get home.

The next day, May 10, was Confederate Memorial Day and the children marched to the cemetery with flowers to decorate the graves. Then they paraded in the courthouse square and sang Southern songs and listened to speeches lauding the Confederacy. Finally they were dismissed, and that was the end of the school year.

Before she left Charlotte, Connie gave Ambrose Miller something to remember her by. "Ambrose," she said, "I'll bet you don't dare jump off the roof of the woodshed."

"Gracious, that roof must be twelve feet high."

"Sissy, wait 'til I go home and tell my brothers about you."

"I'll do it, if you'll do it, Miss Smarty."

"Come on!" said Connie. In a twinkling she scrambled up on the woodshed roof, and Ambrose pulled himself up behind her. Connie was an old hand at jumping. She and Ben and Viv loved to jump out of the barn loft into the sweet-smelling hay.

Ambrose stood with Connie on the corner of the roof, looking over the edge. It was a long way to the ground. He never would have gone up there if she hadn't been leaving the next day; he could not have her gloating over him all summer.

"You count, Ambrose, one-two-three-go. When you say go, we jump."

Ambrose turned pale.

"Don't forget, I *dared* you."

"All right," he gulped. "One, two three, *go!*"

They jumped. Connie, with the sure instinct of a farm child, jumped straight into a pile of garden manure. It was soft and lumpy and she landed with a plop. If Ambrose had been quick enough to think of jumping into the manure, he never could have done it. It was far too smelly for him. He jumped onto the hard ground and landed with a crack. He screamed.

Mrs. Miller came running out of the house. "Ambrose, my dear, what is the matter!" Ambrose was holding his ankle and wailing. She turned on Connie. "What have you done *now*, you dreadful girl?" She sniffed the air. "And you smell, too. Don't you dare put a foot in my house with manure all over you."

Ambrose Miller had broken his ankle and Connie left for home the next day under a cloud of disapproval. But she did not care a whit. It wasn't her fault Ambrose Miller did not have enough gumption to jump into a manure pile. Gaily she kissed Laura good-by and hopped on the train. The pouring rain didn't dampen her spirit. She was going home.

"Morning, Miss Connie," said the conductor. "Going back to Lincolnton?"

"You bet," crowed Connie. "Ain't this a *grand* day?"

✳ 6 ✳

Wedding Bells

✳✳

THE TRAIN RIDE was a jolly one. It took two hours to go thirty miles because, as Connie told her family, "that durn train halted at every old backyard." Connie knew many of the people who got on and off and she talked to all of them. At last the engine chugged into Lincolnton. The minute Connie saw her mother's face her heart sank. "What's happened, Mama?" she said, hugging her with all her might.

"Oh, Connie, I have so much to tell you. I should have written you, but I've been too busy. I don't know where to begin."

"What is it? Lord's sake, stop talking and tell me!"

"Kate's going to be married to a wonderful man, Papa isn't well and has to stop work for good and," she paused, "we're going to rent the plantation."

"Rent the plantation!" Connie sat down on her suitcase. "Oh, no, you can't. All I've been livin' for is to come back here. We just can't leave now."

"We have to, Con. There're no two ways about it. I can't keep the farm going any longer. We're moving to Charlotte."

Connie could not believe what she heard. "Did you say Charlotte?"

"Yes, Charlotte. We're going as soon as the wedding's over. All except Kate. She's marrying Dr. James Babcock —

he's a grand fellow, Connie, the head of the State Hospital — and they will live in South Carolina."

"We'll all go to Charlotte — the boys, Cousin Alice, Elsie, everybody?"

Her mother nodded. Connie thought for a moment, then she brightened. "That's too many to live at the boarding house, isn't it?"

"Heavens, yes. We'll have to find a house to rent."

"Praise be," said Connie. Then something caught her eye. "There's Kit!" The old mouse-colored mule was harnessed to the shafts of the Studebaker wagon. Connie ran up and hugged her, rubbing the cropped mane that felt as stiff as a brush. "Oh, Kit, I'm glad to see you."

As soon as Connie and her mother drove Kit round the bend in the Big Road, Ben and Viv ran to meet them. "Hey, Con," shouted Viv, "you look like a million!"

Mary Wood and the Light Brigade smothered Connie with their welcome. The minute she could escape, Connie ran up to her room. She unlaced her shoes and kicked them into the air. She took off what Elsie called her "glad rags" and slipped into the patched gingham dress she left hanging in the closet. Then she streaked out into the fields to find Ben and Viv. Now she was really home.

Connie had been away only five months, but in that time her father had turned into an old man. It was not his sixty-six years that weighed on him; it was the hard times. The South was in the grip of a depression. Even Mr. Rhinehart's factory, which was the backbone of Lincolnton, had shut down. Like many other farmers, the Guions simply could not make ends meet. Mrs. Guion managed to rent the plantation for a year to a man named Lackey, which gave them enough money for the move to Charlotte.

The misery of moving away was lessened by the commotion of Kate's wedding. Ef came home from New York, Laura from Charlotte and Louis from the University of North Carolina. Excitement ran high when Kate arrived from Columbia, South Carolina, where she ran a school to train nurses in psychiatric care.

"What's Dr. Babcock like, Kate?" demanded Connie. "Tell us all about him."

Kate's hazel eyes sparkled and she took a deep breath. "Well — he's wonderful. He's a Southerner, of course. He's handsome and shy and smart. He graduated from Exeter and Harvard and Harvard Medical School and now he's an alienist."

"My land," said Mrs. Guion, "what's an alienist?"

"It's what you call a doctor who treats mental illness, Mama."

"Alienist," repeated Connie, trying out the word. "Sounds awful. That's one kind of doctor I don't want to be."

When Connie met her brother-in-law-to-be she liked him at once. Dr. James Babcock was a tall, straight man with big brown eyes, dark skin and a heavy moustache. Connie could have done without the moustache, but the rest of him was fine. He was the kind of man who always had a twinkle in his eye and knew just how to talk to children. He was ill at ease with Kate's many relatives who gathered for the wedding, but the minute he was alone with the children he told them stories and jokes and had a good time.

"Connie," he said, "Kate tells me you want to be a doctor. Do you know what a doctor is?" Connie shook her head. "A person who has inside information. And do you know what a bridegroom is?"

"No."

"Something they use at weddings."

"Oh, Dr. Babcock, you're a caution."

All the Guions — Connie in first row at left

The day before the wedding the Guions posed by the farmyard fence for a family picture, taken by Tom Wetmore, which shows them all together for almost the last time. All the older ones have hats, to mark the importance of the occasion; the six younger ones are barefoot. Dominating the group is Mr. Guion, whose bushy hair and beard make him look like Walt Whitman. On his right is Mrs. Guion in a white shirtwaist, wearing a crocheted cap trimmed with rosettes; on the other side is Ben, gravely holding his fingertips together in imitation of his father. Next to Ben sits Cousin Alice, easily the dressiest one, with her hair done in tight curls and a shiny new straw hat on her lap. Leaning against her is her pet, Viv, tow-headed and mischievous. Louis, now six feet four, is sporting his grandfather Caldwell's watch chain, even though he does not own a watch. He towers over his five sisters: Mary Wood wearing a new hat; Laura, her blond curls aglow; Kate, the bride, whose new dress and earrings set her off from the others; Alice, in her homemade dress, standing next to Ef, who is stylish and slim-waisted in her New York clothes. Seated on the grass are Connie and Ridie and Alex, with identical boy-haircuts, and baby Jo, patting one of Cardell's pups. Jo looks pensive, Ridie wistful, Alex quizzical, but Connie, even at that early age, seems to have a kind of inner peace.

August 17, 1892, was a perfect day for a wedding, warm and sunny, with a slight breeze ruffling the shade trees. Dr. and Mrs. Richardson lent their carriage and horses to take Kate and her parents to the church. The rest of the family piled into the wagon and Kit pulled them to St. Luke's in Lincolnton, where Mr. and Mrs. Guion had been married thirty years before.

It was the first wedding the children had ever seen. The church was crowded with friends who realized the importance of this event in the Guion family. The younger Guions sat in the front row with their mother and Cousin Alice, and the older ones sat in the second row with Elsie and Oaf. Miss Azzie struck up "Here Comes the Bride" on the organ and everyone looked anxiously around. Up the aisle came Kate and her father. Kate, tall, thin and handsome, with an abundance of brown hair at the back of her neck, wore a dress of white "nun's veiling" with a tucked bodice, leg-o'-mutton sleeves, and a long, full skirt. In one hand she carried a homemade bouquet of white snowballs. Her other hand rested lightly on her father's sleeve. Mr. Guion, pale and handsome, had tears in his blue eyes. Kate's leaving would be the first break in the family.

Mr. Wetmore, who had married Mr. and Mrs. Guion and baptized all twelve children, stepped forward in his flowing robes. "Dearly beloved, we are gathered here in the sight of God . . ." The ceremony rolled along smoothly until Mr.

Wetmore said, "Who giveth this woman to be married to this man?"

"I do," said Mr. Guion.

"Mama!" said Connie in a whisper that could be heard all over the church, "Stop him! Don't let him give Kate away!"

"Hush," said her mother, "that's what he's supposed to do."

After the ceremony, everyone went back to River Bend. Mrs. Guion and Elsie and the older girls had prepared a feast for the large gathering — fried chicken and hot biscuits and ice cream and cake. The wedding supper had to be served on boxes and barrels because the family had already started packing for the move to Charlotte.

"My arms still ache from cranking the ice cream freezers," said Ben.

"That's good for your muscles," said Louis, who had grown almost a foot since leaving home and was now a tackle on the University football team.

"Everybody sing," called Cousin Alice, sitting down at the piano. She played "Just a Song at Twilight" and "Genevieve, Sweet Genevieve," and everyone, old and young, sang along with her. As always, she ended with "Onward, Christian Soldiers."

Louis drove up in the Richardson's black and yellow phaeton to take the bride and groom to the railroad station. They were going on a wedding trip through the North before settling down in Columbia, which was to be their new home.

"Come on!" called Louis. "You'll miss your train."

There was a flurry of hugs and kisses and good-bys. "Come to see us, Connie, and we'll talk about medicine," said Dr. Babcock. "Allow me, Mrs. Babcock." He helped Kate into the carriage and off they drove, looking backward and waving.

Connie watched them disappear down the Big Road. "I

don't care *what* Mama says," she muttered. "Papa ought not to go around giving away his daughters."

The wedding over, packing proceeded rapidly. At first the children thought playing among the boxes and barrels was a lark, but as the time neared for them to depart their spirits drooped. It was heart-breaking to leave River Bend Plantation, especially for Connie, who knew too well what life in Charlotte was like. On the last day Connie and Ben and Viv went around the barn saying good-by to all the animals. "Please, can't we take Kit with us?" Connie begged her mother.

"We'll be lucky if all of us can squeeze into that place in Charlotte, let alone a mule."

The family possessions were packed into two big wagons, lent by the neighbors. The children wanted to ride to Charlotte in the wagons, but Mr. Guion put his foot down. "I haven't worked forty years on the railroad for nothing. We will all ride the train and use my free pass."

As the family drove away from River Bend, Connie looked backward. "Promise me we'll come back after Mr. Lackey's year is up, Mama."

Mrs. Guion herself was twisted around, looking. "I can't promise anything, Con."

"One thing about Mama," observed Viv, "she never goes at anything crawfish fashion. She tells you straight out."

"Well, *I'm* coming back," said Connie. "I'm not going to be a prisoner in Charlotte for the rest of my life."

Laura had rented a house for the family on West Fifth Street, near the post office. When Connie and her brothers saw it they were shocked. It looked like a cracker box and the yard seemed non-existent to children used to running and playing in fields. "Gosh," said Viv, "it *is* a prison."

The good neighbors who had driven the wagons stayed and

helped unpack and settle the house. If the house had seemed small at first, after the furniture was in it, it was jam-packed.

Since there was no question of Mr. Guion's being able to work, Alice decided to leave her domestic chores to Mary Wood and go out to look for a job. "But what can you do, Allo?" asked Ben. "Nobody wants to hire a woman, do they?"

"I'll bet I find something."

That night Alice came home triumphant. "I've got it! I'm employed! You'll never guess how I did it!"

"Tell," said Connie. "Tell!"

"I marched into the Western Union office and said to the manager, 'I'm a telegrapher and I'd like to work for you,' and he said, 'So? Where did you learn the trade?' And I said, 'Oh, up at the Lincolnton telegraph station' — I didn't tell him it was in our front hall — and he said, 'If you can send thirty words a minute, I'll hire you.' So I did, and he did, and now I'm a *real* telegrapher. Isn't that amazing?"

But even with Laura's and Alice's weekly checks, and Ef sending every penny she could spare, the Guions were hard pressed. There were nine children living at home, and with Mr. and Mrs. Guion and Cousin Alice and Elsie that meant thirteen mouths to feed, or 273 meals a week.

Connie and Ben and Viv tried to help by going into the poultry business. They scavenged around town until they found enough lumber to build coops for the hens their mother had brought down from Lincolnton. They peddled eggs and chickens and were very proud when they could contribute a dollar to the family budget. They all took their pennies to Laura, the family banker. "Take care of the pennies," Laura would say, "and the dollars will take care of themselves." This was far from the case, but it had a comfortable sound.

One day the Richardson family came for a surprise visit. Hospitality was important to the Guions and when Alice found the cupboard was bare, she took Connie aside. It would be unthinkable not to offer the guests something. "Here, Con, run to the post office and give Laura this note. Hurry."

Connie went to the stamp window and poked the note through to Laura. Laura read it and burst out laughing. "What does it say?" asked Connie.

" 'Send me the jawbone of an ass. The Philistines are upon us,' " read Laura. She pushed a dime over to Connie. "Go buy a soup bone. Allo can feed an army with that." In the Guion family no one wasted time bewailing the lack of funds. They *did* something about it, and with as light a touch as possible.

The Guions soon adapted themselves to their new life. Mary Wood, Ben, Viv, Connie and Alex all went to the graded school but Ridie and Jo were still too young. Connie began to enjoy school, now that she had her family with her. The Charlotte children did not understand the Guions' independence, their boisterous games, or their odd clothes, but they accepted them, all except Ambrose Miller.

One day Mrs. Miller marched in to see Mrs. Guion and said, "Did you know four of your children are walking on the ridge pole of your roof? Ambrose saw them and ran to tell me. It's that girl Connie and her brothers. She always seems to be up on a roof. Do make them come down, before they break their necks."

"Mrs. Miller," said Mrs. Guion, "those children have to learn to walk ridge poles sometime, and they might as well do it now. They won't dare break their necks because I don't allow that. May I pour you a cup of tea?"

Mrs. Miller departed in a huff. That night she said, "Ambrose, I don't want you to play with the Guions, ever. They are much too rough."

"Yes, Mother, they're impossible, aren't they?"

The Guions found many exciting new things in Charlotte, carbon street lights that burned all night, gas lights in the houses, indoor bathrooms, and — wonder of wonders — electric street cars. They walked three miles to the graded school, but if they were lucky enough to encounter a rainstorm they could spend a nickel and ride on the thrilling electric car. Snow, unfortunately, did not have the same effect. In North Carolina, the lightest snowstorm closed the schools and the cars stopped running altogether.

With all the distractions of her new life, Connie did not forget her determination to become a doctor. She seized every opportunity she could find to "practice" medicine. One day her mother said, "Connie, I have a headache. Please take Ridie and Jo outside and amuse them, so I can rest."

"I know a new headache remedy, Mama. You take a large silver spoon and —"

"Thank you, no. I just want to lie down."

Connie did not find it easy to amuse two little girls in the small backyard. She believed in wide open spaces. To make matters worse, part of the yard was fenced off for the chickens.

"Let's play circus," said Ridie.

"How?" demanded Jo.

Connie's imagination took off. "I know! We'll balance the long ladder on top of the chicken fence. You two be trained fox terriers who walk up one side of the ladder, tip it, and go down the other. Hop on your hind legs and hold up your front paws."

"If we're fox terriers, what are you?" asked Ridie.

"Ringmaster. I'll go get my whip." Connie ran into the house and came out wearing her father's high hat and waving a buggy whip. "Ladies and gentlemen! Right this way for the Big Show! See the Tiny Trained Fox Terriers! First up the ladder, Miss Ridie Woof-Woof."

She cracked the whip and Ridie, her hands cupped close to her chest, started up the ladder.

"Bark!" said Connie.

"Bow-wow-wow." Ridie reached the balance point, tipped the ladder, and fell to the ground. She screamed, Jo screamed, and Connie dashed to her side.

"My head, my head! I hit my head!" yelled Ridie.

"I can fix that." Connie ran into the house and came out with a large silver spoon. She put the bowl of the spoon over the goose egg swelling out on Ridie's forehead and pressed as hard as she could.

"Con-Con fix," said Jo. Ridie began to cry again.

Elsie appeared at the kitchen door. "Connie Guion, if you don't stop persecutin' that chile, I'll fetch your mother off her sick bed."

"Elsie, I'm not persecutin' her. I'm doctoring her." Louder screams from Ridie.

"Same thing," said Elsie, slamming the door.

"Some people around here have a lot to learn about medicine," said Connie. "Including me."

✳ 7 ✳

"In My Father's House Are
Many Mansions"

Left foot, right foot,
Hay foot, straw foot,
Paddy's got a cut foot,
Belly full of bean soup — MARCH!

Connie was drilling the Guion Volunteers in the back yard. She snapped to attention as her blond "army" marched by. Cousin Alice stuck her head out the window. "Connie, how many times have I told you never to say 'belly'? Ladies don't have bellies."

"What do they have?"

"Abdomens."

"I can't say 'abdomen full of bean soup.'"

"Don't say anything then. Please remember the word 'belly' is expressly forbidden."

Connie thought for a minute, then she tried again:

Left foot, right foot,
Hay foot, straw foot,
Paddy's got a cut foot,
Bucket full of bean soup — MARCH!

The children stepped briskly about the small yard. "There, that ought to hold them," said Connie.

"Hold what?" asked Alex. "The beans?"

"No. The ladies what haven't got bellies."

More and more Connie was called upon to keep her younger brothers and sisters out of the crowded house because her father was resting. Since leaving Lincolnton, Mr. Guion's health had gone steadily downhill.

There was one thing about Mr. Guion's failing health that particularly upset his wife: he had never been confirmed. A staunch Episcopalian, it distressed her beyond words that her frail husband was not a confirmed member of the church. She kept after him until he said, "All right, Kate, I'll be confirmed — if you can arrange to have it done privately. At the age of sixty-seven, I am not going to stand up there with a lot of little girls in white dresses."

Mrs. Guion lost no time making the arrangements. Bishop Cheshire quickly and quietly conducted a private confirmation, with only the older Guions present. After the service Laura said, "Papa, now that you're a member of the church, will you please stop swearing?"

"Yes," said Mr. Guion, thumping the table, "by God I will."

Nobody liked the crowded house on Fifth Street, and it was a great relief when Mrs. Guion announced one morning at breakfast, "The time has come for us to move out of this house."

"Where can we go, Mama?" asked Ben. Then he added hopefully, "Back to the plantation?"

"No, your father and Laura and I have decided to buy the new house at the corner of Ninth and Brevard Street."

"Buy?" cried Connie, sensing danger. She knew there was only one way her parents could afford to buy anything, and that would be to sell the plantation. "Oh, Mama, you aren't going to sell River Bend, are you?"

"We've already sold it, Con. Mr. Lackey wanted to buy it and we couldn't afford to keep it. It was the only thing to do. River Bend belongs to him now."

"Oh, Mama." Connie's voice was weak with despair.

"Cheer up, Con. With that money, and some help from the Building and Loan, we'll start a new life here in Charlotte in our own house."

"Do you mean we're going to live in that place on Ninth Street, with the dirt yard full of lumber and junk the carpenters left?" asked Mary Wood.

"We'll clean it up," said Mrs. Guion. "Yes, that's the one."

Connie did not say anything at first. She couldn't. She had hated having the Lackeys rent the plantation in the first place; now it was theirs. Mr. Lackey was uneducated and fat and never wore a tie. It did not seem fair for someone like that to own her apple tree and Cousin Alice's hyacinth bed and their dear old house, full of Guion memories.

"Old Kit," she said in a strained voice, "what's going to happen to Rock and Old Kit, Mama?"

"We have to sell them, too, Con. I'll get someone to drive them to Charlotte. Mr. Wadsworth, your friend at the livery stable, thinks we can get a good price for them."

"You *can't* sell Kit and Rock. They're part of the family."

Mrs. Guion fixed Connie with a level gaze. "We need the money, my girl. That's all there is to it."

In September the Guions moved to 313 East Ninth Street. Although the new house was not in Stumptown, the stylish part of Charlotte where Mrs. Guion lived as a girl, it was only a block away from Caldwell Street, named in honor of her father. The house, typical of the 1890's, had a broad porch around three sides, a bay window in the parlor, and a steeple on the roof. It was trimmed with fancy "gingerbread" woodwork and surrounded by an ungraded, unplanted yard. Although it was fairly large, the Guions filled it to overflowing and Connie found it too close for comfort.

"Don't complain," her mother told her. "Why don't you do something about it?"

Connie enjoyed a challenge, but how could she do something about this? It seemed impossible. She turned the idea over in her mind and at last hit upon a plan. She decided to build a room for herself.

"My land," said Mrs. Guion. "Where can you find the space to build a room in this house?"

"At the end of the upstairs hall, over the front door. I'd even have a window. Please let me."

"Go right ahead. If there's anything I enjoy, it's a resourceful child. You'll have to earn the money to buy your materials, of course."

Connie enlisted Ben and Viv, who always responded to her ideas, to help her peddle eggs for the money. When she had saved up a dollar, Connie was ready to start her project. She and Ben and Viv got enough scrap lumber to make a framework. They hammered it into place, and then the boys helped Connie stretch and nail brown sailcloth over it and hang up a brown sailcloth curtain for a door.

"This looks like a real room!" said Viv.

"It's not a room, it's a house. Connie's house," said Ben. And from then on, it was called Connie's House. There was just enough space to hold her bed, desk and dresser. Here Connie slept, studied and amused herself until the family moved away, thirteen years later.

In addition to her "house," Connie had an "office" beneath the front porch. She was a master at inventing games, but her favorite was still "Doctor." Instead of losing interest in it as she grew older, her improvisations became more elaborate. "Doctor" Connie cared for the sick, whether they were "stick horses," dogs, chickens, dolls or baby sisters, dispensing imaginary potions of every drug she had ever heard of; quinine, whisky, calomel, salts, and goose grease.

Gradually, the Guions got their new house in shape, but the yard remained a mess. Whenever it rained, a torrent of water poured off the neighbor's lot and washed away their soil. To remedy this, Mr. Guion invented a family engineering project; many wagonloads of red dirt were dumped in the street and the children had to cart it in wheelbarrows to the yard. "We'll make our place higher than theirs," he said. "Then the water will run the other way." This turned out to be impossible. "What we need," announced Mr. Guion, "is a drain to carry the water out to the street." The children groaned. They knew who would be expected to put in the drain.

Ben and Viv dug the trench and Connie and Mary Wood helped lay the brick. Much to their surprise, the homemade drain worked. Next, Mr. Guion had them haul topsoil into the yard and plant rye, in preparation for grass. Cousin Alice planted roses and white jasmine around the house and Mrs. Guion put in hyacinth bulbs, to bloom the following spring. Cousin Alice, as usual, knew a poem to suit the occasion:

> *If of thy store there be*
> *Left but two loaves for thee,*
> *Sell one, and with the dole*
> *Buy hyacinths to feed thy soul.*

Mrs. Guion installed one improvement which Connie hated. She built a lye hopper to make soap. "Gee whilligers," said Connie, "how will I ever collect enough Octagon soap wrappers for a watch? Why can't we *buy* soap, like other people?"

"There are three things I cannot live without," said her mother. "A woodshed, a workshop, and a lye hopper. Get Cousin Connie to save her soap wrappers for you."

"She is, so are all the neighbors, but I need two hundred. At this rate, I'll be ninety years old before I own a watch."

"Maybe you're better off if you don't know the time," laughed Mrs. Guion. "Time is like money, Con. The less you have, the further you can make it go."

Despite all the improvements in the house on Ninth Street, the tang of autumn made Connie yearn for the free life of the farm. She remembered the thrill of rabbit-hunting with her brothers through woods turning bright with frost. After the leaves fell you could stand on the front porch and see the bend in the river, and from the backyard you could even see the other bend. You couldn't see them at all in summer.

Connie still cherished the hope that some miracle would take them all back to River Bend. To ease her longing, she visited Rock and Old Kit in Mr. Wadsworth's stable. She fed them apples and sugar and they nuzzled her open palm.

Then one day Ben said, "I wouldn't go over to Wadsworth's today, Con. They had an auction there yesterday."

"Oh, Ben, he didn't sell Rock and Kit?"

"Yes, he did, but don't feel too bad. He got a hundred dollars for each one. Whoever bought them must know they're valuable and will take good care of them. We need the money, Con, with Papa not well and . . ."

Connie wasn't even listening. Rock and Kit were gone! That brought home one terrible fact: her dream of returning to River Bend was dashed to bits. The happy plantation days were gone forever. She trudged upstairs to her brown sailcloth house. She was glad she had somewhere to go.

Connie could not understand how her father adjusted so easily to the loss of the plantation, for she knew he loved the outdoor life. The truth was that Benjamin Guion was worn out. But he had long cultivated the art of leisure and he was content to sit by the fire and read novels or history or poetry. Sometimes he just sat and chewed a plug of tobacco. He never smoked, but he enjoyed the then popular habit of chewing and his children scrambled to collect the colorful tin tags from his tobacco plugs.

Mr. Guion's greatest pleasure was Louis's success on the University of North Carolina football team. Louis was no great shakes as a student, but as a tackle he was hard to beat. "My boy Louis is making football history," Mr. Guion would tell people. "His team beat Auburn 64-0, Vanderbilt 24-0, and Virginia 26-0. With Louis in the line, the enemy never gets to score. Louis loves the University as much as I did. It's been forty-five years since I graduated but I still dream about Chapel Hill."

That fall Louis's team was scheduled to play Rutgers at New Brunswick, New Jersey. Few, if any, Southern football teams made forays that far north in 1893, so the game took on the aspect of a battle between the States. All North Carolinians were excited about it. Then a shocking thing happened: Louis appeared at home.

"Louis Guion," demanded his father, "what are you doing here? Why aren't you practicing for the Rutgers game?"

"Got a boil on my bottom, Papa."

"Oh my God! *Kate!*" Mr. Guion bellowed for his wife. "Come quick and repair Louis's bottom." Mr. Guion firmly believed his wife could do anything.

"Con-Con fix," said Jo, and Connie did fix Louis's boil. She treated it day and night with a bread poultice — bread soaked in hot water and wrapped in cloth — and with mustard plaster. When the boil finally came to a head, Connie experienced for the first time the satisfaction of making a patient comfortable. It was a good feeling.

Louis rejoined his team in time for the Rutgers game. Ef and Alice traveled to New Jersey to see him play, and the rest of the family longed to go, too. North Carolina won, to the glory and wonder of the South. Connie joined with gusto in the Charlotte celebration. She felt that she had a share in the victory.

Mrs. Guion was happy in her new house with the lye hopper and back porch workshop, but she still lacked a woodshed. "If you want a woodshed, Kate, you shall have one," said her husband. "We'll build it near the street so the wood can be dumped right into it."

"Oh, Mr. Guion, please don't worry your head about that. All I *really* need to make me happy is for you to keep well." Kate Guion knew her husband was incapable of letting a construction job go on without his supervision, and she also knew he was not up to that now.

"Nonsense. I'm feeling better all the time. We must begin building the woodshed at once, before winter is upon us."

Just as his wife had feared, Mr. Guion spent many hours out in the damp autumn air, directing the workmen. The October winds and rain grew cold, but he insisted on going out. "I'll only be a few minutes, Kate. I want to look over the job."

"Oh, Marse Ben," begged Elsie, "don't go out there. I saw the new moon over my right shoulder last night and you know that's bad luck. You jus' stay in here by the fire, Marse Ben." Mr. Guion had bought Elsie at a slave auction forty years before, and though slavery had ended, the bond between the two of them had grown stronger with the passing years.

"Why, Elsie," laughed Mr. Guion, "I saw the same moon over my *left* shoulder. I reckon my good luck will cancel out your bad luck."

Moon or no moon, Mr. Guion did catch cold. Dr. Mc-Combs put him to bed at once and called in Dr. Brevard. Dr. Parks McCombs, who was the foremost doctor in Charlotte, was the Guions' dear friend. Years before, when Mrs. Guion was a little girl, he had studied medicine with her father, Dr. Pinckney Colesworth Caldwell, and he had great loyalty and devotion for Kate Caldwell Guion and all her family.

Dr. McCombs examined Mr. Guion carefully. Then he said, "I'd like a word with you in the parlor, Miss Kate."

"It's pneumonia, isn't it, Dr. McCombs?" said Mrs. Guion, when they were alone.

"Yes. He's very ill. I think you'd better send for Ef to come home from New York and nurse him. Keep him swathed in flaxseed poultices, with hot bricks at his feet, and give him whisky and quinine every two hours. We must do all we can."

Connie stood in the drafty hall, listening. She fingered the "O.H.M. Whisky" knife in her pocket and tried to think how she could help. Then she put on her coat and hat and went out into the gray November twilight. She knew just where to find the low wintergreen bushes with the spicy red berries. With her knife, she cut off the aromatic leaves and hurried home. "Here," she said to her mother, "stew these up for Papa."

"Why, Connie, thank you. I will." Connie had seen her mother cook up wintergreen leaves on the plantation. They made a strong solution of sodium salicylate that relieved aches and pains. Neither Connie nor Mrs. Guion had any idea this common remedy would one day be used in aspirin.

When Ef returned to Charlotte, Dr. McCombs drove to the station to meet her with his beautiful horse and buggy. He had been fond of Ef since she was a little girl, but when he saw the small, determined young woman step off the train, he was almost bowled over.

"My word, Effie, you've grown into a handsome young lady."

"Thank you, Uncle Parks. How is my Papa?"

"Very sick. I'm afraid it will take all the new things you have learned at St. Luke's to help him. At sixty-seven, pneumonia is critical."

Even with Ef's nursing and Dr. McComb's skillful care, Mr. Guion grew worse. As his breathing became more difficult, the boys made a backrest to try to relieve it. His devoted friend Elsie Guion sat in a rocker by the bed day and night fanning and crooning to him.

When Louis and Kate were sent for, everyone knew the end was near. On the ninth day of his illness, all twelve children were called to their father's bedside. Connie looked at him and was surprised he had changed so little. Even in illness he was handsome, with his wavy hair and beard, his expressive brown eyes and fine features. But the eyes that always held a twinkle looked sadly at the children. He said nothing.

In the morning, Mrs. Guion told them their father had died at daybreak. It was November 9, 1893.

To the older children, the father's death was a grievous blow. To Connie and the younger ones it brought more mystery than sorrow. He had been away from home so much they hardly knew his gentle charm. But they always remembered how he and their mother used to enjoy themselves talking and laughing and reading aloud.

On the day of their father's death the children hardly saw

their mother at all. She would come out of the bedroom going very fast, so they could not tell she had been crying. The
house was strangely silent. Neighbors came and went quietly,
bringing food and murmuring words of comfort. The undertaker, Mr. Harry, arrived with the wooden coffin. Mrs. Guion
and the girls put on the black dresses and black veils of deep
mourning. The girls began wearing colors again the following
summer, but Mrs. Guion wore her widow's veil the rest of
her long life.

Mr. Guion was buried on Friday. Elsie said it was bad
luck to begin anything on Friday, but Mrs. Guion said they
weren't beginning something — they were ending it. When
it was time for the funeral, Connie drove the three younger
children to St. Peter's Church in Cousin Connie Jones's cart.
They associated the pony cart with happy times and it was
hard to realize they were now riding in it to their father's
funeral.

As the ancient words of the burial service from the Book
of Common Prayer flowed over Connie, one part stayed in
her mind: "In my Father's house are many mansions: if it
were not so, I would have told you. I go to prepare a place
for you . . . that where I am, there may you be also."

It made her feel, somehow, closer to her father than ever before.

✳ 8 ✳

If You Can't Pay For It, You Don't Need It

MANY sad adjustments had to be made by the family after Mr. Guion's death, but the worst one was Louis's leaving college. After Louis finished the fall term, he came home and went to work in Lidell's Foundry, making machinery for cotton mills. He earned only a few dollars a week but the experience proved invaluable, as he and his younger brothers later went into the cotton mill business.

When people asked Mrs. Guion how she made her children work so hard she said, "I don't make them. They just know if we don't work, we'll starve." Her motto was "If you can't pay for it, you don't need it," and the family lived by it.

Soon after "Marse Ben" died, Elsie departed. "I hanker to stay with you all, Miss Kate," she said, "but I got to go where they needs me most. Mister Farr, his wife up and died in chilebirth, and I got to bring up his chilluns."

There was much wailing and hugging and kissing when Elsie left, even though she was going to work only a few blocks away. "First Papa dies," moaned Ridie, "then Elsie goes. Who's gonna be next?"

Thrifty as they were, it never occurred to the Guions to go without help. Everybody in Charlotte had a "washerwoman" who fetched the laundry on Monday and brought it back at the end of the week. Washerwomen were paid a dollar a week and even the Guions could afford that. Most families had a cook as well.

The Guions' new cook was a tall, thin woman named Annie. The day she arrived, Connie, Ridie, Jo and Alex tiptoed into the kitchen to get a look at her. She was standing by the big wood-burning stove, stirring a pot of soup, wearing a long blue dress, a white apron, and a red bandana around her head. Without turning around she said in a low voice, "You wormy rascals, get out of here." They got. For the next ten years Annie ruled the Guion kitchen with an iron hand, and the whole family loved her.

Annie and Connie were two of a kind, both full of energy and ideas.

"Now, Missy," said Annie. "I'm goin' to teach you to be a sure 'nuff cook." Connie spent many hours in Annie's self-styled cooking school. She enjoyed measuring and mixing and baking. "It's almost like science, isn't it Annie?"

"I don't know nothin' about science, honey, but someday you'll be powerful glad old Annie taught you to bake a honey cake."

"Annie, let's make a four-layer chocolate cake for the Mecklenburg picnic."

"I'll make the cake if you'll explain to me 'bout them Mecklenburgs. I like the parade, but what it's all about is a mystery to me."

Annie wasn't the only one who did not understand the misty origins of Mecklenburg Independence Day. North Carolinians refused to recognize the Fourth of July; they celebrated instead May 20. On that date in 1775, a group of citizens in Mecklenburg County, North Carolina, declared their independence from England, preceding the Declaration of Independence by more than a year. Every May 20 in

Charlotte scaffolding was erected in Mecklenburg Square and decorated with red, white and blue bunting. The band played and important men made speeches about North Carolina's always leading the way. Children in colonial costumes marched past while the crowd sang "Dixie," and in the afternoon everybody had a picnic.

The Guions always had their picnic at a cousin's farm which, happily, was located at the end of the electric street car line. This meant they could all climb aboard the magical dark red car and enjoy a long ride out into the country on the slippery straw seats. The sides of the street car would be off for summer and young men would hang on the outside, with the breeze blowing in and the motorman clanging the bell with his foot. Connie would sniff the warm air and gaze at the open fields. School was over and the long summer days stretched ahead in endless delight.

She was thinking about her chocolate cake in the picnic hamper when her mother broke in with an abrupt question. "Con, how would you like to take a trip?"

"Oh, Mama! Could I?" She longed to see the whole world and everything in it.

"The Babcocks want you to come to Columbia and visit them. I think you could be a help to Kate."

"You mean I'd go to another state? What's South Carolina like, Mama?"

"Like North Carolina, only more so."

When Connie saw Columbia, South Carolina, she was disappointed. "I declare," she said to Dr. Babcock, who met her at the station, "you got sand streets down here! In Charlotte our streets are paved."

Dr. Babcock threw back his head and laughed. He found his little sister-in-law endlessly amusing. "Now don't make fun of us, Con, just because we're sand-lappers."

"Sand-lappers," Connie laughed. "What a wonderful word."

Dr. Babcock was proud to be the superintendent of South Carolina's State Hospital for the Insane. "Except for Bellevue in New York," he told her, "this is the oldest mental hospital in the country."

Connie looked at the vacant-eyed men and women, dressed in shapeless blue demin, who stood about the yard or sat on the wooden benches. "Are those your patients?"

"Some of them, the chronic cases. We have to lock up the violent ones."

"Do any of them get well?"

"A few. For most of them it's hopeless."

As they climbed up the circular stairway to the Babcocks' apartment on the second floor of the asylum, Connie stopped and pointed. "Why are those oars up there?"

"They're souvenirs of my rowing days at Harvard. I put them up to remind me of happy hours on the Charles River when my biggest problem was winning the next race."

Kate ran out and hugged Connie; the sisters were over-joyed to see each other. Kate looked thinner and a little tired. "Have you turned into a sand-lapper, Kate?"

"Indeed I have. I love South Carolina almost as much as Dr. Babcock does."

Connie looked around the apartment in amazement. She had never seen a place filled with so many things — old furniture, old books, mugs, pitchers, antique silver. Kate smiled, "Dr. Babcock's a born collector, you know. If you marry a collector, there's nothing to do but relax and enjoy it. They can't help themselves."

Dr. Babcock was also a natural teacher. He gave Connie a big stamp book and started her on a lifelong hobby of collect-ing stamps. He taught her many things about old silver and antique furniture and medicine. In Connie, Dr. Babcock found an eager mind that soaked up information as quickly as a sponge does water. He became to her part brother, part father and part teacher, and she adored him.

James Babcock was, by any standards, an unusual man. When he wasn't caring for patients, he sat in his wingback chair and read, wearing eye glasses which he bought by the dozen at the five-and-ten-cent store. He read everything, and — thanks to a photographic memory — forgot nothing. Sometimes he would jump up from studying the writings of a young doctor named Sigmund Freud and go out to talk with a patient. He never stopped trying to unlock the mysteries of personality, and he was far ahead of his time in understanding Freud's revolutionary ideas.

Connie often went with Dr. Babcock on hospital rounds and although she was only twelve, she could tell he was a good alienist. He was interested in every detail of his patients' lives. He treated them as normal people and listened carefully to their stories, no matter how fantastic, always trying to give them some feeling of reality. Dr. Babcock told Connie, "Look your patient right in the eye and listen to every word he says. If you *really* listen, you'll find he's telling you more than he himself realizes."

Although Connie was fascinated by Dr. Babcock, psychiatry did not appeal to her. She thought the greatest satisfaction in medicine would be helping people to get well, and in the 1890's caring for mental patients was more custodial than anything else. Few of Dr. Babcock's patients ever left the hospital, and those who did often had to return.

One of Dr. Babcock's pleasures was reading aloud and he often read to Connie and the children of his asylum helpers. His favorite author was Rudyard Kipling and Connie loved to hear him read from the *Just So Stories* about the great gray-green greasy Limpopo River and the cat who walked by his wild lone in the Wet Wild Woods.

One day he said, "Connie, here's a poem about psychiatry:

> *The Camel's hump is an ugly lump*
> *Which well you may see at the Zoo*
> *But uglier yet is the Hump we get*
> *From having too little to do.*

"What does that have to do with psychiatry?"

"People who have nothing to do spend their time thinking about themselves, and if they concentrate on themselves long enough and hard enough, before long they'll need a psychiatrist."

Connie returned to Charlotte bursting with news of the Babcocks, but to her surprise the day she got home the family was too excited to listen to her.

"Wait 'til you see what we've got, Con!" yelled Viv.

"You turn the crank and it goes ding, ding," said Ridie.

"What is it?" demanded Connie.

"Our *telephone!*" they shouted.

"Telephone?" Connie turned to her mother. "I thought you said if we can't pay for it, we don't need it."

"The phone's not expensive, Con. It's only a local line. The boys need it to get their odd jobs, and Laura and Alice use it a lot, too."

Connie followed her excited family into the back hall to look at the wonderful new instrument. It was a golden-oak telephone, fastened to the wall, with a shelf at the bottom for pad and pencil. "Wait till I write Dr. Babcock! How do you work it?"

"Sit on the stool," said Louis. "Turn the crank and when central answers, just tell her the number."

Connie was about to make her first, historic phone call when the doorbell rang and in walked an old friend from Lincolnton, Miss Christine Tethero. Miss Christine was a tiny woman, all sunburned and wrinkled, who might have been only eighty, but who looked a hundred years old. To Connie's dismay, the family insisted Miss Christine make *her* first phone call. Reluctantly, Connie stepped aside. But, alas, Miss Christine could not telephone after all. She was too short to reach the crank. Everyone talked at once, telling her what to do. Finally, Connie and the boys helped the tiny old lady up on the stool. Now Miss Christine could reach the phone, but there was another, greater problem. Whom should she call? What should she say?

"Call Laura at the post office," suggested Mrs. Guion. "Her number is 14."

When Laura's cheery voice came over the wire, Miss Christine was thunderstruck. She took down the receiver from her ear and looked into it. "That's you, Laura, is it?"

"I can't hear you, Miss Christine. Say something."

Miss Christine looked around at the family, stricken. Clearly she was trying to think of something of importance to say, something suitable for her first telephone conversation. Then her face lit up. She had it! "Laura," shouted Miss Christine triumphantly, "that's really you? Is it Laura?"

The family collapsed into gales of laughter. They helped Miss Christine down from her perch and gave her a glass of port to steady her nerves. By the time Connie got to the phone to make her first call, it was an anticlimax, thanks to the commotion generated by Miss Christine Tethero.

Connie had several opportunities to practice medicine that summer. First Alex got typhoid fever from eating a hokey-pokey block, as ice cream on a stick was called, which he bought from a man who wheeled a tin container around town. The typhoid fever epidemic that swept Charlotte was traced to that man's poorly refrigerated hokey-pokeys. When Alex's fever reached 104, Dr. McCombs said, "Send for Ef." He told Mrs. Guion to give Alex ice water baths and she sent Louis and Connie to Mr. Carmichael's ice house for a hundred-pound block of ice. They chopped it up in the tub, poured water over it, and then lifted Alex in. He yelled bloody murder, but his fever came down.

"It's hard to treat a patient rough, Con," said her mother, "but sometimes it's the only way."

Mrs. Guion and Cousin Alice took Alex to the mountains to recuperate and the younger children went along, too, leaving Connie to keep house for Ben and Viv and Louis. Laura had gone to Wrightsville Beach for her vacation and Annie was away at camp meeting. Connie was enjoying her independence when, without warning, Laura suddenly reappeared.

"Laura, what's the matter?"

"I'm sick, Connie. I could hardly make it home. Help me to bed."

Connie cranked the phone and called Dr. McCombs again. He examined Laura and said, "Typhoid fever. Your mother and the younger children must be kept away. Send for Ef."

"Dr. McCombs never misses a chance to send for Ef," Connie told Viv. "I'm beginning to think he's sweet on her."

"Ho," laughed Viv. "An old man like that. I'll bet he's thirty years older than Ef."

"Men are queer, and old men are the queerest of all."

"Keep talking that way, missy, and you'll end up an old maid."

"Maybe I want to be an old maid. Dr. Babcock says marriage is an institution based on love and love is blind, and therefore marriage is an institution for the blind."

Connie nursed Laura until Ef got home; she gave her sponge baths and brought her the bedpan and fixed her meals. Although she was worried to death about Laura, she enjoyed being a nurse. She gave Laura only pap to eat, as the doctor directed — oatmeal, mashed potatoes and custard — but when she raised her big blue eyes and whispered, "Oh, Con, I do want a bite of raw sweet potato," it was more than the young nurse could stand. She went right out in the garden and dug up a sweet potato for Laura. Afterward Connie felt awful because she knew she had done the wrong thing — chewing on a raw potato could kill Laura. Connie worried herself sick until she discovered Laura had not eaten the sweet potato. She had thought better of it and put it under her mattress to keep from hurting Connie's feelings. "From now on," Connie said, "I'm going to be tougher with my patients. As Mama says, sometimes it's the only way."

Connie sat down on her bed and counted the Octagon soap wrappers once more. "A hundred and ninety-eight, a hundred and ninety-nine, *two hundred!* I've got it! I've got it!" She reached under her pillow and pulled out a well-thumbed picture catalogue. She flipped past pages of bicycles (four thousand coupons — she'd never be able to own a bike), celluloid dresser sets, and black Bibles, to the page of watches. There it was, her watch: *Silver watch with hinged cover, two hundred coupons.* Carefully she cut out the order blank, filled in her name and address, and attached it to the coupons she had cut off the soap wrappers. She ran all the way to the post office.

A month went by but no package came in the mail. William Jennings Bryan, the young congressman from Illinois who was running for President, came to Charlotte to speak.

Everybody was excited to have such a famous man come to town. Everybody, except Connie. By now, all she could think about was that watch.

"Mr. Bryan is going to speak in the post office yard," Laura said at breakfast. "I know you're too busy to go, Mama, but you can hear him over the telephone."

"Think of that. I can sit at home and listen to the 'Peerless Leader of the Democratic Party' talking way downtown." Even though women were not allowed to vote, Mrs. Guion was an enthusiastic Democrat and Bryan, who was running against William McKinley, was her candidate.

Connie stood in the crowd and tried to listen as Mr. Bryan's rich voice rolled on and on, but she had no idea what he was talking about. As soon as he finished, she ran inside the post office to Laura's window.

"What do you think of Mr. Bryan?" asked Laura.

"Smooth talker but awful sissy looking. Laura, hasn't my watch come? Please look again."

"Sorry, Con. No sign of it."

"Maybe the Octagon soap people have gone out of business, and I'll never get my watch."

Connie's patience had long since run out. She was so obsessed that the family began to tease her. "Hey, Con," Viv would say, grinning, "could you please tell me the time?"

"I wouldn't give you the time of day even if I had it, Vivian Guion."

And then one Saturday evening Laura came home from work with a small brown parcel tucked in her purse. "Something in the mail for you, Connie," she called. "Wonder what it is."

"Yip-pee!" Connie ripped off the paper and held up a man's pocket watch, the size of a small alarm clock. "Oh,

Lordy, isn't it beautiful! Lookit! The front cover opens up and so does the back. This little key's the winder, and this one's the setter."

"Looks like a man's watch to me," said Mary Wood. "How will you ever wear it?"

Connie glared at her. "I shall simply put a shoestring through the handle and tie it to whatever part of my anatomy is available."

The next morning the Guions marched as usual in a body to St. Peter's Episcopal Church, a large red brick building with small stained glass windows, a wine-colored carpet, and heavy oak pews. The atmosphere was lugubrious; even the minister was dreary. Listening to his droning voice, Connie wished he would be made a bishop.

That Sunday Connie wore her usual white shirtwaist and black broadcloth skirt, but suspended from her patent leather belt, on a black shoestring, was the watch. She felt as though she were wearing a diamond necklace. The family filed into their two customary pews and Connie sat between her mother and Viv. The choir marched in, led by Cousin Connie; when their singing stopped, the church was silent. Silent, except for the *clang, clang, clang,* of Connie's watch. The people in front of the Guions turned around to see where the noise was coming from. Connie stared straight ahead. *Clang, clang,* went the watch.

"Connie," whispered Viv, "take off that watch, it's a disgrace. You can hear it all over the church."

Connie shook her head.

"Mama," said Viv, louder, "make her stop wearing that town clock."

"That's Connie's business and none of yours."

"Let us pray," said the minister.

On her knees, Connie held the watch in the palm of her

hand. *Clang, clang, clang.* Viv groaned. When they got up Viv said, out loud this time, "Mama, I can't sit here and listen to her clank."

"Maybe you'd better move, Connie," whispered her mother. "Viv is making such a fuss I can't worship the Lord."

Connie rose and walked to the back of the church, clanking as she went. Every eye was on her. People simply did not get up and move around in St. Peter's. Connie's face was bright red, but her step was resolute. She settled down in the last pew, alone with her thoughts and her Octagon soap watch. *I know the Lord likes my watch, even if Viv don't,* she thought. After that Connie wore her beloved watch every day of the week, except between nine and noon on Sundays.

A few weeks later when Connie came home from school, with her new watch dangling from her belt, she was met by Dr. McCombs. He took her hand in his and told her that her mother was very sick. Fear gripped Connie's heart. Her mother was never sick. Other people might get sick, but not her mother.

Dr. McCombs said Mrs. Guion had erysipelas, a serious skin infection, on her face and scalp. As usual in a crisis, he recommended sending for Ef. "This disease is contagious," he said, "but I don't think it's fatal."

Fatal! The very word terrified the children. They had seen their mother sick in bed only once, long ago, when she had typhoid. Having babies, of course, didn't count. To make matters worse, Dr. McCombs would not let any of them go near her; they could only stand at her door for a minute. One evening when they came to say good night they got a fearful shock. The doctor had ordered all of Mrs. Guion's coal black hair shaved off. The sight of their mother's bare head, covered with black salve, was heartbreaking.

Connie went to Dr. McCombs and begged him to tell her

something she could do to help her mother. Dr. McCombs had little time for children's questions. "Oh, she'll get well," he chuckled. "Just feed her chicken brains."

This prescription did not seem odd to Connie. Goose grease was used for mumps and mustard plaster for asthma, why not chicken brains for erysipelas? Resolutely, she went from house to house, collecting chicken heads. When she got home she sat down and dissected out the tiny brains with her O.H.M. Whisky knife. Then she gave them to Annie, who cooked them for her mother.

Eventually, Mrs. Guion recovered from her illness, but it left its mark, for when her hair grew in again it was pure white. At first Connie proudly took some of the credit for her mother's cure, until one day she discovered Dr. McCombs had been joking with her. Although her mother had eaten the hard-earned chicken brains, they were useless. Connie was furious.

"Don't be too hard on Uncle Parks," said Mrs. Guion. "He doesn't understand children."

"And I don't understand him. Remember that time I swallowed my tooth and imagined it was stuck in my throat? I told Uncle Parks about it, and he laughed. But when I told Dr. Brevard, he swabbed out my throat and I felt better."

Mrs. Guion nodded. "My father was like that. When I was a little girl, an old man kept coming to him and saying he had bullfrogs in his stomach — he could hear them every time he belched — and he wanted to get rid of them."

"What did Grandfather do? I bet he didn't laugh."

"No, he didn't. He told the old man to come back in a week. Then he sent one of his slaves down to the pond to collect bullfrogs, and the next time the old man came, my father said, 'Today we're going to get rid of those bullfrogs in your stomach.' Papa gave him a big dose of ipecac to make him throw up and every time the old man gagged, Papa slipped another bullfrog into the slop bucket. By the time the poor fellow finished vomiting, he was cured."

Connie clapped her hands. "I want to be a doctor just like Grandfather."

Each summer Connie's best friend, Rosa Bland, came up from Georgia to live with the Guions. Rosa's mother was dead and she lived with her aunt, but during the summer vacation she came to Charlotte to be near her father. One June evening when they were all sitting on the front porch Dr. Bland said, "Connie, have you ever seen the ocean?"

"No, sir, but Papa used to talk about it. He loved the ocean."

"How would you like to go with Rosa and me to Wrightsville Beach?"

"Oh, Mama, *could* I?"

Mrs. Guion frowned. "We don't have a pass on the railroad any more, Con, and that's a long trip."

"But Miss Kate," said the doctor, "I want Connie to go as my guest."

"I'm afraid you do too much for us, Dr. Bland."

"Nonsense. It's not a patch on what you do for us, taking Rosa into your family. Pack your duds, girls. We're off to the beach tomorrow."

Traveling to Wrightsville Beach on the Seaboard Airline Railroad was, in itself, an adventure. Dr. Bland and the girls got on the train early in the morning and rode all day. Because dining cars were unheard of, they took along a box lunch. When evening came, the train stopped at Hamlet, North Carolina, to change engines and everyone — passengers and crew alike — piled into Gresham's Eating House for dinner.

Connie had never eaten in a restaurant before and the

menu dazzled her. "Order anything you like, girls," said Dr. Bland.

"I'll have fried chicken and mashed potatoes and strawberry shortcake," said Connie promptly.

It was almost midnight when they reached Wrightsville Beach, but Connie was too excited to sleep. As soon as daylight streaked the sky she woke Rosa. "Come on! I've got to see the ocean." The two girls dressed quickly, tiptoed out of the silent hotel, and raced, barefoot, down to the beach. Ahead of them, the sun was slowly rising out of the ocean like a red balloon. The tide was high and the blue waves rolled in, one after another, rising in a high crest and suddenly descending with such force they shook the ground. Then, rapidly receding, they left white foam, sea shells and starfish behind them.

"It's the mightiest sight I've ever seen," gasped Connie.

"Run with me to meet your new friend," cried Rosa. "He'll never fail to come to meet you." She took Connie by the hand and they ran toward the incoming waves.

"Young ladies! Young ladies!" yelled a voice. "Don't go any nearer!" The night clerk was running after them. "The ocean is full of danger." The girls laughed at his fearfulness, but they returned with him to the hotel for breakfast. Neither of them ever forgot how the ocean looked that summer morning when they had it all to themselves.

Connie returned to Charlotte with a bag full of sea shells, a sunburned nose, and a lifelong love of the sea. "The big old ocean's my never-failing friend," she told her mother. "He always comes to meet me."

People were always giving the Guions practical things, but it was Dr. Bland who gave Connie the surprise of her life. He appeared at the house one morning pushing two new Waverley bicycles, one for Rosa and one for Connie. "Here you are, girls — your own runabouts."

Connie and Rosa with their bicycles

Connie could not believe her eyes. All her life she had longed for a bicycle and now she was to have one of her very own, a new one at that. Carefully she inspected the shiny, black bike. It had a brown leather seat and pneumatic tires and a wicker basket and a bell, and was easily the most beautiful thing Connie had ever seen.

"It's all yours, Connie," said Dr. Bland. "Do you think you can learn to ride it?"

"Can I!" Connie hopped on the wonderful Waverley and

sailed down the street. She had been practicing on other people's bikes for years.

Overnight Connie became her mother's self-appointed
"runner." No errand was too much trouble for her, as long as
she could do it on her bike. One day she pedaled across town
to take flowers to a Negro funeral; the next day she carried
home an eighteen-pound live turkey on the handlebars. The
greater the challenge, the better she liked it.

When Connie and Rosa went riding together they dressed
alike in costumes provided by Dr. Bland: flat-topped sailor hats,
long-sleeved white blouses, black skirts and wide belts fastened by monogrammed silver buckles. They learned to do
tricks on their bikes, to ride without hands and to stand on
the seats. Sometimes they went bicycling until after dark
and when Connie got home, even though she was now fourteen, she got a "licking" from her mother. She couldn't have
cared less. Connie was still spinning along in the wonderful
world of the Waverley bike.

✳ 9 ✳

Miss Shipp's School

ONE OF the delights of living in Charlotte was the daily newspaper. The Guions never had one before and they could not
get over it. Early each morning the *Charlotte Observer* was
delivered to their house on Ninth Street. Whoever brought
it in called out the headlines to the rest of the family.

On the morning of February 16, 1898, it was Connie who
carried in the paper. The big black headlines jolted her:
U.S.S. MAINE BLOWN UP IN HAVANA HARBOR. DANGER OF
WAR BETWEEN U.S. AND SPAIN.

"War!" yelled Connie. "Paper says war! We're gonna fight
the Spanish."

Two months later, the Spanish-American War began. President McKinley had hoped to avoid it, but the American people
demanded a free Cuba, and Congress mobilized the Army and
Navy to drive the Spanish off the island.

At first the war seemed far away from the Guion family.
Then a letter came from Ef that put them into the thick
of it. She had volunteered as a Navy nurse and was sailing
aboard the hospital ship *Relief* for the Philippines. "Drat it,"
said Connie. "Why can't I go? Ef will get to see everything."

"Ef's thirty-one and you're fifteen," said Mrs. Guion. "Bide
your time, Con. You'll be going places, too."

Dr. McCombs, who stopped by as soon as he heard the
news, was upset. "I don't like it. War is no place for a

Ferebe (Ef) in nurse's uniform

woman. Dysentery, syphilis, smallpox — that's what Ef's patients will have."

"Don't you worry about Ef, Uncle Parks," said Connie. "She can take care of herself, and everybody else, too."

On August 12, two weeks before Connie's sixteenth birthday, the war ended. "Four months of fighting, all those men dead, and what does it prove? Nothing." Mrs. Guion shook her head in disgust.

"We got Puerto Rico and the Philippines and Guam," said Louis, "and we made the Spanish vamoose out of Cuba."

"Seems to me we have enough problems here at home," said Mrs. Guion, "without taking on Cuba."

That summer Connie went to Marietta, Georgia, to visit Rosa Bland. Rosa took her to lots of parties and introduced her to tennis. They spent hours playing in the heat, dressed in shirtwaists, full skirts, ruffled petticoats, black stockings and sneakers.

One day Connie received a surprising letter from Laura, telling of a whole new plan for her future. "Now that you've finished the graded school, I've made arrangements for you to go on studying at Miss Kate Shipp's School in Lincolnton," Laura wrote. "Miss Kate will give you free tuition and board, in exchange for your taking care of her two little nephews, William Ewen Shipp, age four, and Fabius Busbee Shipp, age two. If you study hard, Con, I feel sure you can go to college directly from Miss Shipp's and will I be proud! Alex Haskell's sisters have been to college, one to Wellesley and one to Radcliffe, and Alex says Wellesley is the best of all women's colleges. It's way up in Massachusetts, and that adds to the expense, but I want only the best for you, Connie."

Imagine, thought Connie, *me in college — and the best one, too!*

Just before Connie was to leave to go to Miss Shipp's School, mumps struck the house on Ninth Street. The Guions never did anything halfway and when they got the mumps, they did it eight strong. The siege lasted for a month. When it was all over, Mrs. Guion dusted off her hands and said cheerfully, "Well, that's the end of *that* disease."

Connie looked forward to Miss Shipp's because it meant returning to the Lincolnton country she loved. But when her mother took her there they did not even stop to look at River Bend Plantation. It was sold now, and those days were gone forever. They stopped instead at Woodside to see the Richardsons. Julia Richardson was going to Miss Shipp's School, too, and the girls chatted and giggled excitedly over their new adventure.

When Connie saw Miss Kate Shipp, she whispered to her mother, "She looks like an ocean liner sailing out to sea."

"Hush," said Mrs. Guion, but she couldn't help smiling. Miss Kate Shipp was a tall, fat woman with large arms, heavy bosom and a thick, corseted waist. She moved in a slow stately manner that was not so much a walk as an advance. Miss Shipp's hair and eyes were gray, and her round, intelligent face was punctuated with moles and whiskers. She looked Connie over with a calculating eye.

"Your daughter's small, Mrs. Guion. Do you think she can manage my two nephews?"

"Yes, indeed. Connie has a gift for getting along with children."

"I hope she's a good student. I expect the best, you know." Miss Shipp's father was a judge, and she had studied at Cambridge University in England and prided herself on her high standards.

The new nursemaid got off to a slow start with William and Fabius Shipp. The little boys hid behind their mother's skirts and peeked out at her; when she said hello to them, they ran away. Their mother, who was very young, had a woeful expression and Connie soon found out why she looked so sad. Her husband, Lt. William Ewen Shipp, had charged up San Juan Hill with Colonel Teddy Roosevelt's Rough Riders and had been killed in action. His widow and small sons moved in with his sister, Miss Kate, and because Mrs. Shipp was helping with the school, the little boys would have to spend a lot of time with Connie.

It took Connie exactly one day to make friends with them. She knew that with small boys it's action that counts, not words. In the barn she found a little cart, which she rigged

Connie with the boys in Miss Shipp's goat cart

up with a harness and hitched to one of Miss Shipp's goats. As soon as the boys saw the goat cart they left their mother and asked "Nonnie" if they could ride in it.

"Yes, indeed," Connie beamed. "William, you drive and Fabius can ride in back. I'll trot alongside and keep the goat from eating grass."

As the boys started off in their small chariot, they turned and waved to their all-but-forgotten mother. She and Miss Kate watched the colorful procession of goat, girl, cart and small boys disappear down the road. "One thing seems evident," said Miss Kate Shipp. "This little Connie Guion is resourceful."

Miss Kate's school, which was supposed to prepare boys and girls for college, was in a red brick building surrounded by old trees. Connie was one of only six boarders, but fifty day students came from all over Lincoln County. Classes began at 8:30 and ran until 2:30, when the day students went home to help on the farms.

Every morning a tall lad with dark red hair and a friendly smile made a point of sitting next to Connie. "My name is Caleb Motz," he said, grinning. "What's yours?"

"Connie Guion."

"Bunyan Womble and my other friends are studying to go to U.N.C., but not me. I'm going to Vanderbilt."

"I hope to go to college, too, but all this Latin and algebra makes my head ache."

"That's funny. Most girls don't go to college. Where're you going?"

"Wellesley, near Boston."

"What do you want to go up to a Yankee school for?"

"My sister Laura says Wellesley's the best there is."

"Some people think girls don't need all that much education."

"Well, I reckon I do. I'm going to be a doctor."

"A *doctor*? A pretty girl like you? Don't make me laugh."

"You wait. I'll be the one who laughs."

The studies at Miss Shipp's School were hard, but Connie worked industriously on algebra and Caesar and her skills increased. Because the classes were small and informal, the relationship between pupil and teacher was close and learning was fun.

The school's social life was delightful, too. The boys and girls played tennis and rode the farm horses together. On moonlight nights they would have a "straw ride" with a picnic at the end of it, and sing their way home as the wagon jolted along under the stars.

Dances were held regularly in the school auditorium and everyone joined in — pupils, teachers and townsfolk. The three colored men who played the piano, banjo and violin were rolling in rhythm and Connie was glad her brothers had taught her the waltz, polka, and schottische, but her favorite dance was the glide. The couples would start at one end of the room and, after a few swirls, glide the length of the hall. "If you could do Latin the way you do the glide," Caleb told her, "you'd be a Phi Beta Kappa. It's a sin for a girl who can dance the way you do to talk about being a doctor."

Connie looked up at him, a laughing light in her gray eyes. "Don't doctors dance?"

"Not women doctors. They just sit home and write prescriptions."

Interesting as Miss Shipp's was, Connie rejoiced when the time came to return to the family in Charlotte. Caleb drove her to the station and gaped as she swung herself up into the cab of the locomotive to ride with her old friend the engineer. "Why don't you sit in the parlor car like a lady?" called Caleb.

"I don't want to be a lady. I want to be a doctor."

"Will you write to me, Connie?"

"Maybe."

"If you don't, I'll come right down to Charlotte and find out why."

"Good. You come."

The locomotive blew out a cloud of steam and started chugging slowly down the track. With an impish smile, Connie blew Caleb a kiss. He pretended to catch it and staggered backward as though overcome. Connie laughed. It was glorious to be sixteen and to have a good-looking beau and to be riding through the blooming Maytime of North Carolina on your way *home*.

Connie returned to her brown sailcoth room at the end of the hall, and to her many household chores, with a light heart. Everyone was happy to have her back, particularly Alex and Ridie and Jo, who had sorely missed their leader. "Con is like sunshine in the family," Cousin Alice remarked.

That summer Connie's godmother, Cousin Connie Jones, made up her mind that Charlotte had to have a hospital. Mecklenburg County had a poorhouse and a pesthouse, but no hospital. But one hospital would not do. It was thought necessary, in the South, to have one for Negroes and one for whites. Cousin Connie got everyone in town excited about those two hospitals. Connie greatly admired her godmother's ability to ignite people's interest by sheer enthusiasm. The way she raised money, and talked doctors into joining her hospital staffs, made a lasting impression on the young girl.

One day in July Connie was weeding the garden when she heard a voice say, "How does your garden grow, ma'am?" She looked up and there was Caleb Motz smiling at her. "I told you I'd come if you didn't write."

"Maybe that's why I didn't write."

"Don't I wish it! I brought you a present, Connie. It's in the buggy."

Caleb disappeared and came back lugging an enormous watermelon. It was so big he could hardly get his arms around it. "Weighs seventy-five pounds. I grew it myself — just for you."

"Oh, Caleb, that's the biggest watermelon in the world. Let's have a party." They put the melon in the bathtub and left the cold water running to chill it. Then they went out and played three sets of tennis, oblivious of the scorching sun. At four o'clock the entire family gathered around Caleb's sensational watermelon. They sat on the grass and cut it as ceremoniously as if it were a roast pig. The pink meat was crisp and juicy and the slick black seeds were perfect for seed-spitting contests. There was no doubt that Connie's beau had scored a hit with her family.

"Anyone who can grow a melon like this should be a

farmer," said Mrs. Guion, eyeing Caleb speculatively. "Is that what you plan to do?"

"No, ma'am. I want to be an architect."

"That's a long row to hoe."

"Architecture's all I care about." He looked over at Connie and added, "Well, almost all."

Alex giggled and Connie jumped up. "I'm going to wash your sassy face with watermelon rind, smart Alex." She chased her little brother and the party broke up in a melee; everyone's face was washed with watermelon.

For Connie, senior year at Miss Shipp's centered on getting into Wellesley College. She studied hard and was doing well when, one bleak morning in March, Miss Kate summoned her to her office. "I have received a letter from Wellesley, Connie. I'm afraid it's bad news."

"Oh, no, Miss Kate."

"They say you do not have enough books of Cicero, Caesar or Virgil, nor have you enough algebra or geometry, to be admitted to Wellesley College. I don't know who they think they are."

Connie was thunderstruck. Laura had been corresponding with the dean at Wellesley and she had assumed everything was all right.

"Connie," said Miss Kate, "I think you should abandon this foolish dream of going to Wellesley. I'll help you get into Converse College, if you will promise to come back here and teach after you graduate."

"Where is Converse College?"

"Spartanburg, South Carolina. It's a good Southern college, much more suitable for you than Wellesley."

Connie thought a minute, then she shook her head. "My sister Laura has her heart set on my going to Wellesley, and I'm going to get there somehow."

Laura wrote more letters about Connie to Miss Pendleton, the Wellesley dean, and Miss Pendleton began to take an interest. "It is my opinion that your sister should come North to prepare for college," she wrote Laura. "Northfield Seminary is an excellent school. Its founder, Reverend Dwight Moody, was a friend of Wellesley's founder, Mr. Durant, and there are close ties between the two institutions. Perhaps we can help your sister obtain a scholarship at Northfield. We do want more Southern girls to come to Wellesley."

Northfield Seminary, it turned out, cost one hundred and ten dollars a year. This, plus the railroad fare, staggered everyone — except Laura. Money was never an obstacle to her. "Ef will soon be home to help us," she said cheerfully, "and she knows how to split a nickel up and down and still have it perfectly legal."

For over a year the family had been receiving letters from Ef about her adventures aboard the Navy hospital ship in the Pacific. She wrote that she had seen Singapore and Japan and Honolulu and Admiral Dewey, as well as many new and interesting diseases.

"I'll be glad when Effie's home," said Uncle Parks Mc-Combs, who always dropped by to hear her letters.

After much discussion, it was decided that Connie would go to Northfield as a special student to prepare for Wellesley. And then something happened that nearly wrecked all of Connie's plans.

Although Miss Kate Shipp was a strict disciplinarian, she did not believe in rules and regulations. On the first day of school she fixed the pupils with her steely eyes and said, "I expect all of you to act like ladies and gentlemen of honor at all times. If you infringe this law, you will be dismissed forthwith."

It was just before graduation that Connie felt the whiplash

of Miss Kate's anger. One balmy April afternoon Caleb whispered to her in class, "Want to go frog-spearing this evening?" He was always thinking up things they could do together. "Frogging" was something new.

"Oh, I'd love it. What time?"

"About sunset. That's when the frogs come out."

The long April twilight was casting a greenish light over the darkening pond when Caleb and Connie got there. The water's edge seemed to be trembling with bass drums. Caleb had brought along lanterns and spears and covered tin buckets. "You stand on this rock, Con. Mind taking off your shoes and socks?"

"Mind? What I mind is wearing the gol-durn things." Connie ripped them off and stuck her toes in the cold water. Caleb looked at her admiringly. "If you weren't so pretty, you'd be a real roughneck."

"Go along. Now what do I do?"

"Hold still. As soon as a frog croaks, shine your lantern at him — that blinds him — then throw your spear, hard as you can, and jerk it back by the cord."

"Great! If I haul in a frog, then what?"

"Wrap him up in this rag. You can't hold a frog in your hands, you know. They're slipperier than eels. Drop him in the bucket, and pop on the lid. I'll take a stand near you and give you a hand if you need it."

"Oh, I'm sure I won't need it."

"Did you know there's such a thing as a girl being too independent?"

"I doubt that."

Soon, frogs were thumping around in the bottom of Connie's bucket. She did wish Ben and Viv could see her. The time slipped by quickly. Suddenly Connie realized darkness had fallen. "It's late, Caleb. We've got to hurry back."

Caleb drove her to the back door of the school. "Wait till Miss Kate sees your catch, Connie. She loves to eat frog legs."

Connie climbed out, bucket and shoes in hand. She pushed a damp blond curl off her face and said, "I had a marvelous time, Caleb. I don't know how to thank you."

Caleb leaned forward and said in a low voice, "You could give me a little kiss. . . ."

Connie's laugh rippled through the darkness as she ran toward the house. "See you in school tomorrow. And thanks a lot — for the frogs, I mean."

She ran into the kitchen, flushed with excitement, and began showing Aunt Line, the cook, her bucket full of frogs. Aunt Line cut her short. "You is in trouble, girl, and you don't even know it. You better be awful perticaler-like, 'cause Miss Kate, she boilin' at you."

Quickly, Connie pulled on her shoes and stockings and went into the dining room. She wanted to bubble over about the frogs, but she realized things were strangely quiet. Miss Kate glared at her icily while everyone else stared down at empty dessert plates. Then Miss Kate rose and slowly left the room, followed by the others.

Connie followed them into the living room. "Miss Kate, if I've done something wrong, I'd like to apologize."

Miss Kate looked straight through her and moved majestically onward. There was nothing for Connie to do except go to her room. On the way she passed Aunt Line, who whispered, "Be keerful. Look in bureau drawer."

Inside the drawer, Connie found a piece of lemon pie and a mug full of cold milk. At least she had one friend left. She sat down to eat, for she was ravenously hungry, and began to mull over her plight. She remembered something her mother had said: "Miss Kate is like Rosa Dartle in *David Copperfield*. She's an edged tool and wants careful handling."

It was a little late in the day to recall that word of warning.

In class the next morning Miss Kate treated Connie and Caleb as though they were invisible. Even their schoolmates seemed to avoid them. "We'll have to try to talk to her after school," whispered Caleb. "We can't stay in limbo forever."

The minute classes were over Caleb addressed the Great Stone Face. "Miss Kate, Connie and I are sorry we were late. In the future, we will give up frogging."

Miss Kate glowered at them. "I have written to your parents, and I am considering expelling you."

"Connie and I think we should both be expelled, even though it *is* only a month before graduation." Connie looked at Caleb with new admiration. What a masterful stroke, to agree with her! Miss Kate's defenses were visibly shaken.

"Depart," she said. "I must think on this."

The next morning before school a mysterious cartoon was placed on Miss Kate Shipp's desk. It showed a tall boy and a short girl going down the steps of Miss Kate Shipp's school, each carrying a bucket full of frogs. Above their heads was a banner which said, "They Sacrificed Diplomas for Frog's Legs."

Miss Kate sailed slowly into the classroom. She picked up the cartoon and studied it for a minute. Not a sound was heard in the room; the pupils seemed made of marble. Then Miss Kate looked up, and her gray eyes twinkled. She threw back her massive head and laughed. The marble melted and the pupils laughed, too. Merriment rocked the classroom. The great frog crisis was dissolved by laughter, and Connie and Caleb were allowed to finish at Miss Shipp's School.

✳ 10 ✳

It's Cold Up North

CHARLOTTE was a small town and news soon spread that Kate Guion was sending her daughter up North to school. All the Guions' friends were full of hopes, questions, advice and criticism. "How *can* you allow your child to associate with Yankees?" one of them demanded.

"My dear," said Mrs. Guion, "I'm sending Connie up North to find the family silver those damyankees stole from us during the War between the States."

The whole family turned loose to get Connie ready to go away. Ef and Alice sewed all day, and as soon as Laura got home from the post office she picked up her needle and went to work, too. Laura was a master fitter. She could cut down old clothes to Connie's size and make them look almost fashionable. Ef ripped up old shirts and dresses and cut the material into underbodies, petticoats and panties. Cousin Alice added tatting and embroidery to the legs of the drawers and the tops of the "bodies." Ridie, Jo and Alex circled around the seamstresses with questions and lamentations. They were dismayed at the thought of having their Connie go "North," wherever that was.

Never a day passed that someone didn't appear with a piece of hand-me-down clothing for Connie. The excitement reached a peak when Miss Annie Lardner arrived carrying a gray blouse, only slightly worn, and a brand *new* skirt. It was an ankle-length gray flannel skirt, with black ric-rac zig-zagging down one side, and to Connie it was the height of elegance, her only new and her most prized possession.

"You're pretty well fixed now, Con," said Laura, "except for a coat. I don't see how you can stand the cold weather without a coat."

"Never mind," said Ef. "I'll take care of the coat."

As the preparations progressed Mrs. Guion said little, but it was easy to see that she had a heavy heart. Going to North-field was a far distant cry from traveling to Miss Shipp's in the cab of the locomotive. It would be a long and expensive trip, and there was no thought that Connie could come home before next summer.

Although she was eighteen, Connie was glad not to have to make the journey alone. Ef was returning to her nursing in New York and Ben was going to work at a cotton mill machinery company in Newton Lower Falls, Massachusetts. When the day came for their departure, Uncle Parks Mc-Combs and his driver Ed took the travelers to the station. As they were leaving, Annie ran out with a big tin box. "Here you are, Miss Effie. Now you all can eat like well-doin' folks."

None of the family went to the train with the travelers; it was hard enough to say good-by at home. As they rode down the shady street in the beautifully shined-up buggy, Uncle Parks tried to make little jokes to cheer up the three long faces, but no one laughed. When the buggy came within a block of the station, they could hear shouting and laughter.

"I hate to put you children on that rowdy train," said Uncle Parks, looking at Ef.

"Poof," said Ef. "I've ridden on excursion trains before. There's nothing to it."

Hordes of people were crowding into the long train and

the din was terrific. Ef led the way to the first day coach beyond the baggage car. "This one's apt to be a little less noisy," she said. "Good-by, Uncle Parks. Don't look so worried. We'll get along all right."

After the train left, Dr. McCombs went back to see Mrs. Guion. He found her looking dejected, too. "Why, Miss Kate, you look like you lost your last friend."

" 'Parting is such sweet sorrow,' " chirped Cousin Alice.

"Oh, Cousin Alice, do be still. I'm not one bit sad. I want my children to see the world. It's just a little quiet around here, that's all."

In later years Connie Guion recalled in detail that trip north on the Seaboard Airline excursion train:

The fare from Charlotte to Norfolk was only two dollars instead of twelve dollars, so everybody went — all kinds of people. Some were drinking, and the rest were drunk, but Ef knew just what to do. She had us sit in the last seat, next to the toilet, and when they began throwing bottles and apple cores, we were safe, though one drunk got locked in the toilet and pounded on the wall all night, like a jungle drummer.

At Rocky Mount, a woman got on with a baby. She sat next to me and handed the baby a banana, then she got sleepy and pushed the baby over on my lap. I told her I didn't want banana all over my chin, and she said if I would change places she'd put the baby next to the window. After three more bananas the baby went to sleep, but next morning the window was so smeared with banana it looked like ivory.

We reached Norfolk in the morning and that afternoon got on board the Old Dominion Line boat bound for New York. It was painted white, with shiny decks and shiny brass, all spanking clean. You could buy a stateroom for a dollar or sit on deck, so we sat on deck. Ef got out Annie's tin box of beaten biscuits and we munched them all night. A man in uniform, who we took to be the captain, brought us pillows to sleep on and told us they were serving dinner inside. Ef told him she crossed the Pacific five times and never got seasick because she kept her stomach filled with beaten biscuits, and we did not need any food.

We steamed into New York Harbor at dawn. The sky was streaked with bright colors and you could see the Statue of Liberty and the Singer Building, the tallest in the world, with the sunrise shining on its windows. Everything was beautiful — until we got off the boat at the Battery.

I was so disappointed in New York City I could have cried. We got on a street car pulled by mules. I said at home we had electrics and Ef said not to talk so loud. The city was dingy and riding that old mule car was the end. Then we climbed up to the Ninth Avenue elevated and had another terrible ride to 110th Street. We could see fat women at the tenement windows, leaning on their elbows and looking lonesome. There were mattresses hanging out and dirty clothes, too. Dirty children played in the streets and trash was everywhere. Ben and I didn't say much, because we knew Ef loved New York, but we were disgusted.

We went to Ef's apartment; then she took Ben and me to a dry goods store. She bought me a long wool cape, blue on the outside and red plaid on the inside, and a red tam-o'-shanter and rubber boots for the snow.

Though I was eighteen, this was the first time I ever had gone into a store and bought something to wear. I enjoyed the sensation.

Ef bought Ben a suit and an overcoat and then we put him on the train for Boston. He looked like a man. The next day Ef took me to St. Luke's Hospital, which was big and impressive and clean and white. She introduced me to all the doctors and nurses and took me to see the sick people in the wards. She even let me peek into the operating room and I thought I was in heaven.

Ef took me to see the Cathedral of St. John the Divine, which was nothing but a big hole in the ground, and to see the zebras in the Bronx Zoo. In New York, even the zebras are dirty. Next morning we went to Grand Central Station, an immense place, like a palace. You couldn't even see any trains and I began to get a little scared. Ef took me down to a restaurant and bought me some oyster stew and I felt better. After we said good-by, I walked alone down the ramp to the train. I felt like I had cut my last tie to civilization. The train was full of noisy boys and girls going to Amherst and Smith and Northfield. I didn't say anything, just listened and ate my beaten biscuits.

We got to South Vernon at ten o'clock that night. It was cold and dark and nobody met us except the stagecoach driver. I gave him the ticket for my trunk, but I could not understand what he said. The people in Massachusetts talk like foreigners.

We jostled over the dark road to Northfield in the three-seated stage. Miss Savage, one of the teachers, met us and took me to my room in Moore Cottage where I met my roommate, a silent fat girl named Alice Hamilton.

I was tired and hungry and far from home. I fell asleep fast.

The next morning we had to be in the dining room by seven o'clock. I was assigned to the table of Miss Mabel Young who called me "Miss Guion." Everything was stiff and formal. It seemed to be the fashion to say "Yes, Miss Young," so I said that a couple of times, just to say something. The Yankee breakfast was pitiful: yellow corn meal mush, with sugar and cream, and light bread instead of hot biscuits.

After breakfast we were given our daily jobs. Mine was to wash the tins. I never saw such a pile of tins as were stacked in that sink. As soon as I could, I walked around the school. It was beautiful, with rolling hills and huge elms and white buildings spread out on green lawns. There was a big classroom building called Stone Hall and a gym and a library. The auditorium had no stage because plays were never permitted at Northfield; they were too sinful. I discovered there were four hundred girls in the school, and outside of the fact that I couldn't understand what the New England girls said, and they couldn't understand me, I liked Northfield fine.

All the new girls had to take examinations in arithmetic, grammar, history, geography, and Latin. The questions aroused only hazy recollections for Connie, and she was quite sure she had failed. The night before classes started Miss Hall, the headmistress, sent for her. Miss Savage, who guided her across the dark campus by lantern light, said, "I'm afraid Miss Hall has bad news for you, Miss Guion."

Connie braced herself for a shock. She knew all the girls

and most of the teachers were in awe of the headmistress. The only light in Miss Hall's office was a kerosene desk lamp that cast flickering shadows around the gloomy room. Miss Hall, a tall woman with soft mousey hair and a sweet face, looked distressed. With Miss Hall, life was a solemn endeavor. She discussed all her problems with God, often in front of the students.

"Miss Guion, I'm sorry to have to tell you that you failed all your examinations, failed them miserably."

Miss Hall appeared so dejected that Connie felt sympathy for her at once. "That's all right, Miss Hall. It doesn't matter. I seem to have forgotten 'most everything I learned at Miss Shipp's. I reckon I'll learn a lot here, too, and forget it by the time I get to Wellesley."

Miss Hall pushed a paper across the desk to Connie, who held it under the kerosene lamp and read, "Civil government, grammar, geography, domestic science, spelling and history."

"What's this, Miss Hall?"

"It is your schedule."

"My schedule?" Connie pushed the paper back to her. "You mean you want me to study these things again?"

Miss Hall nodded.

"No, Miss Hall," Connie said firmly, "I never expect to do that. I have already forgotten them once and that's enough." She pulled a paper out of her pocket. "Here is my plan for the next two years. I drew it up from the Wellesley catalogue before I left home."

Miss Hall read the schedule. "You are not prepared to take these courses."

"I'm not afraid of hard work. I know I can do it."

"This is an excessive amount of science. Why do you think you need physics?"

"To get into college and medical school."

"But, Miss Guion, if you follow this plan, you will never amass enough credits to graduate from Northfield."

"I don't give a hoot whether I graduate or not."

"*Miss Guion!*"

"Since I'm just brushing up for Wellesley, Miss Hall, I don't see why you care what I take."

Miss Hall closed her eyes. She kept them closed so long Connie thought she had gone to sleep. Then she picked up Connie's paper and read it again. "The schedule you have drawn up for yourself is preposterous. Six major subjects!" She studied Connie's face. Clearly, here was an unusual girl. Miss Hall stood up, towering above Connie. "Miss Guion, I shall give you one chance to show me what you can do. For the first six weeks you may take the courses you've chosen. If, at the end of that time, your grades are high enough, I shall allow you to take physics also. But if you don't make good marks, you will have to follow this schedule of mine. I'm willing to take a chance on you, but should you fail, you must suffer the consequences."

Connie thought for a minute. Then she held out her hand. "You're a brick, Miss Hall. Let's shake on it."

Miss Hall looked shocked. No one had ever called her a brick before. The pious New England spinster did not know what to make of this breezy little Southerner. She took Connie's hand and said stiffly, "I wish you success." Then, almost as an afterthought, she added, "I graduated from Wellesley. It's a wonderful place."

Miss Savage and Connie trudged back to Moore Cottage in silence. Connie studied the star-strewn sky, humming to herself. When they reached the door, Miss Savage said, "I think you are the most stubborn student we have ever had." Connie, astounded, could not think of an answer. She just nodded her head in agreement.

When the other girls heard about Connie Guion's six-week bargain with the headmistress, they were dumbfounded. "Gracious," exclaimed Alice Rehbein, "no one ever disagrees with Miss Hall. Didn't you know that?"

"Nope, and I'm glad I didn't."

With ironclad determination, Connie set to work. For six weeks she did nothing except eat and study. Each day she got up at daybreak and went down to the chilly living room to study. When Mrs. Moody, the housemother, came in to supervise breakfast, she would find Connie hard at work.

"What is it today, Miss Guion?"

"English. I don't have what it takes to write a short story. I can think of everything except a beginning, a middle and an end."

Bible was even worse. In despair, Connie went to Miss Headley, the Bible teacher. "I can't remember all those prophets. It's just memory work and I don't see any sense to it."

Miss Headley, shocked, dropped her voice. "Oh, but Miss Guion, you ought to know your Bible."

"I've a lifetime to catch up on the Bible, but I have to pass these subjects in six weeks. Oh, how I wish I'd listened when Mama used to read us the Old Testament."

Connie often thought of home, but at first she was too busy to be homesick. If she wasn't studying, she was doing her job. At Northfield, the students did all the work. The only paid employees on the place were the men who ran the power plant and took care of the grounds. In addition to her daily kitchen chores, Connie did odd jobs to earn a little spending money. She made ten cents an hour addressing envelopes for Mr. Will Moody, Dwight Moody's older son, who did not seem to mind the fact that her handwriting was almost illegible.

As the six-week trial neared an end, Connie increased her efforts. She found it impossible to finish her studies before the ten o'clock lights-out bell. She told her troubles to her hall teacher, Miss Mabel Young, and to her surprise Miss Young said, "You're older than most of the girls and ought to be able to stay up later. Why don't you come to my room every night and study until eleven?" The extra hour each night was a lifesaver. Miss Young, who also was a Wellesley graduate, took great interest in Connie's struggle to get to college.

When the examinations were finally over, Miss Hall again sent for Connie to come to her office. Connie did not scare easily, but that day her knees almost knocked together. What if Miss Hall would not let her pursue her carefully laid plans? "Miss Guion," said Miss Hall, "I have watched you for six weeks, and I have studied your examinations, and I am amazed. It is not brilliance of mind that impresses me, but your remarkable persistence and tenacity. I have prayed to God for guidance and He tells me to let you go ahead with your ambitious plan of trying to squeeze four years into two. You may take the physics course."

"Hooray!" yelled Connie. "Oh, dear me, I didn't mean to shout. Excuse me, Miss Hall. Thank you, Miss Hall, I'll keep up, really I will. Thank *you*, Miss Hall."

Connie's enthusiasm was not shared by Miss Margaret McBain, her physics teacher, who disliked having a student enter her class late. Connie's bench in the laboratory was between two girls she had never seen before, Sarah Conrow and Beth Osborn. Both girls took an immediate interest in Connie and spent hours explaining to her the intricacies of physics. They helped her to set up her apparatus and write up her lab book. With their support, and by struggling to understand a simple physics book she borrowed from Mrs.

Will Moody, Connie finally caught up with the others. It was no small feat.

As the days passed, Connie became more and more aware of the gulf that separated Northfield from Miss Shipp's. Northfield, a church school founded by the popular evangelist Dwight L. Moody, was corseted with rules and regulations, and any infraction of them was deadly serious. Dancing and. card games were considered immoral and the only boys were at the Mount Hermon School, four miles away. Northfield girls were allowed to see them twice a year. The formality of the school was contradicted by a surprising informality in religion. God seemed to be a member of the society and all of the faculty were indeed familiar with Him.

Occasionally Connie would be inundated by waves of homesickness. Sundays were the worst. She hated going to the dreary church, which seemed like a barn — brown on the outside and brown inside, with big windows of plain glass and a fat, pompous minister, dressed in a business suit, who preached hellfire and damnation. Sunday afternoons, too, were bleak because all recreation was forbidden. Connie would sit in her room and study until time for evening chapel. Sometimes she re-read her mother's letters and then she felt worse.

All her life Connie had lived outdoors and she soon found she had to leave her studies a little while each day to get some exercise. During the fall she hiked up into the mountains and drank in the blazing color of the New England autumn. When the weather grew colder and Wanamaker Lake froze, she tried skating on the slick black ice. Much to the merriment of the other girls, she spent most of her time falling down.

And then at Thanksgiving a wonderful thing happened. Snow began to fall, and it kept right on coming down. It did not melt the following day, the way it does in North Carolina. Instead, more snow fell. Connie was ecstatic. Almost every afternoon she and Alice Rehbein and Belle Parker and their chums went bobsledding. Connie was a picture dressed in a heavy white sweater, red tam-o'-shanter and mittens, gray woolen skirt, and long black tights.

The girls would lug the bobsleds to the top of the hill, then run about fifty feet and jump on them. Two or three sleds would start in quick succession, whizzing down over the icy whiteness. Down the hill, across the road, over the tennis court they flew, the girls squealing and shouting as they soared over a six-foot drop and swooped down into a field. They had to make a sharp right turn at the bottom to keep from going into the Connecticut River, and the sense of speed and danger was intoxicating. Sometimes the girls went to other hills to coast and when it grew late, and a big sleigh came by, they would hitch their sleds on behind and glide home through the gathering darkness.

When Christmas came, Connie saw her friends off, then packed her few belongings and moved to East Hall where the girls stayed who were unable to go home. A few teachers stayed, too. "No matter how poor you are," Connie wrote to her mother, "there are plenty of people at Northfield who are poorer. There are missionaries' daughters from China, Japan, India and Brazil, and girls from the frozen backwoods of New England. About fifty of them are spending Christmas here at school, so I have lots of company."

The teachers did all they could to divert the lonely girls. Bounds were lifted and the girls could go where they pleased. They hiked into the town of Northfield and enjoyed the forbidden luxury of visiting the drug store, the bakery and the general store. Mr. Will Moody even gave a Christmas party in the gymnasium. They played games like musical chairs and shuffleboard and Mr. Moody's beautiful wife, Mae Whittle, sang for them in her rich contralto.

On Christmas Day everyone climbed into horse-drawn sleighs and rode over the snow to Mount Hermon to share Christmas dinner with the boys. Christmas was a soberly religious day, with none of the fireworks and gaiety Connie loved. After dinner they sang the old carols and a lump rose in Connie's throat. In her mind's eye she pictured home: Cousin Alice at the piano with her mother and Laura and Ef and Louis and Mary Wood and Viv and Alex and Ridie and Jo gathered around her. The Babcocks might be there, and Alice and her new husband, Sidney Vason, too. Annie would be standing in the doorway smiling, and the smell of roast turkey and hot biscuits would float in from the kitchen, and they would all sing:

> *O, little town of Bethlehem,*
> *How still we see thee lie,*
> *Above thy deep and dreamless sleep,*
> *The silent stars go by.* . . .

Connie Guion knew she was a long, long way from home.

* 11 *

The Mischief Maker

EVERYONE knew that Rhoda Baker did not like Connie. The first day they met at Northfield Rhoda said, "That Connie Guion is nothing but a mush-mouthed backslapper. She'd better keep out of my way." Rhoda was an odd, discontented girl and Connie's gaiety infuriated her. The two of them worked side by side in the kitchen at Moore Cottage washing dishes. Connie washed the pots and pans and Rhoda the glasses and silver. At first, Connie tried to talk but Rhoda refused to answer, so they washed in silence, an unnatural climate for a girl who was as gregarious as Connie. It was so unpleasant that she hurried to get through and always finished first, which made Rhoda more surly than ever.

One morning as Connie was getting ready to leave, Rhoda glowered at her and began slopping water on the floor. Miss Smith, the housekeeper, walked up quickly. "Miss Baker, do you realize that some poor girl will have to mop up that water?"

"What do I care?" said Rhoda, sloshing more water on the floor.

"Rhoda Baker," said Connie, "are you clean out of your head?"

Without warning, Rhoda whirled around and threw a glass of dirty water into Connie's face. Connie spluttered, shook off the water, and laughed. "You've got good aim, Rhoda." Rhoda's face darkend; her eyes were red coals.

"Please leave, Connie," said Miss Smith. "I'll take care of this."

The next morning Miss Smith moved Connie to a new job. She was to cook breakfast at Moore Cottage, a job she did for two years at Northfield. "Wouldn't Rhoda Baker be miffed if she knew how much I prefer cooking to scrubbing?" laughed Connie. "That little crab apple did me a good turn."

"I don't see how you can laugh about her," said Alice Rehbein indignantly. "I hate the way she treats you."

Connie shrugged. "I haven't got time to hate."

"Oh, Connie, you're a star! I can't wait to take you home with me at Easter. My family will love you, especially my older brother. He's crazy about pretty girls."

"I can't wait either. Brooklyn — a brand new city!"

The prospect of a new adventure helped Connie struggle through the rugged winter term. Each morning she had to climb out of bed at 5 A.M. to cook breakfast for sixty girls. Getting up early is no chore for a farm girl, but the bitter cold on those dark mornings was bone-chilling. Sometimes the temperature dropped to 30 below zero and one morning when it hit 40 below the mercury in the thermometers froze. Soon after Connie lit the kerosene lamps in the frigid kitchen, the janitor stoked the coal furnace and the house began to warm up. Promptly at six, Connie clanged the rising bell, which gave the other girls time to dress and spend fifteen minutes praying in the parlor before breakfast.

Connie cooked hot cereal and muffins every morning and on Saturdays she made coffee, following the school recipe, which she considered a great joke. She mixed a bushel of bran, a quart of molasses and a little sugar with a pint of coffee and roasted it in the oven. The girls thought this strange brew was the height of sophistication, but Connie never touched it.

Connie made delicious muffins with ease — until one morning calamity set in. She and her assistant, Elsie Frank, made the muffins as usual and sniffed the fragrance as it floated from the big wood-burning stove. As soon as they were done, Connie broke one open and gave half to Elsie. It was steaming and fluffy and looked enticing. Connie took a bite. *"George!"* she said, spitting it out. "That's awful!"

"Tastes salty," said Elsie.

"Salty as the briny deep! What did you put in it?"

"Sugar." Elsie pointed to the sugar crock.

Connie stuck in her finger, then licked it. "Straight salt. Some brat put salt in place of the sugar."

"No one would be that mean, except Rhoda Baker."

"Never mind who did it. Quick, poke up the fire. We'll burn these and make another batch."

"Make a hundred and twenty more muffins? We haven't time. We can't do it, Connie."

"Oh, yes, we can. We have to. Dump those in the fire before Miss Smith comes. Hurry."

Twenty minutes later, Connie and Elsie served the girls a brand new batch of hot muffins. "Won't you have one?" Connie grinned at Rhoda Baker. "They're sweet as sugar."

"No, thank you." Rhoda turned her head away. "I'd rather eat dirt."

"Did you ever try eating crow?" laughed Connie.

"The breakfasts here are poisonous," said Rhoda. "We need a new cook."

"Why didn't you brain her?" asked Alice Rehbein afterward.

"She can't help it. People like Rhoda Baker are born

cranky. If it wasn't me, it'd be somebody else. As my brother Louis says, 'you have to roll with the punches.'"

Spring vacation came at last, although spring did not. "It's durn funny," said Connie peering out the train window. "Down home the jonquils and hyacinths have come and gone. Up here it's all March wind and pussy willows and bare branches. When will it warm up?"

"'If winter comes, can spring be far behind?' unquote Percy Bysshe Shelley," said Alice breezily.

"You sound like my Cousin Alice. She pops out a poem on every occasion. Cousin Alice is the frosting on the cake at our house."

Connie enjoyed the ferry ride from Manhattan to Brooklyn. "There's the new Brooklyn Bridge," Mr. Rehbein pointed out proudly. "Next time you come we'll drive our buggy right over it." The Rehbein's four-story frame house, with a garden in the back, was located in Williamsburg, then the fashionable part of Brooklyn. Mr. Rehbein had come over from Germany with Mr. Steinway to make pianos, and in the living room was a Rehbein piano. All the Rehbeins played and sang and the household seemed to revolve around that piano.

As Alice had predicted, her bother Alpheus was captivated by Connie. A blond young man in his late twenties who had a receding hairline and a twinkle in his eye, Al Rehbein worked on Wall Street and studied at Brooklyn Polytechnic Institute at night, but he managed to find plenty of time to entertain the two "fresh pieces" from Northfield, as he called them. He took the girls to visit the Stock Exchange and up to the top of the Singer Building, and to see the Statue of Liberty. Everywhere they went, Connie snapped pictures with her prized possession, a new box camera, and Al Rehbein enjoyed her enthusiasm.

One morning Al took Connie and Alice buggy-riding out

to the New Rochelle Yacht Club for lunch. "Fancy me in a yacht club," said Connie. "I wish the Guions could see me now."

" 'Scuse me miss," said the waiter, "are you kin to the New Rochelle Guions?"

"Could be. I'm a Tarheel from North Carolina but my family goes way back."

The waiter went away and returned with a picture of an old house on a glass plate. "Here's where all them Guions used to live. The old Guion house is a landstone around here."

Much to Connie's delight, the waiter presented her with the glass plate. After lunch Al drove them into New Rochelle to see the "landstone" built by the first Guion, who came to America in 1685 with the French Huguenots. The place was now dilapidated and on the glass oval in the front door was the word *Dressmaking*.

"Dressmakers!" exclaimed Connie. "They're no ancestors of mine. I can't sew a stitch."

The last night of Easter vacation was the most exciting of all. Al Rehbein and his friend Jim DeNyse took Connie and Alice to the theater. For the occasion, Connie borrowed a white silk evening gown and long kid gloves and piled her hair on top of her head. When she came downstairs, Al Rehbein gasped. "You look as lovely as a lily, Miss Connie." Connie did not know what to say; she just beamed.

Connie had never been to the theater before and she was almost overcome with excitement. The play was a new one by James M. Barrie, *The Little Minister,* starring a twenty-year-old girl named Maude Adams. Connie thought she had never seen any human being as fascinating as Maude Adams, and the play, with its poetic fancy and fey humor, was delightful. To cap everything, Al Rehbein took them to the McAlpin Hotel for a midnight supper. Connie felt she was in a

Maria and Louis Isaac Guion, the first Guions to come to America

dream, surrounded by soft music and potted palms and eating lobster.

"This whole evening is full of firsts for me," she said. "I never tasted lobster before."

"Do you like it?"

She tried to think of an apt comparison. "It's even better than spareribs."

"And did you enjoy your first play, Miss Connie?"

"*Did* I? You know what I liked best? Where the man said 'Has it ever struck you that trouts bite best on the Sabbath — God's critters tempting decent men!' It made me think of Northfield. We can't do anything on Sunday and they think things like dancing and playing cards and going to the theater are sinful. I wish they could see Alice and me cutting loose."

"Surely dancing's not a sin."

"Once Mr. Dwight Moody's daughter rebelled and went to

a dance and when she came back it was late and Mr. Moody was standing at the door. He said sarcastically, 'Good morning, *daughter of Satan!*' And do you know what she answered?"

"I couldn't guess."

Connie raised her voice and cooed sweetly, "Good morning, *my Father.*"

Al Rehbein laughed, then he leaned forward and said in a low voice, "It's a good thing you're going back to Northfield tomorrow, Connie. If you stayed much longer, I might fall in love with you."

"Good gracious! What in the world are you talking about?" Connie looked at him with wide eyes. It had never occurred to her that a man ten years older than she could take a fancy to her.

"Do you think you could ever be interested in me?"

"No," said Connie flatly.

"Well, I must say you're frank."

"To tell the truth, there's only one thing I'm interested in and that's being a doctor."

"You'll never make it. You're too saucy to be preserved in formaldehyde."

"Oh, I'll make it." Connie raised her chin slightly. *"Nothing* is going to stop me from being a doctor."

After the giddy delights of Brooklyn and New York it was hard for Connie to settle down to work at school. In fact, she did not settle down completely. She enlivened her studies with hi-jinks, much to the distress of her teachers. Connie was not used to rules and breaking one for an occasional prank did not seem serious to her. To the faculty of Northfield, breaking a rule was a sin.

One dreary day Connie decided to try making fudge in her room. She made an illegal trip to town to buy a cheap pan and "borrowed" some cocoa and butter from the kitchen.

Connie, second from left, upper row, at Northfield

Then she and two friends, Helen Brown and Eliza Short, began cooking the fudge over the chimney of Connie's lamp. They were so busy mixing and giggling they did not hear footsteps coming down the corridor. Suddenly, the door swung open and there stood Miss Savage.

"May I ask *what* you are doing?" Miss Savage was a huge, brusque woman with hair pulled straight back into a hard knot, giving her a masculine appearance.

"We're making fudge, Miss Savage," said Connie. "Won't you have some?" She held out the pan with an innocent smile. "It's delicious."

"Miss Connie Guion, I've tried to make allowances for you because I consider you a lightweight and a greenhorn, but this is the last straw. You could have set Moore Cottage on fire. Hand me that pan of fudge."

"Yes, Miss Savage."

"And don't ever let this happen again. If it does, I shall punish you severely."

She left, taking the candy with her, and the girls collapsed with laughter. "I'll bet she eats all of it herself," said Eliza.

"Next time I'll make enough for the Savage, too," Connie giggled.

But Miss Savage had shocked Connie by calling her a lightweight and a greenhorn; she had never thought of herself that way. Resolutely, she made up her mind to reform. She studied harder than ever and, for a while, managed to stay out of mischief; then one Saturday she ran afoul of Miss Savage again.

Miss Savage announced that no one was allowed to enter Eliza Short's room because she was sick. To ignore a sick friend was beyond Connie's comprehension. She slipped off to the village bakery and spent her hard-earned dimes on an apple pie for Eliza. When the coast was clear, Connie sneaked into Eliza's room with her present. The two girls were about to cut the pie when they recognized the swish of Miss Savage's skirts in the hall.

"She's coming!" whispered Eliza. "Hide in the closet!"

In a flash Connie shoved the pie under the covers and ducked behind the curtains of the closet. She took off her shoes, stuck her feet into Eliza's shoes, and stood behind a long dress. The door opened and in marched Miss Savage. She walked over to the bed and sat down, flat, on the pie. Her back straightened, but no flicker passed over her face. "How do you feel, Eliza?"

"A little better, thank you."

"Good. You haven't let any girls come in your room, have you? We wouldn't want others to catch your cold, would we?"

"No, Miss Savage."

Miss Savage looked around the room suspiciously. "You're alone, Eliza?" Eliza nodded her head.

Miss Savage rose and straightened her skirts, brushing one hand across her back several times. She walked over to the closet, pulled the curtain aside and glanced in. Eliza sneezed violently. Miss Savage dropped the curtain.

"I must hurry to chapel," she said. "Good day, Eliza. Be sure no one enters this room."

The minute the door closed, Connie stuck her head out. "Did she mash it?"

"It looks like applesauce," laughed Eliza.

"She knew I was in here but she didn't have the nerve to find me and go through with the punishment. Her bark's always worse than her bite."

"She's gone to chapel."

"I'm late!" Connie raced out the door.

"Take the short cut," called Eliza. "You can beat her."

Holding up her skirts, Connie ran across the field, up hill and down hill, until she reached the chapel. Just as she plopped down in her seat, puffing and blowing, Miss Savage walked down the aisle to check attendance. She also was out of breath. She stopped and squinted at Connie with a baffled expression. Connie lowered her head in pious prayer. Miss Savage hesitated, and then moved on. "Praise the Lord," murmured Connie.

A few weeks later Connie received a letter from her mother that made her forget all about pranks. She read and re-read it, but she could not take it in. Like all of Mrs. Guion's letters, it was short and to the point. She wrote that Uncle Parks had been ill and had sent for Ef to come home and nurse him. He recovered, but Ef was not going back to New York. She was going to marry Uncle Parks.

Connie was flabbergasted. She simply could not picture her sister as Mrs. Parks McCombs. She closed her eyes and tried to imagine them as man and wife. Of course they did have two things in common: the healing of the sick and the enjoyment of laughter.

At last the day Connie longed for arrived, the June day when she returned to her family in Charlotte. She bubbled over with the joy of being at home. Everyone gathered around to hear about her adventures up North: her mother, Laura, Louis, Ben, Viv, Cousin Alice, old Annie, Ridie, Jo and Alex. Connie looked affectionately around the family circle. She was glad Ben's apprenticeship in Boston was over. Only four were missing — Ef, who was already married and living in the big frame house Dr. McCombs had bought for her; Kate, who was busy with her two little girls, Margaret, five, and Fercbc, age three; Mary Wood, who was living with Kate and working as Dr. Babcock's secretary; and Alice, who, with her husband Sidney Vason, now lived in Augusta, Georgia. No one had changed much in the ten months Connie had been away.

"I've had good reports on your work at school," said Mrs. Guion, "but Miss Hall says sometimes you're a mischief-maker."

"Now isn't that silly?" Connie grinned broadly.

"Tell us the worst thing you did," demanded Alex.

Connie thought a minute. "One snowy day we borrowed the tin trays from the dining room and sat on them and went coasting, and when we got hungry we ate sap out of the buckets on the sugar maple trees. Miss Hall heard about it and made us kneel on the floor while she prayed over us. She said stealing was a sin and she prayed to God that we wouldn't become criminals."

"Stealing!" Mrs. Guion was indignant. "No child of mine ever stole anything. I don't call that foolishness stealing. Stealing is what those damyankees did when they took my horse."

"Shucks," said Viv, "don't you ever do anything worse?"

"Sometimes we hitch a ride into town on the back of a wood wagon and we hop off at the bake shop and buy chocolate cream puffs and ride back to school, swinging our legs and munching the cream puffs, and no one ever knows the difference."

"Man," laughed Louis, "that's *really* sinning."

As soon as Connie could get away, she rode her bicycle over to see Mrs. McCombs. "How do you like being an old married lady, Ef?"

"Just fine. Uncle Parks and I have good times together."

The summer vacation was far from gay for Connie. She was still struggling to catch up at Northfield and she studied every day. She was trying to write a five-hundred-page notebook on English history for Miss Bassett, with lots of maps and charts. If Miss Bassett excused her from history, she could spend more time on math and science.

Rosa Bland came to see Connie and so did Julia Richardson, and there were plenty of beaus around, too — the Irwin brothers and George Graham and Fred Nash. They played tennis and danced and went buggy-riding. The boys teased Connie about wanting to go to college. In North Carolina in 1901, young girls did not turn into eager scholars. Connie was an enigma to them.

To Connie's regret, Caleb Motz was still in Tennessee. He wrote her a long letter telling about his work at Vanderbilt and asking if she had changed her mind about being a lady doctor. Connie wrote back: "Wild horses couldn't change my mind, but I want you to know I am not going to be a lady doctor. I'm going to be a doctor."

And then one day something happened that shattered the whole Guion family. Dr. McCombs collapsed with a stroke and was carried home unconscious to Ef, his bride of five months.

For three weeks, he lay in a coma and everyone felt sure he would never get well. Connie went to live with Ef and took over all the shopping and housekeeping.

Silently, Ef nursed her sick husband. Nobody knew what was going on in her head. She never saw anyone except her family and Dr. McCombs's devoted friends, the sad-faced gentlemen who took turns sitting with him all night. On July 23, 1901, Dr. Parks McCombs died. The Guions felt as though a prop had been knocked out from under them. All their lives they had relied on Uncle Parks as physician, counselor, and friend. Kate and Mary Wood came home for the funeral, but Alice could not come because she was expecting a baby and didn't dare travel.

Dr. McCombs was not only the foremost doctor in Charlotte; he was beloved by everybody. When his faithful Ed used to drive him through the streets, all the children would cheer him. Many of those who crowded into St. Peter's Church for the big funeral were children who remembered how Uncle Parks used to give them a riddle along with their medicine.

After the service the family went back to Ef's for lunch and it hurt Connie to see her looking so woebegone. She greeted her family with an attempt at a smile, which was the saddest thing of all.

"Do you think you'll go back to nursing in New York?" asked Kate.

"No, I don't," Ef said in a small voice.

"Why not?"

"Oh, there are too many things to straighten out here."

Connie glanced at her sister in surprise. Everyone assumed Ef would return to her highly successful nursing career. Connie shrugged. It would not enter her head to worry about Ef; she was the epitome of self-reliance.

When the time came for Connie to return to Northfield she was more than ready to go. On this trip she had company all the way to South Vernon, for Alex went along with her. Through the magic of Laura's financing, he was to enter Mount Hermon School as a sophomore.

✳ 12 ✳

Connie Stands Her Ground

THE NEW SCHOOL year at Northfield began with prayers for President McKinley, who had just been assassinated, and for his successor, Theodore Roosevelt. Along with the rest of the world, the teachers and students of Northfield were shocked by the murder of the President.

On the first day of classes Connie presented her carefully prepared history notebook to Miss Bassett. She was surprised when Miss Bassett returned it with an "A" and said, "Miss Guion, you could easily make history your field."

"Thank you, Miss Bassett. I aim to take as little history as possible. I'm going to concentrate on medicine."

"Well, the more things a doctor knows, the better the doctor." Years later, when Dr. Connie Guion established a relationship with a difficult, withdrawn patient by discussing ancient history, she was to recall Miss Bassett's remark.

Connie attacked her final year at Northfield (not her senior year; she never did graduate, although she was adopted by the class of 1903) with zest. She wrote her mother a letter telling about her struggles with French and algebra and about her jolly new friend, Ruth Smith, from Japan.

Connie's first encounter with Ruth Smith was typical of both girls. Ruth, a tall, attractive girl with a lot of blond hair, was sizzling with high spirits. She sat at Connie's table and her job was to keep the water glasses filled.

"Say, Ruth," said Connie one morning, "my water glass is empty. Will you get me some more?"

"Sure thing." Ruth jumped up and went toward the kitchen with a quick, light step.

"She walks like a dancer," said Eliza Short.

"Quick, hand me a pitcher." Connie winked at Eliza. "I'm going to trick her." She hid the empty pitcher in her lap and covered it with a napkin.

Ruth filled Connie's glass first. While she was filling the other glasses, Connie dumped her water into the hidden pitcher and asked for more.

"You drink a lot of water, don't you?" observed Ruth, filling Connie's glass again.

"It's the New England air," said Connie. "After you've been here awhile, you'll get thirsty, too. May I have some more?"

"Gracious!" Ruth stared at the empty glass. "I can't believe it."

All during the meal Connie kept Ruth running to fill her glass. Ruth's good humor never flagged, but she whispered to Eliza Short, "Does Connie Guion have some kind of strange illness?"

Finally when Ruth was pouring "one more," Connie jerked her napkin off the hidden pitcher and said, "Just put it in here, Ruth, and save your energy."

Ruth stood still a moment, then she threw back her head and laughed. She had a contagious laugh and everyone in the room laughed with her. "Connie Guion," she cried, "you're my Waterloo!"

One day that fall Mr. Moody stopped by Connie's desk when she was addressing envelopes, and asked how she liked the school. "Oh, it's fine, Mr. Moody, but I can think of one way to make it better."

Mr. Moody looked surprised. "How is that, Miss Guion?"

Connie cleared her throat. "A lot of us girls wonder why we always go to Mount Hermon for Thanksgiving and Christmas, but we never invite the boys over here."

"Well, now, why should that be? Why don't you girls set up a plan and we'll see what we can do."

Connie and her friends were amazed at Mr. Moody's response to the new idea. After endless conversations, they decided on the kind of party they wished to have for the mysterious young men from Mount Hermon. Naturally, Connie was chosen to present their plan.

"Well, Miss Guion," said Mr. Moody, "what have you girls come up with?"

Connie took a deep breath. "We want to have a Hallowe'en party and invite as many Hermonites as we possibly can. We want to give a picnic first at the gym and everybody'll wear fancy costumes, and we'll have witches and trickery and games and everything that goes with Hallowe'en, and we'll pay for it out of our own money. How does that strike you, Mr. Moody?"

There was a pause. Connie crossed her fingers and held her breath. This daring suggestion amounted to a revolution at Northfield. At last Mr. Will Moody spoke. "An imaginative plan indeed, Miss Guion. You are quite an innovator. By all means, let us have the Hallowe'en party. And don't worry about the money. The school will pay for it — somehow."

For years afterward Connie Guion was known at Northfield as the Girl Who Invented The Hallowe'en Party. The party was a howling success. The boys and girls played all kinds of games, such as eating doughnuts off a string and hunting for peanuts. Connie and Alex tied for first in the bobbing-for-apples contest, both of them choking with water and laughter. Mrs. Will Moody played the piano and sang for the

Connie in "the only low-necked dress in Northfield"

guests, but of course there was no thought of anything as radical as dancing.

The only other excitement that term was a sleigh ride to Brattleboro, Vermont, to visit Mr. Howe's Photographic Studio. Connie and her friends took turns posing for their picture in Eliza Short's best dress, the only low-necked dress in all Northfield. Mr. Howe mailed them the proofs with a note: "Keep these hidden. The winds of Northfield blow cold on bare shoulders."

At Christmas Connie visited Eliza Short in Milford, Delaware. It was a gay holiday with lots of dances. As Connie wrote her mother, "Eliza is as pretty as a peach and always ready for a fire or a fight. She has loads of beaus and doesn't care a whit whether school keeps or not." A handsome boy named Will Marshall gave Connie a rush. He was going to Jefferson Medical School, but he refused to discuss medicine with her. Like everyone else, he laughed at her talk of being a doctor.

One Saturday afternoon in January Alex got permission to come over from Mount Hermon to Northfield to see Connie. She took one look at him and said, "Alex Guion, you need a haircut."

"Shucks, Con, you might say you're glad to see me."

"I'm glad to see you. But you need a haircut. You look like William Jennings Bryan. Sit right down in the dining room and wait till I get a comb and scissors."

Connie was placing a school smock over her brother's stiff collar and flowing tie, when they looked at each other and began to laugh. "Don't you dare set *this* smock on fire."

"That reminds me of a riddle, Con. What is a fireman?"

"I dunno."

"A man with a burning ambition to get ahead."

"I guess that makes me a fireman. People snort when I talk about going into medicine, but I'm just smoldering with ambition, Alex."

"Keep the home fires burning, Con. I'm sure you'll make it, by spontaneous combustion if necessary."

Miss Margaret McBain celebrated the arrival of spring by informing Connie she was going to fail in physics. "That's all right, Miss McBain," Connie said cheerfully. "It doesn't matter a bit so long as I pass that Wellesley physics exam."

"If you do," snapped Miss McBain, "it will be a miracle."

Connie asked Miss Hall's permission to drop her laboratory work and spend those three hours studying physics in the library. By now, the headmistress was interested in getting Connie to Wellesley and the permission was granted. Connie spent many hours studying in the library, digging out facts and making them her own.

Miss Mabel Young, who was incensed because Miss Mc-

Bain would not give Connie a passing certificate, wrote to a friend at Wellesley for copies of old physics examinations that Connie could study. Miss Young was a sweet-looking spinster with a thin, angular face and pince-nez glasses and many of the girls had a crush on her. To Connie she was a friendly guidepost on the road to Wellesley; without her help, she would have been lost.

As Connie left to go to Wellesley to take the examination, Miss McBain said, grudgingly, "Good luck, Miss Guion. I'm afraid you're going to need it."

Miss Hall said, "If you pass Wellesley's test, Miss Guion, I will see that you get the same grade in the physics course here." Miss McBain glared at the headmistress.

Miss Mabel Young said, "Give this letter to Dean Pendleton. We were at Wellesley together."

Connie's first glimpse of Wellesley was disappointing. She had dreamed of it for so long that in her mind it was more desirable than paradise, but at first glance the campus seemed vast and unfriendly, a far cry from the charm of Northfield. Hesitantly, she walked into College Hall. This was more like it. In the center of the open rotunda was a marble flower bed filled with delicate ferns and spreading palms. Near it sat an old man selling bunches of flowers from a tiny cart. Connie walked around the marble colonnade surrounding the court and examined the gold-framed pictures and the white statues. Then she leaned her head back and looked up four flights of balconies to the skylight. It was elegant!

Dean Pendleton, a formidable woman with a cloud of white hair and an icy smile, read Miss Young's letter and said, "Well, Miss Guion, you come well recommended. I hope you can pass the examination and be with us next September."

When Connie read over the questions, she recognized them

all, thanks to Miss Mabel Young, and she wrote off the answers exactly as she had memorized them. Then she said goodby to Miss Pendleton and hurried back to Northfield. She found some tension at school over the outcome of her examination. Miss McBain, who was apparently on pins and needles, told Miss Young, "I am certain Connie Guion will fail."

Miss Young smiled and handed her a telegram. "Look at this. I asked my friend at Wellesley to wire me." Connie had passed! Everyone was surprised except Connie and Miss Young. Miss Hall said she was very proud. Miss Margaret McBain said nothing.

On March 2 another, more important telegram arrived, this one addressed to Connie. It was from her mother and it contained wonderful news: ANNIE PARKS MC COMBS BORN TODAY. EF AND BABY DOING WELL. LOVE. GRANNY.

"I'm an aunt to the fifth power," Connie announced to Ruth Smith.

"Impossible," said Ruth. "You're only nineteen and that's too young."

"Aunt Connie, that's me. The Babcocks have three girls, and last summer Alice and Sidney Vason had a son they named James Babcock Vason. And now Ef has a little girl. No wonder she didn't want to go back to nursing in New York. Annie Parks McCombs. I can't wait to see her!"

As the school year drew to a close, Connie worried more and more about financing her college education. She knew Laura would help her. But could Laura manage it? Wellesley cost four hundred dollars a year, and with Alex at Mount Hermon and Ridie entering Northfield in the fall, Laura's hands were full.

About a week before commencement, Miss Hall told Connie she had been awarded the Northfield scholarship to

Wellesley College. This meant one hundred dollars, a great windfall. But on commencement morning the whole picture suddenly changed. Connie was summoned to Miss Hall's residence.

"Miss Guion," the headmistress started off briskly, "Fanny Upham was the girl we first selected for our Wellesley scholarship. She refused it, in favor of a four-year scholarship at Mount Holyoke." Miss Hall hesitated. "Now she has changed her mind. She wants to take the Wellesley scholarship. Fanny is graduating today — and of course you are not. Miss Guion, will you accept the *four*-year scholarship to Mount Holyoke and give Fanny Upham your *one*-year scholarship to Wellesley?"

Connie cleared her throat. "Miss Hall, I want to go to Wellesley. I don't even know what Mount Holyoke is."

"Mount Holyoke is an excellent college and you would have a *four*-year scholarship."

"I can't picture myself going to Mount Holyoke, Miss Hall. I haven't anything against it, but I set my heart on Wellesley."

"You must not be stubborn, Miss Guion. Think of the heartache and worry a four-year scholarship will save your family."

"You don't understand my family. My sisters themselves decided Wellesley was the only place they wanted me to go. They would never accept a substitute."

Miss Hall looked out the window. "Fanny Upham was awarded the Wellesley scholarship before you were."

"Then let her have it. I am perfectly willing to give it up, but I am *not* going to Mount Holyoke."

"But why?"

Connie thought for a minute. "Because I will not sacrifice my sisters' dream for a scholarship."

Miss Hall glanced at her watch. It was time to get ready for commencement. "That is your final decision?" Connie nodded and Miss Hall shrugged sadly. "Then there is nothing more I can do. Since the other girl did refuse the Wellesley scholarship at first, it's yours, of course." She held out her hand. "I have every confidence you will succeed at Wellesley, Miss Guion." Connie was confused by this sudden turn of events. She nodded her head hopefully.

Because she was not graduating, Connie did not go to commencement. She had in her pocket a card from Dean Pendleton which read:

Connie M. Guion has presented satisfactory credits in the following subjects:

English: Rhetoric, composition, literature
History: English, Greek, Roman
Mathematics: Algebra and plane geometry
Latin: Grammar, prose composition, Caesar, Virgil, Cicero
Greek: No
French: Minimum
Physics: Maximum

She may enter Wellesley College, in the class of 1906, this September.

Connie told herself this was more important than any diploma, but she felt wistful when she saw her friends in their splendid caps and gowns, and she took pictures of them with her box camera. Then she went around to say good-by to her teachers. Miss Savage congratulated her on getting into

Wellesley and then said, "Will you tell me one thing, Miss Guion? How did you get from Eliza Short's closet to your seat in chapel so quickly? I went as fast as I could, but you beat me."

"Then you knew I was there all the time?"

"I knew that and a lot more. It will be more peaceful at Moore Cottage next year, but I'll miss you."

Connie's French teacher said, *"Au revoir,* Mademoiselle Guion. Before you go, will you promise me one thing? I passed you in French, *n'est-ce-pas?* I want you to promise *nevaire, nevaire* to take French *encore.* You have the worst pronunciation I have ever heard."

"Madame, I give you my word, *avec plaisir."*

Miss Thompson looked at Connie with her quizzical expression and said, "I felt victimized when I found you sitting in my algebra class. I'd never seen you do anything except trip up some other girl, or slide down a snowbank on your bag of books. But I was mistaken. You have the makings of a real mathematician, Miss Guion."

It was Miss Mabel Young who summed up Connie's career at Northfield. "I've watched with interest your drive to get into Wellesley College. You have a determination and persistence which in the long run may be a greater asset than brilliance."

"Thank you, Miss Young."

"I shall see you at Wellesley. I have been asked to go back there to teach."

"Capital! Won't we have a great time!"

"Yes, I think we will. You know, Connie, you make me think of my favorite aphorism from Henry James."

"What is that, Miss Young?" Connie asked politely.

"He said, 'Be bold, be delicate, and pursue the prize.' That's you to a T, Connie Guion. God bless you!"

* 13 *

Wellesley! O, Wellesley!

CONNIE GUION may be the only girl who ever entered Wellesley College with just two dresses. One was a navy blue skirt, with two white shirtwaists. The other was a wool suit from Sears, Roebuck. To Connie, two dresses seemed quite sufficient. Her mind was on other things: she was going to college at last!

Clothes had never mattered to the Guions. Mrs. Guion used to tell the girls when they went to a dance, "Just wear a pretty smile and give others a good time; and nobody will notice what you have on." If Mrs. Guion ever thought wistfully of the beautiful pink merino gown she had worn to balls in the golden days before the War, no one knew about it.

For the family to send Connie to Wellesley was far from simple. Of the four hundred dollars that was needed for room, board and tuition, Connie had one hundred from the Northfield scholarship and Wellesley would allow her two hundred dollars for working in the self-help dormitory. This left one hundred dollars for the family to scrape up, a challenge which the Guions met enthusiastically, as they put education before everything else. Kate, Louis and Mary Wood sent checks home each month and Laura used their money, along with her own, to support the family and pay for the schooling of Connie, Viv, Alex and Ridie. For the past ten years Laura had been engaged to a young cotton broker, but

Connie, the year she entered Wellesley

she would not consider getting married until her brothers and sisters were educated.

Ef longed to help, too, but she had her own problems. To everyone's surprise, Dr. McCombs had left her little except their house and a desk stuffed with uncollected bills. If a patient did not pay, it had been Dr. McCombs's habit to forget the whole thing. Since Ef now had a daughter to look after, she abandoned her nursing career and took in boarders.

Ef's new baby was the bright spot for Connie that summer before college. Parkie, as Annie Parks McCombs was called, was a chubby little girl of three months when Connie first saw her. They took to each other at once and Aunt Connie loved to care for the baby and play with her.

Three weeks before Connie was to leave for college, Laura came home from the post office with a Wellesley freshman manual, which she threw down on the table. "Will you look at that?" She pointed to a description of the "Wellesley gymnasium and field costume" and read aloud:

" 'For physical education each student needs the following:

" '1. Union underwear

2. Loose, unboned cotton underwaist

3. Dark blue serge kilted skirt, reaching just below knee

4. Dark blue serge scant bloomers, buttoned on waist, with drop seat in rear

5. Dark blue serge blouse, without trimming, to button on waist over bloomers.

6. Rubber soled shoes, without heels.' "

"Oh gosh, Laura, I can get along without that stuff."

"You didn't read what it says at the bottom." Laura took the booklet. " 'The above is required and must be ready for immediate use on the opening of college.' "

"Maybe we can buy it secondhand," said Connie, trying to soften the blow.

"Or I could make some of it. I'll write the college tonight," said Laura.

The answer came back firm and clear. The outfit was to be purchased, new, from A. G. Spalding & Co. in Boston at a cost of sixteen dollars and fifty cents. "Well," said Laura cheerfully, "that's that. We'll get it somehow, Con."

Laura not only produced the money for the gym suit, she bought Connie a ticket to Boston on the Fall River Steamship Line. On her way north, Connie stopped in Delaware to visit Eliza Short. Eliza was as gay and giddy as ever and she and Connie had good times with their beaus Will and Tom Marshall. The weather was still warm and the peach orchards were heavy with ripe fruit. One of their favorite pastimes was driving a buggy between the rows of peach trees, picking the fruit and eating it as they went. Connie inhaled the fragrance of the orchard and thought of the old days on the plantation when she used to drive wagonloads of peaches into market.

One day the boys took them in the buggy to Rehoboth Beach for a picnic. Rehoboth was a wide expanse of sea-washed sand, without one house to mar its open sweep down to the pounding surf. They swam in the waves and lolled on the beach. Connie looked fetching in the dark blue taffeta bathing suit Laura had made in the latest style, with sleeves and bloomers and a knee-length pleated skirt. Will Marshall gazed admiringly at the damp curls escaping from Connie's ruffled bathing cap and said, "What a waste!"

"What are you talking about?" demanded Connie.

"What a waste to send a pretty girl like you to college. None of the girls I know go. You ought to be like Eliza, Connie — just have fun and decorate the world with your shining presence."

"Women aren't supposed to be ornamental only. Didn't you read in the newspapers about Anna Taylor?"

"Who's Anna Taylor?"

"Oh, heavens, you don't read anything. Anna Taylor was the first woman to go over Niagara Falls in a barrel. And you know what the editor of a New York paper said about her?"

"That she was daft?"

"No, silly. He said, 'Anna Taylor took a lot of the credit that belonged to the barrel.' "

Will Marshall laughed. "Oh, you women have a tough time. Promise me one thing, will you Con?"

"I will if I can."

"I don't mind your going to college, if you have to, but please promise you'll never go over Niagara in a barrel. It'd be just like you to try it."

When Connie got to Wellesley she was assigned to the Eliot, a rambling dormitory in the village that housed sixty scholarship students. All the freshmen lived in village houses, about a mile from campus, and trudged up to classes in their long skirts. In stormy weather the wealthier girls rode in old Tom Griffin's horse-drawn cab, a luxury Connie never considered.

After the coziness and fun of Northfield, Connie's new room and roommate were discouraging. The room was barren. The roommate had dark hair and dark eyes and a pinched expression; she wore a man's shirt and necktie and a long black skirt. "Hello. I'm Bessie Wilson. I'm from Beverly, Massachusetts." She spoke in a dry voice with a sharp New England accent.

"I'm glad to know you," Connie grinned. "Gracious, don't they give us beds?"

"The beds are behind those curtains."

Connie peered behind the calico curtains. The beds were folded up against the wall.

"How about desks?"

"We have to buy them, of course."

"Oh. Are they expensive?"

"No, we can purchase hand-me-downs, I believe."

Connie laughed. "In the South we're used to hand-me-downs, but I thought you Yankees would be more particular."

Bessie Wilson did not smile. *Oh, murder,* thought Connie, *this girl isn't going to stand for any foolishness.*

As soon as she could, Connie explored the Wellesley

campus with two new friends, Elsie Goddard and Olive Hunter. They strolled through the grove of copper beeches at the East Gate and walked down to Tupelo Point to gaze at Lake Waban, circled by the flaming trees of autumn. Then they went past the new Houghton Memorial Chapel and Rhododendron Hollow to Longfellow Pond, where a fountain misted down on floating yellow elm leaves. They ended by climbing around the half-finished, raw-looking Quadrangle dormitories. "I think Wellesley College is smashing," Connie announced.

Classes started the next day and Connie attacked her courses head on. She took English, math, Latin, chemistry, Bible and hygiene. Her first course in chemistry, taught by a young Wellesley graduate named Miss Penny, was almost unbearably exciting to Connie. "I'm so wild over chemistry, I want to major in it," she told her faculty advisor, Dr. Charlotte Roberts.

"You couldn't pick a better subject, Miss Guion," beamed Miss Roberts, who happened to be the head of the department.

Classes were held in College Hall, which also housed all upperclassmen, all administrative offices, and the library. One September afternoon, when Connie was on her way to math class, a sophomore named Juliet Poynter stopped her near one of the white statues in College Hall's palm-filled center and asked her if she knew who the heroic-sized woman was seated on the marble chair.

"I haven't the slightest idea," said Connie.

"Gracious, you freshmen are ignorant! That's Harriet Martineau, the famous English writer who helped the American Abolitionists. She's supposed to represent the ideal modern woman, well educated and forthright. Now, Miss Connie from North Carolina, I want you to climb through the rungs of Harriet's marble chair. That's a little agility test we give freshmen."

Connie, always the tomboy, put down her books, scrambled up on the pedestal of the statue, and wriggled nimbly under the chair and out the other side. Juliet Poynter watched in admiration. "I declare! That was good. Why I've seen freshmen get stuck under Harriet's chair and stay there. You must be an athlete, Connie. I hope you'll come out for crew." Connie beamed at this unexpected praise from the willowy upperclassman. It was the beginning of a lifelong friendship.

Connie made friends easily, but living with Bessie Wilson took some doing. Bessie always finished her work early and was ready for bed at nine. Connie, determined to excel, wanted to study late. When Bessie complained that the light kept her awake, Connie quietly put a kerosene lamp under her black umbrella and studied flat on the floor.

"I think you're half cracked," said Bessie irritably.

"Could be, but don't forget I come from a long line of people who think it's bad luck to put up an umbrella in the house. I'm tempting fate, just so you can sleep, Bessie."

"Tut, tut," said Bessie, not knowing what else to say.

The two girls lived on the third floor and Bessie, of course, used the staircase. Not Connie. She preferred to climb out the window and let herself down by the fire escape rope. She slipped the halter at the end of the rope under her arms, picked up her bag full of books, and lowered herself by the pulley. It was a rapid and exciting way to travel, but Bessie refused to try it. She stayed in their room and pulled the rope back up, to be ready in case of fire.

One day Dr. Emily Barker, the housemother, happened to catch Connie making her perilous descent. She summoned Connie to her office. "Miss Guion, I do not want you coming down from the third floor by rope."

Connie's eyes opened wide. "Why, Dr. Barker, what if there's a fire? Up on that third floor we'd be stranded. I have to keep in practice."

Baffled, Dr. Barker changed the subject. "I understand you want to study medicine, Miss Guion. Where do you plan to take your training?"

"I've already registered at Johns Hopkins. Where did you study, Dr. Barker?"

"At the University of Michigan Medical School, thirty-five years ago. Thank goodness it's easier for women to become doctors now, but it's still a struggle. I hope you can see it through."

"I mean to. I want to be doctor more than anything in the world."

The Eliot was one of two houses at Wellesley that did not have maids to wait on the students. The scholarship girls did all the work. Connie got up early each morning to make the desserts, an easy task compared to getting breakfast for sixty at Northfield. She usually baked six cakes, one for each table in the dining room, and hurried back after class to ice them. "Tell Annie," she wrote her mother, "I'd be up the creek if she hadn't taught me to make a cake."

Only one other Northfield girl went to Wellesley with Connie, and that was, of all people, Rhoda Baker. Rhoda lived at the Eliot, too, and once again she and Connie worked side by side in the kitchen. Rhoda was as disagreeable as ever, but Connie paid her no heed.

Each month Laura sent Connie a dollar for spending money. This she changed into ten dimes and kept under her dresser scarf for emergencies. Imitating her mother's thrifty habits, she never spent the last dime until the next dollar arrived. To earn a little extra, Connie ironed the girls' ruffled shirtwaists or baked cakes for teachers' parties or addressed envelopes for the *Wellesley News* at the usual fee of ten cents an hour.

One rainy autumn afternoon Connie was surprised to receive a mysterious note asking her to come to President Hazard's house at 4 P.M.

"Why would the president of Wellesley want to see you?" demanded Bessie Wilson.

"She probably wants my advice on how to run the college."

"That hardly seems likely."

"I was *joking*, Bessie."

"Don't you ever take anything seriously, Connie Guion? If President Hazard sent for me, I'd be worried sick."

Connie had seen Miss Caroline Hazard in chapel and around the campus, a dignified, handsome woman with dark hair and classic features. Her composure at first seemed almost pompous, but actually it stemmed from an inner serenity nothing could disturb. She was a cultured woman, musical and literary, but vague about the students. When she passed them on campus she bowed and said, "How do you do, dear girls?" She never knew their names; she just knew they were dear Wellesley girls who deserved the best.

Connie walked in the rain up to the home President Hazard had built on the campus. She was shown into a charming room filled with books and flowers and mementos of world travel. A fire burned in the fireplace and carved on the mantel were the words *Give me my scallop shell of quiet . . . Sir Walter Raleigh.*

"I'm happy to see you," said Miss Hazard. "Won't you join me in a cup of tea by the fire?"

"Thank you, Miss Hazard, I'd love to."

Miss Hazard poured steaming tea from the blue Wedgwood teapot, added a slice of lemon, and handed the fragile cup to Connie. "My dear girl, how well do you know Rhoda Baker? I understand you were together at Northfield."

"Yes, Miss Hazard, we were. I guess I know her pretty well. She's smart, but she's a little odd."

"Do you think she would steal a watch?"

"Rhoda Baker? Never."

"What makes you so positive?"

"Miss Hazard, Rhoda Baker doesn't know whether it's 4 A.M. or 6 P.M. and she doesn't care. A watch wouldn't mean anything to that girl."

Miss Hazard sipped her tea thoughtfully. "A valuable watch has disappeared from a girl's room at the Eliot. Dr. Barker thinks Rhoda took it. She says the girl has been acting queerly."

Connie glanced at the Octagon soap watch hanging from her belt. She hoped no one would want to steal it. "Rhoda's queer, all right. She doesn't have enough common sense to grease a gimlet, but she's not a thief. I'm sure of it, Miss Hazard."

"I have a feeling you are right. I shall call Dr. Barker at once. Will you excuse me?"

Miss Hazard disappeared into the hall. Connie could hear her talking into the wall telephone. "Dr. Barker, I have interviewed a number of people in an effort to evaluate Rhoda Baker's background and personality. I've come to the conclusion she's erratic, but I do not believe she would steal."

There was a pause while Dr. Barker replied at the other end.

"Yes, Dr. Barker, but since it was the housekeeper who was so swift to accuse Rhoda, I am inclined to be suspicious of her. I want you to send the housekeeper to town on some pretext and while she is gone, search her room for the watch. Do you understand? Thank you, Dr. Barker. Good-by."

When the president returned, Connie rose to leave. "My dear girl," said Miss Hazard, taking Connie's hand and looking down at her, "thank you for your help. Please do not mention our discussion to anyone. We must never take the chance of hurting an innocent person."

The minute Connie returned to the Eliot, Bessie said, "What did Miss Hazard want?"

"She wanted me to help her protect the rights of all Wellesley girls."

Bessie looked at her sharply. "Why must you always talk perfect nonsense?"

"Just lucky, I guess," said Connie.

The next day the housekeeper at the Eliot suddenly packed and departed. Everyone was puzzled except Connie, who realized Miss Hazard's suspicion must have been correct. She never forgot the care Wellesley's president took to protect an accused student.

Connie soon discovered that the social life at Wellesley revolved around numerous campus clubs, such as the Mandolin Club, the Scribblers, the Consumers, the Pie Eaters and the Licker Club. The Licker Club took its name from a popular children's book, *The Goops:* "The Goops they lick their fingers; the Goops they lick their knives; they spill their broth on the tablecloths; they lead disgusting lives."

Connie joined the Southern Club, a small, enthusiastic group devoted to being proud you were a Southerner. She was proud to be the only girl from North Carolina at Wellesley. At their meetings they sang "Dixie" and eulogized Robert E. Lee and made chocolate peppermints. (All of the clubs were intensely interested in eating.) An upperclassman in the Southern Club named Carrie Nelson from Warrenton, Virginia, went out of her way to be nice to Connie. Carrie Nelson also came from an impoverished and aristocratic Southern family and was on a scholarship. Her friendship was to prove invaluable to Connie.

Class spirit ran high at Wellesley and 1906 was eager to make an impression. Connie and her friends hatched the daring idea of putting their class numerals up on the tower of the new heating plant recently given to the college by John D. Rockefeller. Connie, Elsie Goddard, Alice Ames and Catherine Jones concocted the idea and persuaded their class president, Olive Hunter, to join them.

With great secrecy, they bought a can of black paint and painted a huge 1906 on one of Elsie Goddard's sheets. At 5 o'clock on a cold November morning they climbed out of bed and sneaked up to the campus to scale the tower ladder. They balanced on the scaffolding as they lashed their sheet to the brick tower with heavy cords. A cold wind whipped their long skirts and blew their hair in their eyes, and they were so excited they could hardly tie the knots. As soon as they finished, they scrambled down and raced across the fields to Observatory Hill, where they paused to admire their handiwork.

"What a triumph!" exclaimed Elsie Goddard.

"Nineteen-six forever!" said Connie.

When Dean Pendleton saw the homemade banner she said she would expel those freshmen, if she knew who they were. The workmen said they had taken down some of the scaffolding supports and it was a wonder the girls weren't killed. The president of the sophomore class, deadly rivals of 1906, said she had never seen a stupider trick. The president of the junior class, 1906's sister class, declared the freshman feat ranked in daring and courage with the Rough Riders' attack on San Juan Hill. The five culprits listened and, when no one was looking, laughed. The class of 1906 had arrived.

Elsie Goddard and Connie had lots of laughs together, especially when Elsie took Connie home to Plainfield, New Jersey, for spring vacation. Connie felt very much at home with the Goddards, a large, jolly family. Elsie's sister Margaret was an art student and one night she brought home drawings from "life class." All the Goddards admired the sketches, but Connie blushed crimson and left the room. Afterwards Elsie said, "Why did you act so silly when Margaret showed her sketches? You wouldn't even look at them!"

"How could I look at those naked people when your brother was right there? What do you think I am?"

"I think you're a scream and I can't wait for you to go to medical school."

"Oh, that won't bother me. There's a difference between undressing for a doctor and going naked for an artist."

Connie was especially drawn to Mr. Goddard, a thin, dynamic man with a beaked nose and a sharp wit. One day when he came home from work, Connie rushed out to greet him and gave him such a big hug that she broke two of his ribs. Mr. Goddard, who must have suffered from the accident, made a joke of it. "Next time you bring home a friend, Elsie," he said when he was taking the girls to the train, "try to pick someone who's timid. I'm too old for anyone as enthusiastic as Connie."

"I'm sorry I broke you up, Mr. Goddard," said Connie, eyes twinkling, "but now you're breaking my heart, and that's worse than a couple of ribs."

"Let's kiss and make up," laughed Mr. Goddard, "but, first, put your hands behind your back. You're going to make a great doctor, Connie — if you don't splinter all your patients' bones."

Spring comes late in New England, but when it does come it is an event. In April Connie and her friends went out into the faintly green woods beyond the golf course for an "arbutus hunt." The arbutus, a sweet-smelling pale pink flower that is a harbinger of spring, hides under dry leaves and is difficult to find. As the girls crossed a footbridge, Connie pulled a sprig off a bush and started to chew it. Later, when they came back over the bridge carrying their baskets of arbutus, Connie suddenly stopped in her tracks. There were the whiskers of poison ivy on that same bush!

"Glory be! I've been chewing poison ivy all this time!" She spit it out and ran home to rinse her mouth.

The next morning when she came down to make her cakes, Rhoda Baker said with a sneer, "What's the matter with you? Have you looked at your face?"

Connie looked in a mirror and got a fearful shock — her face was swollen into a round moon. At breakfast she sat next to Dr. Barker, who did not seem to notice her. Finally Connie said, "Well, Dr. Barker, I've got poison ivy."

Dr. Barker looked at her and jumped up from the table. "Come right upstairs and I'll give you some rhus-tox." Connie began eating the little white pills, six at a time. She took rhus-tox all day; she still went to her classes, although she felt terrible. Her Latin teacher stared at the greasy black medicine on her puffy face and said, "Miss Guion, how do you have the nerve to come in here looking like that? You ought to have more respect for me."

"I have poison ivy."

"You have what?"

"I have poison ivy and Dr. Barker painted me with ichthyol."

"Shouldn't you be in bed?"

"Yes, but I came to get my Latin lesson. Just leave me alone until we get through the class and I'll go home."

"You may be contagious and we'll all catch poison ivy."

The class snickered. Connie wished the Latin teacher would catch it, but she knew she couldn't.

Connie was in bed for a month with poison ivy in her mouth and all over her body. Because her itching sores oozed a gummy liquid, she had to sleep on wet sheets; everything else stuck to her. For days she was unable to eat, she could only sip fluids through the straw Juliet Poynter had brought from the chemistry lab. Connie took enough rhus-tox for the whole college. Dr. Barker gave her a dissertation on rhus-tox. She told her the Indians discovered it; they took the tiny buds off the poison ivy plants in the spring and gave it to the warriors to eat so they would not get poison ivy.

"I got into this mess by chewing poison ivy," said Connie, "so why am I taking more of it in these pills?"

"That's what homeopathy is, Miss Guion, and of course you know I'm a homeopath."

"What do you mean, homeopath?"

"A doctor who cures a disease by giving small doses of the thing that caused it. Homeopathy is an ancient and honorable branch of medicine," Dr. Barker said defensively. "You may become a homeopath yourself."

Never, thought Connie. *I mean to be the kind of doctor who makes a patient comfortable and gets him well. That is, if I ever get well.*

Dr. Barker did nothing to make Connie comfortable, but Connie's friends were wonderful to her. They took turns reading to her and helping her memorize the kings in the Old Testament and countless chemistry formulas, and wrote down the solutions to the algebra problems as she figured them out in her head. The Latin teacher was still so afraid of catching poison ivy that she insisted all Connie's assignments had to be recopied.

At last, in May, Connie was able to go out. She was thin and weak and had to wear a green veil to protect her raw skin from the sun. "I feel like I've had scarlet fever, instead of just poison ivy."

"You look it, too," said Bessie.

Connie had missed all the excitement of the student government elections, when the girls paraded over the campus and screamed themselves hoarse, but she received an honor that made up for it. She was chosen to represent the freshmen on Tree Day and to make the speech as Receiver of the Spade.

For Connie, her first Tree Day was a thrilling pageant. First the seniors, in cap and gown, marched down the hill from College Hall, followed by the juniors, dressed in white and wearing purple ribbons, their class color. Down from Shakespeare House came the sophomores in fairy tale costumes, ready to dance "The Romaunce of the Rose," while through the trees on the hillside appeared the freshmen, wearing for the first time the class colors they had been hiding for weeks from the sophomores. Stirring music burst forth and the colorful procession marched across the green. Then the senior president made a speech of welcome; the senior orator doled out humorous advice to the lower classes; and, to Elgar's "Pomp and Circumstance," the Tree Day Mistress and her aides moved majestically across the lawn.

After the dances came Connie's big moment — the receiving of the freshman spade and the making of her speech. She had been practicing the speech for days under the stern direction of Miss Sophie Hart, and it turned out to be a great success, not only because of its content, but because of Connie's Southern drawl. Afterwards, the freshmen sang themselves hoarse and cheered everything and everybody. Then on a signal they raced for their class tree, which they had planted secretly between Longfellow Pond and Rhodendron Hollow. They beat the hated sophomores and were allowed to give their class cheer for the first time. "Rah! Hoorah! Nineteen-six! One-nine-oh-six! *Wellesley!*"

Connie received many compliments on her Tree Day speech, but it quite took her breath away when a note came from Elizabeth Conover, the exalted editor of the *Wellesley News*. "My dear Connie, I don't want to spoil you so early, but of all the 57 varieties I've ever known, you are the best!"

✳ 14 ✳

Connie's First Clinic

TO CONNIE the summer of 1903 was memorable for two things. That August she turned twenty-one, and she saw her first automobile. It belonged to Mr. Roundtree, the agent for Octagon soap, and it was made in the shape of a bar of Octagon soap. It was khaki color and oblong and high off the ground, and it looked like a bar of soap on wheels. When the amazing automobile chugged down Ninth Street Connie ran out to look at it, and Mr. Roundtree invited her to get in and go for a ride around the block.

"Gee whilligers, this is something!" exclaimed Connie. "But don't you miss the horses?"

"Only when I buy gas. A motor car can do a lot of things a horse and buggy can't. Did you hear about those men who drove a Packard car from San Francisco clear to New York?"

"Heavens to Betsy! How long did it take?"

"Only fifty-two days. They set the world's long distance record."

"Do you suppose women will ever be able to drive?"

"Sure, the first one got a driver's license last March. Name's Anne French and she lives in Washington, D.C. Must be some kind of a freak."

Mr. Roundtree slammed on the brakes and the car squeaked to a stop in front of the Guion house. Connie climbed out without opening the door. "Thanks, Mr. Round-tree. My first auto ride was a corker."

"I see you're still wearing your Octagon soap watch, Con-nie. Keep good time?"

"Perfect. I wouldn't trade it for a diamond wristwatch."

"Stick with Octagon and you can't go wrong," beamed Mr. Roundtree.

In her sophomore year at Wellesley, Connie gloried in a course called "The Analysis of Air, Food, and Water," an adventure in chemistry so stimulating to her imagination that she analyzed everything in sight. German was something else again. She took it because German was required for a medical degree, since the best work in medicine was being done in Germany. Her teacher, a Wagnerian type named Dr. Freida Johanna Von Himmelman, had no sense of humor and a short supply of patience. Connie's attempts to mix German with her Southern accent enraged the woman.

"Ach! *Vot* do you talk?"

"Deutsch, Fräulein Doktor," said Connie, hopefully.

"Deutsch! Nein! Ach, mein himmel! You can't effen schpeak English. Vere do you come from? Soch language!"

Connie's Southern blood began to boil. "There are lots of different brogues in Germany. I don't know why we can't have brogues over here, too."

"Vot is brogues, Fräulein Guion? You schpeak nonsens."

Connie gritted her teeth and withstood these Germanic onslaughts for several months. Then she marched in to see the dean. "Miss Pendleton, I *have* to drop German. I can't take any more of that big woman screaming at me."

For a moment, Miss Pendleton looked shocked, but Connie's exasperation was so comical she had to laugh.

"You remind me of the girl who told President Alice Freeman Palmer she wanted to drop English Lit. Mrs. Palmer said, 'If you haven't enough time to say "literature," certainly you must drop something.' "

After Connie passed her German mid-year exam, Dean Pendleton suggested she substitute Miss Sophie Jewett's course in Elizabethan Poetry for the German. Connie, who had been steeped in English literature at her mother's knee, couldn't have been happier. Miss Sophie Jewett, who always dressed in green, wore handsome high-necked shirtwaists and full silk skirts. She was beautiful to look at, with graying, wavy hair and large green eyes, and wonderful to listen to, as she read poetry in her low, thrilling voice. Connie's favorite poet was Sir Philip Sidney and when Miss Jewett read from *Astrophel and Stella*, "Look in thy heart, and write," she suddenly thought of the long unanswered letter from Caleb Motz lying on her desk. Poetry played odd tricks on her; she quickly put the thought away.

Connie liked Wellesley's daily chapel service, perhaps because it was optional. She found refreshing that fifteen minutes of inner quiet early in the morning, fifteen minutes of peace that had to last the rest of the day. The teachers took turns leading the service, and the girls could predict their hymns. The astronomy professor would choose "Spacious Firmament on High" and the botany teacher's standby was "Fairest Lord Jesus, Ruler of All Nature." Connie's eyes often strayed to the Wellesley motto in bronze letters above the Tiffany windows, *Non Ministrari, Sed Ministrare* — not to be ministered unto, but to minister. These ideals of service were made to order for a girl heading down the long road toward the practice of medicine.

The harder Connie studied that fall, the more the words in her books blurred. She began to have frequent headaches and finally consulted Dr. Barker, who sent her to see Miss Sherrard in the Department of Hygiene. Miss Sherrard gave

Connie an eye-chart test and said, "Well, Miss Guion, you certainly need glasses."

"Rats," said Connie. "I suppose they cost a fortune."

"Not at all. You can go to the eye clinic in Boston. It's a wonderful place, the best doctors and no charge for their services. I'll give you a letter to the head of the clinic. You can get your glasses there in one day."

Connie took the early train to Boston and reached the clinic before it opened. She handed the note to a nurse who glanced at it and gave it back. "Sit down and wait," she said.

Connie sat down on a hard bench. The room filled up rapidly; soon all the benches were crowded. Everybody just sat there. In the back room they could see the doctors laughing and joking with the nurses, in no hurry to begin work. Connie had never been in a hospital clinic before. She looked around the dingy, dusty room and thought of the gleaming whiteness Ef had shown her at St. Luke's Hospital in New York.

She waited two hours before her name was called. She handed the young doctor Miss Sherrard's note, but he didn't look at the note and he didn't look at Connie. "Sit," he said. He quickly held one lens after another over her eye and said, "Is this better, or is this better? How's this one? How's this?"

Connie was confused. "You're going too fast. My eyes can't adjust. I don't know which is right."

The doctor did not seem to hear. He sat down and wrote off a prescription and poked it toward her. "Go in there for glasses. Next."

Connie was stunned. She felt she was being shunted about like a piece of unclaimed freight. She took the prescription, but she did not stop to get the glasses. Instead, she went straight to the head of the hospital, a Harvard classmate of Dr. Babcock's whom she had met before. "Doctor," she said, "I've just been through your eye clinic and I am amazed. It's shocking."

The doctor looked amazed too. He was not accustomed to being scolded by pert young ladies in Sears, Roebuck suits. "Exactly what is the trouble, may I ask?"

"Back home we treat cows and chickens better than you treat people in your clinic. That eye man has no idea whether the prescription he gave me is right or wrong, and what's more, he doesn't care. He just clicks the lenses back and forth and says 'next.'"

Connie paused for breath. The head of the hospital looked flabbergasted.

"If that's a clinic," Connie went on, "and that's the way poor people get treated, then something has *got* to be done about clinics. Things ought to be decent, or they ought not to exist."

The doctor did his best to placate her, but Connie was still fuming when she left. She knew her tirade would have little effect on the hospital, but she was surprised that it had such a strong effect on her. All the way home on the train her own words rang to the clang of the wheels. *Something has got to be done about clinics. Things ought to be decent, or they ought not to exist.* The more she thought about those words, the more important they seemed. Connie Guion's life had suddenly taken a new direction.

Laura not only sustained Connie with her dollar-a-month allowance; she wrote her wonderful letters, telling all the news. In December of 1903, she wrote saying she was glad to hear Connie had gotten glasses from that doctor in Boston. She said everyone in Charlotte was excited because the Wright Brothers flew an airship at Kitty Hawk. Mr. Orville was up in the air for twelve seconds and Mr. Wilbur was up for fifty-nine seconds, and was North Carolina proud! Laura also said she had broken her engagement of thirteen years' standing to the cotton broker, and guess what, she was going to marry Alex Haskell. She hadn't seen him since Mrs. Miller's boarding house, but when he turned up she realized *he* was the one. They were going to get married in June and go to Boston on their honeymoon and would come out to see Connie and Wellesley.

Every Sunday afternoon Carrie Nelson took Connie to call on Mrs. Durant, the widow of Wellesley's founder. Both girls had meager wardrobes — Carrie usually wore a black cotton shirtwaist and Connie a white one — but being Southern ladies they never went without hats and gloves.

The girls were awed by the Durants' stately white house, which was later to become the residence of Wellesley's presidents. To Connie, the long, curving driveway in front and the green lawns sweeping down to Lake Waban, the delicately carved mantels, the crystal chandeliers, the Oriental rugs and the formal sitting rooms were the height of elegance.

Connie later wrote her mother, "Mrs. Durant is a Southerner and I'm crazy about her. She and her husband started Wellesley in 1875 and he died twenty years ago, but she's still wrapped up in the college. She looks like Queen Victoria with a round face and round bosom and gray hair. She's such a dear little lady I just want to hug her."

While Mrs. Durant's butler served tea, the conversation usually centered on Warrenton, Virginia, where Mrs. Durant had grown up and where she had known Carrie Nelson's family. Later, the plump little lady in heavy black silk would reminisce about her husband. "How I wish you girls had known Mr. Durant. He was so handsome and aristocratic with his Prince Albert coat and courtly manners."

"Wasn't he a friend of Mr. Dwight Moody?" asked Connie, who wanted to keep Mrs. Durant going on her favorite subject.

"Why, yes, my dear. After our children died — Pauline lived only two months and Henry, junior, died when he was eight — my husband became deeply religious and Mr. Moody was an inspiration to him. It was then he founded Wellesley College."

Mrs. Durant gazed out the window. She dabbed her eyes with her lace handkerchief and went on. "How Mr. Durant loved the tree-covered slopes and the daisied meadows of Wellesley. He loved the girls, too, and worried about their health. He told them, 'I am against waists that are too tight, skirts that are too long, hats that don't cover the head, shoes that are too narrow, heels too high and soles too thin.'"

The three women sat in silence in the deepening twilight, sipping tea and thinking of this dynamic man who had had an effect on all their lives. Suddenly Mrs. Durant switched the subject. "Carrie, dear, do you need any money?"

"No, indeed. I don't have anything to spend money on." Connie glanced at Carrie. Connie was frugal, but Carrie Nelson was really spartan. Both girls had long since turned their backs on anything that cost money.

Mrs. Durant turned to Connie, "I am always impressed by the way you Southern girls manage. When Carrie graduates, how would you like to have the Durant scholarship, Connie? It is my privilege to select the girl who receives it."

Connie's jaw dropped. She knew that the Durant scholarship covered both board and tuition. "Oh, Mrs. Durant, that would be wonderful. What it would mean to my family — and to me!"

"Splendid." Mrs. Durant smiled at Connie. "I feel sure you are the kind of girl who will make Wellesley proud."

That night Connie wrote a happy letter to Laura. "I'm glad

you and Alex Haskell are getting married. I remember him well. I have been to a couple of football games at Harvard with his nephews Jim and Sam Haskell. Everybody up here talks about Alex's sister Mary from the class of '97 who started the Barn — 'everybody's club, to be gay in once a week.' We have dances at the Barn all the time, but no men are allowed. Laura, you don't have to worry any more about sending me to college! Mrs. Durant is giving me a complete scholarship. Isn't that stupendous? Now we can all concentrate on getting Ridie and Jo through Northfield and Wellesley."

To receive the Durant scholarship was a high honor. No girl would even be considered for it unless she was an outstanding student. Connie had also won the Fiske scholarship for four hundred dollars in her junior year, and these two awards marked a turning point in Connie's academic career. By steady hard work, she had finally made up for her erratic early education.

When springtime came to Wellesley, Connie occasionally put aside her books to tramp into the woods and paddle on the lake. Her friends who owned their own canoes would invite her to drift and glide across Lake Waban with them. They would take their mandolins and sing Wellesley songs. Connie still could not carry a tune in a bucket, but she joined in with gusto.

One sure sign of spring at Wellesley comes on Patriot's Day, April 19, when the Boston Marathon is run. All the girls gathered along the viaduct to watch the red-faced men huff and puff their way over the grueling twenty-six-mile route.

"The poor simps," said Connie, shaking her head.

"Why do you say that?" asked Elsie Goddard. "I think they're kind of heroic."

"Heroic, my foot. They're as queer as Dick's hatband. Imagine going out and running till you drop. Only a man would think of such a thing."

"Don't you like men, Connie?"

"Of course I do, but they're all spoiled to death by their doting mamas."

Connie allowed little time in her busy life for men, but she objected strenuously to Wellesley's rule forbidding men to set foot on the campus on Sundays, "except fathers, brothers, and unexpected fiancés." When Connie was an officer of Student Government this rule came up for discussion because a reckless girl had gone buggy-riding with her beau on a Sunday afternoon. It was decided that the sinner would have to resign her position as a class officer. Everyone seemed to think the punishment just, but Connie's common sense was offended.

She rose to her feet and said in her slow Southern way, "Is there something inherently evil in the male that makes you forbid him on campus, or is it because his voice carries farther than yours?" Laughter almost broke up the meeting. Before long the rule was changed. By poking fun, Connie had opened a window on an airtight, musty old custom.

Men came out from Harvard and M.I.T. by train and trolley for Glee Club or Mandolin Club concerts, but never for dances. It was not until 1913 that Wellesley girls were allowed to dance with men at college parties, and even then if a girl were caught holding a man's hand she faced serious consequences.

Many proper Bostonians considered Wellesley a radical institution, but in fact the college had many rigid regulations. Girls had to be accompanied by a chaperone if they left campus after 7:30 P.M. At night, a campus policeman escorted them from the library to the dormitory. The students seldom

went away on weekends, although upperclassmen were permitted two overnights a term. No classes were held on Mon-
days because it was improper to study on Sundays. Men could
not appear in college plays and the girls who impersonated
men had to wear long black skirts, as it was undignified to
wear trousers. It was equally unladylike to let your slip show.
When Vassar girls came for a debate, a student government
sign on the bulletin board read: "Any Wellesley girl whose
slip shows will be fined 50¢."

Smoking, of course, was beyond the pale. Connie, as student government representative, had to question a girl named
Freda Simker who broke the no-smoking rule. "Why do you
want to smoke, Freda?" asked Connie. "You smell bad and
so do your clothes and so does your room."

"My mother and father smoke and I'm going to smoke,
too. I don't give a hoot what this stuffy college thinks."

"If your mother and father stole a thousand dollars, that
wouldn't mean you could steal without breaking the law. If
this comes up before the faculty, you'll have to leave." Connie paused, "I'm going to vote for a reprimand instead. I
think we ought to keep you here because you're such a fool
you need an education."

"You don't like me because I'm a Jew."

"I never knew the difference between a Jew and a Gen-
tile until I came to college, and I don't pay any attention to it
now. All I care about is how a person *acts* and, Freda, you're
acting bad."

Next day Freda was summoned before the college government board. She stood at the end of a long table around
which sat solemn-faced students in cap and gown. The student government president rose and read a stern reprimand,
castigating Freda Simker for smoking. It was a painful ordeal
for everyone, especially Connie. She felt sorry for Freda, al-

though she could not understand why any girl would break a college rule for a miserable, smelly, unsanitary cigarette.

Connie drew a new roommate in her junior year, an attractive girl from Detroit named Laura Dwight. She and Connie made a good team, both full of energy and ideas and laughter.

"I'll darn the stockings," said Laura, "and you sew on the buttons. Divide and conquer!"

"That's great. I loathe darning."

"No wonder. Your darning's pitiful. But once you sew on a button, Con, it's on for life. Girl, you've got tenacity."

Their room became a gathering place. A favorite topic for gab fests was "Why Doesn't Connie Guion Wear a Corset?" Most of the girls laced themselves into corsets to achieve the popular hourglass silhouette and because Connie was round and short, they thought she needed one, too. Two of the girls stuffed a pillow into a Ferriss waist and exhibited it around the dormitory as a statue of Connie. Connie paid no attention.

"Say, Con," teased Olive Smith, "why don't you blow yourself to a corset? Look at this ad in the *Wellesley News:* 'You are cordially invited to inspect the stock of the famous Girdliere, Mme. Rat. Stays and girdles to fit all figures. Stout ladies a specialty.' "

"I'm a free woman and I refuse to be cooped up in stays and girdles. Give me the wide open spaces."

One night when Connie went up to study after supper, she found her room jammed with girls holding corsets. Marion Carlisle handed her a suit of long underwear. "Put this on, Connie. We want you to try on all our corsets, till you find one that fits. It's time for you to shape up."

Connie looked at the eager faces and laughed. She had no idea of spending a penny of her hard-earned money on a corset, but she was willing to go along with the fun. She pulled on the union suit and fastened on one corset after another, swaggering around the room in ridiculous poses. As the Foundation Garment Show proceeded, gales of laughter swept down the hall. Suddenly the door swung open and there stood the professor of mathematics, glowering. "Young ladies of elegant leisure, *you* may not have anything to do, but a few people in this college have and I am among the few. *Will you please be quiet?*"

Later, Laura Dwight said, "Connie, what made you act like such a goose?"

"It was easier than explaining that I don't have the cash to buy a corset. They wouldn't even know what I meant."

"Do you wish you could buy one?"

"Me? No, indeed. I've got better things to worry my head about than where my bulges go."

* 15 *

An Opener of Windows

CONNIE'S WORLD was opening up — the farm girl from River Bend Plantation was becoming a woman of the world. She represented Wellesley at a YWCA conference at Lake George. She spent a holiday on Nantucket. She heard Jane Addams of Hull House tell about settlement work in Chicago. She attended a Paderewski concert and visited the Boston Museum of Fine Arts, her first museum. One Christmas Eve in Boston she saw E. H. Sothern and Julia Marlow in *Romeo and Juliet*. She was even becoming politically aware. She led the Wellesley Democrats in their campaign for Alton B. Parker against the Republican Teddy Roosevelt, a doomed but enthusiastic project. Yet no matter how far Connie traveled, her heart was never far from home. Each summer she returned with zest to North Carolina, more a Tarheel than ever.

Like a squirrel who stashes away nuts against the coming winter, Mrs. Guion hoarded her pennies and when her children came home on vacation she was ready. In the summer of 1905 she somehow managed, with the help of Cousin Alice's war pension, to rent a farm house near Black Mountain, North Carolina. Here the family spent a memorable vacation, three generations of Guions working and playing together. They took walks in the woods, climbed mountains, played baseball, swam in the branch and talked for hours under the stars. They had little cash but they didn't need much. They rented a cow, which Connie milked daily, and stored the milk and butter in a spring house. They had a vegetable garden and chickens; the surplus chickens sold for fifteen cents each, or two for a quarter. The cow was fed on carrots and gave yellow milk, much to the delight of the children. The mountains were full of blackberries, raspberries and dewberries and the greatest treat of all for dessert was one of Connie's blackberry tarts.

Each day Connie walked three miles to town to get the mail, with doting nieces and nephews trailing behind her. Aunt Connie, who taught the children how to shoot marbles and spin tops, was their Pied Piper. Parkie McCombs and Jim Vason, Alice's only child, never let her out of their sight. Alice's husband, Sidney Vason, had died earlier that summer of cancer and Alice had come home to live.

On their way, the mail-fetchers had to cross a board stretched over a swift mountain stream. Often by the time they returned, the rains would have begun. Nowhere can it rain the way it rains in the mountains of North Carolina. It pours down from the top of the mountains and gushes into the streams, as though a giant paper bag full of water had burst. The Guions never went far without raincoats and umbrellas.

"Aunt Connie," said Jim during one cloudburst, "how're we going to get over that creek? It'll be rampaging."

"Never mind, Jimbo," said Parkie, "Aunt Con'll get us over."

By the time they reached the stream, the torrent was running high over the rickety plank, carrying with it snakes off the mountain, rattlers, moccasins and black snakes. "I ain't putting my bare foot in that snaky water," Jim announced. "I don't care if I never get home."

"Aunt Con'll get us there," repeated Parkie. And Connie

did. One by one she transported the children across the wild stream on her back. It was a dramatic rescue, but a costly one because when she reached home, Connie discovered her O.H.M. Whisky knife had slipped out of her pocket. She felt as though she had lost a dear friend. She was determined to find it.

As soon as the storm passed, she went back to the stream and started to hunt. She searched endlessly until, miraculously, she found it two hundred yards downstream caught between two rocks. Connie was careful never to let that prized knife get lost again; sixty years later she was still carrying it in her doctor's bag.

That summer a surprising thing happened — Louis Guion decided to get married. A tall, lighthearted young man of thirty-two, he was living with the Babcocks and running a cotton duck mill in Columbia, South Carolina, when he met a handsome girl named Elizabeth Guignard. Louis had always been spoiled by his four adoring older sisters and the family assumed he would be a gay blade bachelor forever, so the news of his engagement caused great excitement. Connie and her mother took Ridie and Jo to South Carolina for the big church wedding. Viv was best man and Ben was an usher, and the Babcocks were there and Mary Wood, who was still working as Dr. Babcock's secretary. Laura and Alex Haskell came up from New Orleans, where Alex was superintendent of a cotton mill, bringing with them Alex, junior, who had been born five months before. Laura had waited until she was thirty-six years old to have a child, and that baby brought stars to her eyes.

"Well, Con," said the bridegroom, "now you're almost out of college, I suppose you'll be the next Guion married."

"Not on your tintype, Louis. You don't get to be a doctor by getting yourself hitched."

Louis Guion

"Atta girl, Con," laughed Viv. "I can see your shingle now: Connie Myers Guion, M.D., The Little Doctor with the Big Heart."

During her four years at Wellesley, Connie took every biology and chemistry course the college had to offer. Dr. Caroline Thompson's course in the Anatomy of the Cat opened up a new field for Connie. Miss Thompson, tall, red-haired, and freckled, was a homely but stimulating teacher. Connie would rush up to the fourth floor of College Hall to anesthetize the cat and stretch it out on the operating table. Then she sharpened the knives and got everything ready for Miss Thompson. She held her breath as this teacher, who was so clever with her hands in dissection, opened the cat's chest while the heart was still beating and explained the intricacies of anatomy. After the lesson, Miss Thompson quickly chloroformed the cat, making sure it did not suffer.

One of Miss Thompson's zoology experiments that had a lasting effect on Connie was a demonstration of the injurious effect of cigarette smoke. She had the girls stretch out the web of a frog's foot under a microscope to observe the blood flowing through the arteries. Then she would place on the web a drop of water containing cigarette smoke. As they watched, the artery would contract until the blood stopped flowing altogether. Once the effect of the smoke wore off, the blood would begin to flow again.

"Girls," said Miss Thompson, "now that you see how smoke contracts the arteries, do you understand why I hope you will never smoke? Only yesterday I read that a woman was arrested in New York City for smoking a cigarette while driving an automobile on Fifth Avenue, so beware!"

Dr. Charlotte Roberts, Connie's chemistry professor, was equally dynamic. On the first day of class she took a piece of coal out of her pocket and held it up. "Young ladies, this is the basis of all organic chemistry and the end of all organic life. If you can understand what produced this lump of coal — and what it in turn can produce — you will understand chemistry."

The most famous teacher Connie had in college was Katharine Lee Bates, a Wellesley graduate of 1880 who wrote "America, the Beautiful." She had gone on a trip up Pike's Peak and the vista from the mountain top inspired her to compose the poem which was hailed as "the new national anthem."

Connie considered Miss Bates most unpoetic in appearance. A heavy woman with thick-lensed glasses, she had a quick, often cutting wit. The girls said you should choose with care the year to take her Shakespeare course. One year Miss Bates would be writing and that would not be the year. On alternate years it would be good.

Miss Bates had an unusual voice, resonant and husky, and she liked to read her own poetry to the class. She would intone heavily:

The rain that fell yesterday makes all the hillside glisten,
Is coral on the laurel and beryl on the grass . . .

Each day Miss Bates required her pupils to stand when the roll was called and recite a verse from Shakespeare. Day after day Connie would rise and rattle off as fast as she could:

Crabbed age and youth cannot live together:
Youth is full of pleasance, age is full of care.

Exasperated, Miss Bates said, "Miss Guion, can't you possibly learn another verse?"

"No, Miss Bates, I'm so busy with science, I'm afraid I can't."

"Don't you know *any* other poem?"

"Of course not, Miss Bates. If I did, I wouldn't say this stupid thing day after day."

"In the future, Miss Guion, you may be excused from reciting. We've heard that verse three times a week for five months, and that's quite enough."

To her surprise, Connie was asked to join Shakespeare Society, a great honor. She refused that and two other society bids because she did not feel she could afford the membership fees. But the Shakespeare president would not take "no" for an answer; she insisted that Connie let the society's special fund take care of her dues. They couldn't find a girl like Connie Guion every day.

Connie threw herself into the activities at Shakespeare with characteristic vigor. Every Sunday evening she attended vesper services in the paneled-oak living room lined with books. A fire would crackle in the stone fireplace as the girls sat on the floor at twilight and sang, "Now the day is over, night is drawing nigh, shadows of the evening fade across the sky." But when Shakespeare put on *As You Like It* and *Much Ado About Nothing,* the director informed Connie that she was too completely herself ever to become an actress. Undaunted, she worked hard back stage and was very much a part of every production.

There were lots of parties at Shakespeare and Connie got to know Dean Ellen Pendleton, who was also a member. Most of the girls loved Miss Pendleton, who did not hesitate to appear on stage in white satin tights, in spite of the fact that she was the dignified dean; but to a few she seemed as cold as the icicle on the end of the barn. She was a big woman with round pink cheeks, white curly hair and blue eyes sparkling behind rimless glasses. A mathematician with a highly trained memory, she prided herself on knowing the name of every student and every shrub at Wellesley. Miss Pendleton was New England to the core, with a love of excellence and a disdain for anything shoddy. When she became president of the college she left an indelible mark on Wellesley.

Connie's college days rolled merrily along toward their inevitable close, the work punctuated by campus frolics. There was Float Night when the students sat on the lantern-lit bank below College Hall waiting for the racing shells, and the canoes decorated with lights and flowers and class numerals, to appear round Tupelo Point, a signal for everyone to burst into song. There were the "Forensic Burnings" when the juniors who had completed the required course in debates, or forensics, piled up everything they had memorized and burned the whole stack in a secret bonfire. There were the May Day festivities, described by Connie's classmate, Ione Morrison, in her diary:

> *Today was a beautiful day for May Day, the beginning of the end for the seniors. We all dressed in cap and gown and rolled our hoops to chapel. We had gotten up early and scrubbed the Backwoodsman statue and decorated all the other statuary. The Backwoodsman looked particularly gay in lavender bloomers and a lavender parasol. In the afternoon the girls, dressed as children, danced around the Maypole and played games on the lawn while a hurdy-gurdy dispensed sweet strains.*

But it wasn't all sunshine and skittles for the class of 1906. The college was stunned one night in April when news came of the cataclysmic earthquake and fire in San Francisco. Some of Connie's classmates from California had families involved in the tragedy and everyone felt the effects of it.

Connie had her own personal tragedy, too. On Easter Sunday, April 15, 1906, she received a telegram from her mother saying that Cousin Alice was dead. Connie did not even know she had been ill and it was a terrible shock. She simply could not believe Cousin Alice was gone forever. She pictured the sprightly little lady, fairy godmother to all the Guions, shaking her tight curls as she played the piano and sang or read poetry aloud. Gentle, impractical, lovable — Cousin Alice was irreplaceable.

Later a letter came from her mother: "Cousin Alice had

cancer, Con, and of course we should be thankful she didn't suffer long. Ef nursed her and we did all we could to ease her pain. She was cheerful and optimistic to the end. Cousin Alice and I lived together for over forty years. Without her I am desolate."

"I dread going home," Connie told Laura Dwight. "With Cousin Alice gone, it won't be home at all."

As graduation drew near, the class of 1906 was a-twit with excitement. They displayed their class flower, white sweet pea; their class colors, baby blue and silver; their motto, "Honor before Honors"; and posed for pictures for *The Legenda*. Connie's was taken in profile, her hair — no longer blond but brown — swept up in a pompadour. She was dressed in a high-necked white shirtwaist and man's necktie, and the dreamy expression on her face contrasted with her turned-up nose and firm chin.

Two hundred girls were graduating, most of them bent on a serious career, although a few were frankly headed for matrimony. Connie was anxious that her first real employment should pay well. "Why don't you take that job teaching at the girls' school in Houston?" asked Laura Dwight. "It has a good salary."

"I'd have to get to Texas and I'd have to get back, that's why. I've applied for a teaching position at Vassar but I don't suppose I'll get it. Myra Kilborn is after it, too."

On a balmy May morning, just as Connie and her friends were setting off in a buggy for a picnic on Pigeon Hill, Dean Pendleton sent word that Dr. Moulton had arrived from Vassar to interview the candidates for his chemistry department. Connie did not want to keep her friends waiting while she went to see Dr. Moulton.

"Piffle," said Olive Hunter, "we'll wait. Think what a lark it would be to have a classmate teach at Vassar."

Connie's graduation picture

Dr. Moulton had just finished talking with Myra Kilborn when Connie arrived. He was a stooped, middle-aged man, almost bald, who kept his hands in his pockets. "Miss Guion, Dean Pendleton tells me you excel at chemistry."

"Well, I work hard at it, because I enjoy it."

"Why do you want to be a teacher?"

"I don't want to be a teacher."

"Oh?"

"I want to be a doctor."

"Then why —"

"Oh, I won't go to medical school for years yet, Dr. Moulton. I'm registered at Johns Hopkins, but first I have to help my two younger sisters get through Northfield and Wellesley."

"Can you typewrite?"

"No, I can't, and I'm not going to learn."

"Why not?"

"Once I learn, I'll just have it all to do."

Dr. Moulton puzzled over that a moment. Then he said,

"Do you think you would like teaching in the lab, setting up experiments, correcting examinations, all that?"

"Oh, yes, indeed, that's not humdrum like typing."

"Can you show me around your chemistry building, Miss Guion? I'd like to look at it."

Connie glanced at the Octagon watch hanging from her patent leather belt. Her friends would be waiting. "I'd be glad to, Dr. Moulton."

But when they reached the chemistry building, it was locked. "I'm disappointed," said Dr. Moulton. "I did want to go inside."

"Just wait a little bit and I'll see what I can do."

Connie tried every door and window, but all of them were locked. Then she disappeared around the building and came back lugging a ladder. Dr. Moulton was amazed to see her prop it against the wall and climb up to the second floor. His jaw dropped when she opened a window and climbed inside. A moment later the front door opened and Connie said with a grin, "Won't you come in, Dr. Moulton?"

Nonplussed, Dr. Moulton rubbed his bald head. "Well, I never." He walked around the laboratory, still shaking his head, and finally said, "Well, that's all I wanted to see."

"I'll let you out the front door and lock it." Connie retraced her steps and put the ladder away.

When she rejoined Dr. Moulton he said, "Dean Pendleton suggested I should hire Myra Kilborn because she is a brilliant student. She told me, 'That Connie Guion is all right, but she's a diamond in the rough.'"

"Myra is much smarter than I am."

"Perhaps, but when I asked Miss Kilborn to show me this building she said it was impossible because everything was locked. I admire your ingenuity, Miss Guion. The job is yours."

"And the salary?"

"Vassar pays new teachers four hundred dollars a year."

"Grand! Thanks, Dr. Moulton. The girls are waiting for me to start on a picnic, and if you'll excuse me I'll have to run along. Good-by, Dr. Moulton. I'll see you in the fall." Connie picked up her long skirt and started to run toward College Hall. Breathless, she told her chums what had happened, ending with, " — and you know what Miss Pendleton called me — a diamond in the rough!"

"There's an ancient Hindu saying," laughed Elsie Goddard, "I read it in Kipling: 'Who, having known the diamond, will concern himself with glass?' "

"That's our Connie," said Olive Hunter, "all diamond and a yard wide."

Connie's first commencement, at the age of twenty-four, was a little disappointing. She had not graduated from the graded school or Miss Shipp's or Northfield, and she hoped so much that her mother would be able to come to see the first of her twelve children graduate from college. But neither her mother nor any of her older brothers and sisters could afford the trip. The only one there was Ridie, who came down from Northfield.

Showing Ridie around Wellesley, which she planned to enter the following year, was fun. Connie was proud of her pretty, bright sister. Someone gave them two tickets for *Agamemnon* which was playing in Boston. Neither she nor Ridie knew a word of Greek, but they went anyway. Ridie, the poetic one, was so overcome by the beauty of the production she could hardly speak, and Connie shocked her by saying she couldn't see any sense in all that jibber-jabber.

The girls enjoyed the traditional events of graduation, the garden party on College Hall green, the play at Tupelo Point, the glee club concert at the edge of Longfellow Pond, and the class dinner. But the actual commencement exercises were miserable. Governor Giles of Massachusetts was to be the speaker, a poor choice. Everyone gathered in the warm, crowded chapel and the graduating class filed in solemnly in long black robes, high, boned collars and mortar board hats. All was in readiness, but the governor did not arrive. They waited and waited, but no speaker. At last he came, very late, and added insult to injury by making a windy, political speech that did not interest anyone, not even himself.

Afterward, President Hazard addressed the class of 1906 in Latin and they proudly responded in well-rehearsed Latin phrases. She conferred upon them the degree of Bachelor of Arts and handed them their diplomas. The girls shook hands with the president and moved the tassels from the right to the left side of their mortar boards, to signify their new, exalted position in the groves of academe.

When, for the last time as a student, Connie sang Wellesley's *Alma Mater* — "through all her wealth of woods and waters, let your happy voices ring" — she felt her throat tighten. The bright college years were behind her. What lay ahead?

✳ 16 ✳

The Case of the Black Spot

AFTER the Wellesley commencement Connie and Ridie returned to Charlotte. As they rode past the post office where Laura had worked for so many years, Connie looked at the monument erected in memory of Lt. William Ewen Shipp, killed in action in the Spanish-American War. How time evaporated! Just a short while ago she was the little Shipp boys' "Nonnie." Now here she was with her Wellesley degree, a member of the Vassar faculty.

To Connie every room of the Ninth Street house seemed haunted. "This place makes me miss Cousin Alice worse than ever," she told her mother.

"The spirit has gone out of it, but we won't be here long, Con. The time has come for us to move."

"Mama, what do you mean?"

"I mean to face the facts. Cousin Alice is gone . . . Jo enters Northfield in September. Everyone has left and I don't want to live here alone. What's more, I can't afford to."

Connie sat quietly for a moment, trying to take in her mother's words. "Leave Ninth Street . . . but where will you live, Mama?"

"I'll move in with Ef. She can fit me into her boarding house without too much trouble. Isn't it odd that Ef, Alice, and I are all widows?"

"Are you going to sell the house?"

"No, Ef thinks we should divide it into apartments and rent them. That will give us a regular monthly income."

Connie sighed. "I suppose you're right. It's a blow, that's all." She looked around the living room and recalled the shows they used to put on there with improvised curtains, cardboard tickets and slapdash costumes. She looked at Cousin Alice's piano, closed up and silent.

"What will you do with all these things?"

"I'll ask everyone in the family to tell me what they want. Then we'll just divide it up, that's all."

In the end Connie and Ben closed the house while their mother was away visiting in Saluda. Ben, now twenty-eight and unmarried, was selling cotton mill machinery in Charlotte. They were glad to spare their mother the heartbreaking task of dividing up the possessions of a lifetime. Louis wanted the two mahogany dining room tables and sideboard. Laura took their mother and father's big walnut bed. Alice took the mirrors and the mahogany bed she and Laura used to share. The pictures went to Kate, whose house was already loaded with furniture, and Ef got the firescreens.

Working ruthlessly, it took Ben and Connie just three days to clean out the house. Under every window they placed a barrel which had the name of a member of the family painted on it, and they tossed the smaller items out the windows into the barrels. Mrs. Guion was not sentimental; the only things she took to Ef's were a small bed, a mahogany wardrobe, an antique rocker, and a little writing desk made for her by an old carpenter on the plantation. Of course she included Ridie's and Jo's things, for they had always shared her room. Connie took nothing. She had no place of her own and knew she would be on the move from now on.

At last the house was empty, mopped and swept. "We forgot one thing, Con," said Ben.

"What's that?"

"Taking down your sailcloth room at the end of the hall."

"You do it, Ben. I can't. I feel like I'm being torn up by the roots as it is."

Mrs. Guion moved into Ef's house, briskly determined to make a go of her new situation, but it was far from easy. "Connie," she said one day, "what was that poem you used to rattle off every day at Wellesley?"

" 'Crabbed age and youth cannot live together. Youth is —' "

"Yes, that's it. I think that's why Ef and I sometimes have tiffs."

"What about Parkie? She's pretty young."

"Ah, but she's my little granddaughter, and that, my dear, makes all the difference."

Mrs. Guion adored Parkie and so did Connie. She was a round, saucy five-year-old who wore middy blouses and a big hair ribbon on her straight white-blond hair. She was very bright and Connie had high ambitions for her. "Ef," asked Connie, "can't you read to Parkie every day? She ought to be more interested in books."

"I suppose your children will be born with Wellesley diplomas in their mouths," said Ef, who felt she had too much to do already.

Connie prepared for her new life at Vassar by buying herself a corset and she wished her Wellesley friends could see how trim she looked in it. Unfortunately, it was uncomfortable and she seldom wore it, but it made her feel rich to own one.

On that September day in 1906 when Connie first rode through the stone gates of Vassar and saw the rectangular red brick buildings connected by cement walks, she was surprised at how flat and cramped the campus seemed compared to the rolling hills of Wellesley. She wrote her mother:

Vassar was founded by Matthew Vassar, a brewer, and this place is as different from Wellesley as a mug of beer is from a cup of tea. Main Hall has none of the charm and elegance of College Hall. Vassar's rules are much stricter and the girls are more cliquey. They seem happy and gay but they go by tables and most of them worry about where they are going to sit. Daily chapel is required, not voluntary, and the girls are not eager to go, as we were at Wellesley. I met the president, Dr. James Taylor, a nice fatherly gentleman who loves the girls and runs everything. He doesn't believe in leaving things to the students, the way Miss Hazard does, and the student government has little to do. I can't understand why a woman's college should have a man president, can you?

Only twenty-four and full of enthusiasm, Connie was amused to find herself sitting at the formal faculty table in Strong Hall with teachers who were much older. Some of them were prim old maids who did not respond to Connie's exuberance. One said every time she passed the rolls, "Remember, Miss Guion, the piece you touch is the piece you take." There was little of the lively discussion Connie was used to, although she enjoyed the dry wit of Miss Louisa Stevenson, a no-nonsense New Englander who was very friendly. She taught chemistry also and was endlessly curious about Connie's friendships with the students. "How do you find so much to talk about with the girls?" she would ask.

"That's no problem," said Miss Fiske, the English teacher called Fiskabell by the girls because of the way she switched her skirts back and forth. "Miss Guion's the same age as her pupils."

There was no foolishness about Connie in her teaching. She not only did her work to perfection, she exacted perfection from her students. Dr. Moulton was pleased to have an eager young assistant who was engrossed in her work. On the day she received her first pay check, Connie climbed aboard a trolley and went into Poughkeepsie to buy her mother a present. Her mother had had few new possessions in her life. Cousin Connie used to say, "You ought to buy yourself something, Kate. You look like a rag bag."

"What do I care how I look?" Mrs. Guion would reply. "I'll just tie a ribbon in my hair and have a good time."

Connie knew her mother liked nice things and it was exhilarating to be able to buy her a handsome black leather handbag with lots of pockets inside it. "My lands of mercy, Con," her mother wrote, "this is the most beautiful pocketbook in all the world. I'll never set foot outside without it."

Mrs. Guion was the family message center; she forwarded to Connie letters from Ridie and Jo and relayed news from all the others. Once she sent Connie one of her own chicken-scratched letters and wrote on it, "Dear Con, I am returning your note. Please send me a short explanation of what is in it. With love from your Mother."

One of Connie's friends on the Vassar faculty was Elizabeth Beard, the pretty, witty French teacher. Both of them loved the outdoors and they took long walks together. After supper they often strolled to a big elm tree on campus to hear the evening song of a thrush. One night Miss Beard found Connie in her room hunched over something and frowning.

"What ever are you doing?"

"I'm supposed to chaperone some girls to West Point this weekend, but my dress is torn and mending it is impossible. I don't think I can go. Would you go in my place?"

"Substitute for you? Heavens no, the girls would never forgive me. But I'll fix your dress. Let me have it."

Vassar girls could not leave campus without a chaperone, and Connie was easily the most popular one. She had no idea what a chaperone was supposed to do, never having had one, but she took the girls on weekends to New York and Harvard and Yale and had a grand time. It was customary for the students to pay the chaperone's way, and Connie had more gaiety than she ever had had at college, where she had not been able to afford to go trekking off on weekends.

During the autumn when there were football games at the Military Academy, Connie and the girls went by train from Poughkeepsie to Garrison and ferried across the Hudson River to West Point. The girls were proud of their pretty chaperone. Connie had bought for these occasions a new emerald green dress, a black broadcloth coat and a black tricorn hat with a white feather in it. Except for the heavy Spalding sweater she had bought senior year, these were the only new purchases she had made since leaving home.

The girls usually arranged a date for Connie, but at West Point she went out with Sumner McBee Williams, a harum-scarum lad she had known at Miss Shipp's School. He was often in trouble, and when they arrived he was usually marching up and down "the area" on a punishment tour and could not join Connie until later. The girls and their escorts would stroll around the Academy grounds before the game, sometimes exploring the foundations of the huge new chapel that was being built on the mountainside above the plain.

After the football game they would have dinner at the old West Point Hotel near Trophy Point and then dance. Connie was a beautiful dancer, and, quite against the rules for Vassar chaperones, she danced every dance. Some of the names Sumner Williams wrote on her "hop card" — George Goethals, Hap Arnold, Georgie Patton — later became famous. At 8:30 the band played "Army Blue" and all girls had to be off the post by nine o'clock. Connie and her charges returned to Vassar via boat, train, and trolley, getting there after eleven, tired but still full of laughter.

One of Connie's more serious students, Inez Milholland, was considered a radical because she was the militant leader of the votes-for-women movement in the class of 1909. The Vassar authorities considered woman suffrage a subject too hot to handle and prohibited all meetings about it. Inez conducted lively rallies in a graveyard just off campus. To Connie their agitated approach seemed a waste of time.

In December Connie got a letter from Mary Wood asking her to come down to New York to meet her fiancé. It did not surprise Connie that Mary Wood was engaged to be married. Happy-go-lucky and pretty as a Gibson girl, she was crazy about the boys and they were crazy about her. Mary Wood's schooling had been sketchy, and it wasn't until she worked for Dr. Babcock that she settled down. Under his influence she went to Presbyterian Hospital in New York to study nursing and graduated at the top of her class.

Connie liked her new brother-in-law right off. He was a good-looking man with light hair and blue eyes and a long face. "This is Donald Newton, Con," said Mary Wood proudly. "I met him at the Southern Club here in New York."

"Pleased to meet you," said Connie, shaking his hand warmly, "and glad to hear you're a Southerner. Where do you come from?"

"Ooltewah, Tennessee," said the young man, smiling at her broadly.

"Why, I used to know a man from Ooltewah, back at Mrs. Miller's boarding house in Charlotte."

"Did you now?"

Suddenly a bell rang in Connie's head. "You're not the same one, are you?"

" 'Deed I am, Connie, and I'm dashed that you forgot me. Don't you remember how you and I used to talk about *Ivanhoe* and *David Copperfield* and I taught you to spell Ooltewah?"

"Land, how could I forget!"

"Think of it, that both Laura and I should marry men from that boarding house!" said Mary Wood. "Maybe the same thing will happen to you, Connie."

"Who would I marry? Ambrose Miller?"

"Sure, and spend the rest of your days teaching your children how to jump into manure piles," laughed Donald Newton, recalling Connie's famous escapade.

Connie's days at Vassar were filled with hard work and long hours. The teaching was quite different from Wellesley. It was all demonstrations in the lab before one big class, instead of working in small groups. In addition she multigraphed exams and formulas, corrected papers and helped Dr. Moulton in countless ways. She even made him a piece of apparatus that saved him fifty dollars.

After mid-year exams, when every one was worn out from studying, Connie chaperoned some of the girls on a holiday to Mohonk Mountain House, an immense hotel hidden in the Catskills. A nature lover's retreat, founded by a devout Quaker, Mohonk was devoted to quiet and contemplation. Here, climbing among the rocks at Sky Top and Eagle Cliff, tramping through the forest or ice skating on the lake, Connie felt at one with nature as she had not since she was a child at River Bend.

Connie also broke the routine of teaching by inviting some of her Wellesley classmates to visit her. She put mattresses on the floor of her room for them to sleep on and cooked their meals in a copper chafing dish.

"You know what Mark Twain said about this chafing-dish-fish-stew?"

"Couldn't guess," said Laura Dwight.

"He said it's as delicious as the less conventional forms of sin."

"You know, Connie, you look a lot more like a student than a teacher. How long do you plan to teach at Vassar?" asked Olive Hunter.

"I dunno. I'm already thinking of moving on."

"But why?" demanded Elsie Goddard. "This is a beautiful spot and the girls are crazy about you."

"I enjoy Vassar, but I want to do more teaching and less lab work."

"What about medical school?"

"I figure it will be seven years before I can start on that."

"*Seven years?* Why so long?"

"That's how long it will take to get Ridie and Jo through Wellesley, and I'd like to help Alex, too. He's at V.P.I. now."

Ridie also came to Vassar to see Connie. Now a Wellesley freshman, she looked quite grown up with her long blond hair piled high on her head. She had a poetic face with greenish eyes and was small, graceful and athletic. At Northfield she and Jo were known as the Heavenly Twins because they excelled at sports and starred on all the winning teams.

Ridie sat with her sister at the faculty table and all during the meal Connie kept everyone in gales of laughter, describing the adventures of the Guions at River Bend Plantation. Miss Stevenson said to Ridie, "Could it possibly be true there are twelve children in your family?"

"Why, of course. I'm number eleven and Jo makes twelve."

"Connie tells so many incredible tales we don't know when to believe her."

Afterwards Ridie said, "Con, I think you're a little too breezy for those ladies."

"I like to keep 'em stirred up."

"What's the news from home, Con? I haven't heard in weeks."

"Well, Laura's decided to name her second son after Papa and Mama's gone to visit the Babcocks because she says Dr. Babcock has time to listen to her, but Ef's too busy. Parkie loves the graded school and Margaret Babcock is preparing for Wellesley, and the big news is Alex is leaving V.P.I. to take a good job with an engineering firm in the Philippines."

"Good for Alex! Con, don't you feel you're kind of wasting your time here? This is a far cry from medical school."

"Not a bit. Everything I'm teaching will be helpful to me later, but I would like a chance to do more creative chemistry. Right now I'm nothing but a lab technician."

Connie's opportunity came in her second year at Vassar, in a surprising way. One day at table Miss Beard said, "Miss Guion, I want you to meet Miss Mary Benedict from Virginia. She and I were classmates here in '97."

"How do you do, Miss Guion?" said Miss Benedict with a shy smile.

"I'm glad to know you," said Connie. "I don't see many Southerners around here."

"I'm afraid I'm not a real one. I was transplanted to Lynchburg two years ago from the Middle West."

"Miss Benedict used to be head of the philosophy department at Warrensburg College in Missouri," said Miss Stevenson. "Now she is the first president of a new college called Sweet Briar."

"Oh, Louisa," said Miss Beard, "you make it sound so *fait*

accompli. She was only thirty-two when she went to Sweet Briar. She found only one student registered and two professors hired, the buildings weren't finished, and the college was supposed to open in September."

"And did it?" asked Connie.

"Right on schedule."

"That took some doing." Connie was impressed. "What brings you up North, Miss Bendict?"

"I came to raid Vassar for teachers," she said, smiling.

"Oh?" Connie looked at her with new interest. Miss Benedict appeared to be a quiet, forceful woman with very little taste in clothes. Her hair was blond, her eyes blue and her figure slender.

"I'm interested in promoting education for women in the South," said Connie, "because I know how much it's needed. There's a lot to be done."

"Yes," said Miss Benedict, looking Connie in the eye, "and it's very exciting work."

After Miss Benedict left, Connie kept turning over in her mind the things she had said. Finally she went to Dr. Moulton and asked if he would recommend her for a job at Sweet Briar. Dr. Moulton was shocked. "But, Miss Guion, I don't want you to leave. We need you at Vassar. *I* need you."

"Thank you, Dr. Moulton. I've come to love Vassar, and I like working for you, but your department is crowded and I don't see much chance for advancement. I really don't want to keep doing the same thing over and over, and the idea of helping to start a new Southern college is irresistible."

Still protesting, Dr. Moulton wrote to Sweet Briar in Connie's behalf and Miss Benedict immediately wrote to Connie inviting her to meet her in New York for an interview. Elated, Connie put on her chaperoning outfit, picked up two raw eggs from the kitchen for her lunch, and took a train to the city.

When she got to Grand Central Station, Connie went into the ladies' room to clean up and eat her lunch. She was sucking on her second raw egg when, somehow, the shell cut into her lip. Quickly, she washed the cut and pressed paper against it, but it would not stop bleeding. She could never face Miss Benedict with bloody lips. But time was short; she would have to act fast. She ran to a drug store in the station and said to the clerk, "What have you got to stop my lip from bleeding?"

He tried two preparations, but neither worked. "I've *got* to find something," said Connie. "This is an emergency. I'm due at the Manhattan Hotel in ten minutes. Have you got a basement?"

"Yes."

"Does it have cobwebs?"

"I supposed so." The clerk was bewildered.

"Let's go see."

Clearly the clerk thought he had a crazy woman on his hands. "A job hangs on this bleeding lip," explained Connie.

"Uh-hunh," the clerk nodded his head slowly up and down. "Uh-hunh, uh-hunh."

In a dusty corner of the basement they found a cobweb. Connie deftly removed it from the wall and placed part of it on her lip. "There! That ought to do it!"

"Uh-hunh," said the glassy-eyed clerk.

Connie looked at him sharply. "Well, that sticky cobweb stopped the bleeding. The trouble with you druggists is you don't know your medicine."

The Manhattan Hotel was next to Grand Central and Connie was able to reach Miss Benedict on time. Their interview went smoothly until Miss Benedict interrupted herself to say, "Miss Guion, there's something black on your lip."

"Yes, I know, I put it there."

Miss Benedict looked puzzled. Then she continued, "We have twenty on the faculty now and one hundred and ten students. Since Sweet Briar is only two years old, most of the girls are classed as sub-freshmen, but twelve have qualified as college students."

"How big is the campus, Miss Benedict?"

"So far, we have only four buildings, but we plan many more — we own twenty-eight hundred acres. It was all left by Mrs. Indiana Fletcher Williams in memory of her only child, Daisy Williams. I've brought along some pictures. . . ."

As Miss Benedict talked, Connie was caught up in her enthusiasm. Here was a woman with the zeal of a true pioneer.

"It sounds great, Miss Benedict."

"Yes, and everyone who works there is involved in the adventure. But if you come, you'll have to teach not only chemistry but algebra and physics as well. Could you do that?"

"The algebra would be easy, but I haven't had physics since Northfield."

"Then you'd have to take a course during the summer."

"I wouldn't mind that. Louisa Stevenson is working on her Ph.D. at Cornell. I could go to summer school in Ithaca with her."

"Fine, my brother Stanley teaches at Cornell Medical College. You'll get excellent training there. In the beginning, Miss Guion, I can't offer you any more money than you're making at Vassar, but the chance of advancement is excellent. If all goes well, you might even become head of our chemistry department. Do you think you'd like to join us?"

"Miss Benedict, I'll take the job."

"Splendid. Do you mind if I ask you a personal question, Miss Guion?"

"Of course not."

"What is that black spot you said you put on your lip?"

"Well, to tell you the truth, I split my lip on an eggshell and mended it with a cobweb."

"Oh." Miss Benedict was silent a moment. Then she said, "I know you'll bring many fresh ideas to our new college, Miss Guion."

"I'll sure try," said Connie. "On to Sweet Briar!"

✳ 17 ✳

Pistols, Plays and Possums

✳✳

As THE horse-drawn stage jostled down the red clay road toward Sweet Briar College, Connie felt a mounting excitement. Through the tall woods on either side of the road she caught glimpses of fields that stretched into the distance. Real country! Already she felt at home in the Virginia hills. When the omnibus pulled over a rise, Connie could see the Blue Ridge Mountains looming on the horizon, a deep violet in the September sunshine.

At the end of the long driveway stood the college itself, four handsome brick buildings of Georgian design. She recognized them from the pictures Miss Benedict had shown her in New York: on the right, the dining hall with its white cupola and the graceful arcade that connected it to the two dormitories; and to the left the academic building with tall white columns across the front. The unlandscaped buildings rose out of raw, red soil that revealed the infancy of the college.

It was President Benedict who first showed Connie her new chemistry lab and when Connie saw it she almost gasped out loud. The entire furnishings consisted of one heavy laboratory table, a bench and a few chairs.

"How do you like it, Miss Guion?"

"It's a fine room, Miss Benedict, with lots of windows and

plenty of space, but I'm afraid I'll need some equipment for the chemistry classes."

"What kind of equipment?"

"Well, I think we should have some sinks and Bunsen burners and a hood to take off the fumes and a counter we can work on. This table is too high to be any good. It should be ten inches lower."

"Could you make some sketches of what you need?"

"I'm no artist, but I'll try."

Miss Benedict took Connie's drawings to Mr. Charles Heald, one of the trustees, who said the alterations were out of the question; they would be much too expensive.

"Well," said Connie, trying not to show her frustration, "would it be all right if I sawed ten inches off that table myself?"

Miss Benedict's answer was typical. It was her style to steer people into making their own decisions, rather than imposing her ideas. "Use your own judgment, Miss Guion."

Connie consulted Mr. Watts, the college carpenter, and he was flabbergasted.

"Take a peep at that table, Miss Guion. It must be fourteen feet long, and the sides are solid to the ground. You'd have to saw the whole piece."

"I know it, but I've sawed wood since I was a kid. If you'll draw the lines for me, Mr. Watts, I can do it."

Mr. Watts looked at the new teacher admiringly. "I'll come over to the epidemic building with you right now, Miss Guion."

"The what building?"

"The epidemic building. You know, where they teach epidemics."

"Oh. Oh, yes."

Connie started sawing at once because she was eager to get

her lab in order before classes started. She worked long into the night. When the electricity was shut off, she lit a kerosene lamp and kept sawing. She had no idea what time it was because her faithful Octagon watch was still in an unpacked carton.

The next night Mr. Heald, the trustee, came out from Lynchburg to go over college business with Miss Benedict. It was almost midnight when they finished, and as he was leaving Sweet Briar House, Mr. Heald exclaimed, "Why there's a light in one of the classrooms. Someone must be up there."

"I wonder who it could be," replied Miss Benedict, knowing exactly who it was. "Perhaps we should find out."

Connie was sawing intently by lamplight, too absorbed to notice the visitors in the doorway. As she rounded the last corner, she broke off the bottom section of the table and, smiling to herself, began pushing on her cumbersome new prize to set it upright.

"Wait! Let me help you!" Mr. Heald rushed in and grabbed one end of the table. Together they turned it over.

"Look at that," exclaimed Connie, "it doesn't even wobble!"

"Miss Guion, for a physics teacher, you're quite a carpenter. May I congratulate you?"

"Thank you, Mr. Heald."

"What other equipment did you say you needed for this laboratory?"

"I happen to have the drawings right here," smiled Miss Benedict. "I'll be glad to go over them with you."

The next morning Miss Benedict told Connie the trustees had decided the lab was to be equipped exactly as she had specified. Connie heaved a sigh of relief. *Now,* she thought, *I can begin to unpack my boxes from home. First of all, I've got to get my watch. I'm lost without it.*

Connie knew just where the box was. She had packed it carefully in her linen sewing bag, which she knew was in a large, square box on top of her other cartons. She hurried to her room. What she saw made her stop in her tracks. The box containing her most precious possession was gone! Stunned, she searched her room, thinking it might have been misplaced. But there was no box. Maybe it was mixed up with the confusion of luggage in the hall. Connie looked everywhere. No square box.

How could I lose my Octagon watch? What miserable creature could have taken that box? Tears of anger welled in her eyes. Connie went over to the window and looked at the mountains looming against the sky. She recalled the years of collecting soap coupons, and the day that Viv made her leave the family pew because of the way the watch clanked. Material things meant little to Connie, but her watch was more than a possession, it was a trusted companion. Grimly she picked up a hammer and attacked the wooden packing cases. By the time she had unpacked, the crates were in splinters.

Twelve girls were enrolled in Miss Guion's first physics class. She greeted them with a warm smile and began by saying, "Did you realize that every day in many ways you use the principles of physics?" She put a chunk of ice in hot water and thawed it; she floated a cork in the sink; she pulled a chain and the electric light went on. "Why do these things happen?" The girls looked interested; it had never occurred to them to ask why. Miss Guion's physics course was off to a good start.

"Before our next class, please read chapter one in our textbook, Millikan's *Physics*."

"But Miss Guion," said "Jim" Hayes, "we won't even get our books for two weeks."

"What do you mean, two weeks?"

"We have to order them from J. P. Bell's Bookstore in Lynchburg and the man doesn't even come to take our orders till Friday."

As soon as class was over, Connie went to see Miss Benedict. "Is it true we have to wait around for some fellow to come out from Lynchburg before we get any books?"

"I'm afraid it is, Miss Guion."

"What am I to do in the meantime?"

"What the rest of us do, I suppose — just wait."

"But what a waste of time!"

"Well, Miss Guion, you could get on the train and go to town yourself . . ."

"That's a good idea, I'll go this afternoon."

Mr. Barnhart, the manager of J. P. Bell's, was taken aback when the young teacher from Sweet Briar sailed into his quiet store and asked to see the science books.

"Well, er, we have only two on hand."

"This is absurd. Isn't there any way I can order text books in advance?"

"Do you know what you want?"

"Of course I know what I want. Here is the list."

"Yes, ma'am. I'll wire for them at once." Mr. Barnhart was galvanized into action.

At dinner that evening Connie asked the other teachers if they would like to have her get their books, and they were delighted with the idea. Connie could hardly wait to talk to Miss Benedict. "Would you care if I had all the textbooks sent directly to me? I could sell them in my spare time and, who knows, we might even make a little profit for the college."

"That's a splendid idea." President Benedict was beginning to realize there was more to her new chemistry teacher than met the eye. "You could use the faculty office on the second floor as a store."

The Sweet Briar Bookshop opened the following week. Connie sold books from 12 to 1 and from 5 to 6 P.M. daily. The girls were fascinated. They swarmed around the new Dutch door, while Connie stood behind an improvised counter and made change from a cigar box.

A month later Connie went to see Miss Benedict to report on the success of the bookshop. She felt lighthearted and the catbirds singing in the tall boxwood around Sweet Briar House seemed to share her joy. The handsome yellow house, with its galleried porches and square brick towers, was the original home of the Fletchers and the Williamses. Elijah Fletcher had renovated it in the 1840's and planted three hundred boxwood bushes about the grounds. The place still had the air of an old plantation with the log cabin office and slave quarters, peacocks strolling on the lawn and, down by the lake, a herd of cattle grazing as they had in Elijah's day.

Connie's enthusiasm for the bookshop was contagious. "I want to start selling post cards and candy and stationery and before long, Miss Benedict, I think we can hire a scholarship girl to run the whole thing."

"You're quite a doer, Miss Guion. It must seem to you that we move slowly here, but at Sweet Briar speed is not important. It's the development of each girl that counts."

"I just love this place, Miss Benedict. The girls all feel they have a stake in the college and the student government really governs."

"That's because we had no rules until the students wrote them. This year the girls want to start our extra-curricular program. I hope you will organize the dramatic club, Miss Guion. I know you acted in the Shakespeare Society."

Connie in the laboratory at Sweet Briar

"I'm not an actress — a clown, maybe — but I'd love to help."

It was several months before Connie was able to think about putting on a play. Between her heavy schedule — teaching chemistry, algebra and physics — and her hours at the bookshop, there was little time left over. Many mornings she got up at five to prepare the laboratory. Even without her Octagon watch she knew the time, for a noisy mockingbird gave pre-dawn solos outside her window, always at 5 A.M.

On Sundays she took time off to go horseback riding with her friend Martha Plaisted, the energetic young English teacher from Bryn Mawr. They would canter over the beautiful Virginia countryside to Paul's Mountain, ten miles away, with picnics packed in their knapsacks. Mounted on a chest-

Connie on Red Jacket, with Jessica Chapman

nut hunter named Red Jacket, Connie looked more like sixteen than twenty-six, with her curly hair brushed back and tied in a ribbon. She wore a khaki riding habit, with a divided skirt, made years before by the ever faithful Laura.

The young teachers met some strange characters in the sparsely settled back country. One day they shared Sunday dinner with a family who appeared to operate a headquarters for hookworms. The meal consisted of a hunk of pig, boiled in its hide of black and white bristles, together with potatoes and cabbage swimming in grease. Later Connie and Martha asked the college overseer about the people of the hills. He said they were a mixture of Indian, Negro, and white ancestry, called "Issues" by the local people, and he warned that they might be degenerate and dangerous. "We'd be dangerous, too, if we were as poor as those folks," said Connie.

For Connie's first venture in dramatics she selected a popular play, Sir James Barrie's *Quality Street*. In typical Sweet Briar fashion a large crowd showed up for try-outs and Connie skillfully made use of every girl. Since the college had no auditorium and no stage, she decided to have the play in the dining hall. Again she took her problem to the resourceful Mr. Watts.

"That's a cinch, Miss Guion. I'll just build you a flatform," he said. The girls made curtains from old draperies, painted the scenery, assembled their costumes, including two suits belonging to the college farmer, Mr. Martindale, and everything appeared in readiness. But just before the dress rehearsal Miss Benedict summoned Connie to her office.

"Miss Guion, do I understand our girls plan to wear men's clothing in your play?"

"Yes, indeed."

"Surely you know it's customary for young ladies to wear bloomers when they impersonate men."

"They do at Vassar and Wellesley, but Sweet Briar is a twentieth-century college, Miss Benedict. There's no place for old-fashioned notions here."

Miss Benedict walked to the window and stood for a long time with her back to Connie, thinking. Finally she turned around. "I don't want to hamper you — I'm glad you're bringing dramatics to Sweet Briar — but, Miss Guion, we must maintain modesty."

"Yes, ma'am."

"If the girls are to wear men's clothing, the audience must be limited to ladies only."

"Mr. Watts and Mr. Martindale will be mighty disappointed," laughed Connie.

Miss Benedict did not laugh. The interview was ended. Trousers replaced bloomers on the "flatform" and the twentieth century rolled on. *Quality Street* was a great success and with Miss Benedict's encouragement, Connie organized the "Merry Jesters," Sweet Briar's first theatrical group.

Because of her reputation as an innovator, Connie was the faculty member the girls turned to with new ideas. One February night a student named Alma Booth approached her with a bold suggestion. "Miss Guion, don't you think it would be fun to sleep out on the roof of the arcade? The stars are so bright you can almost touch them."

"What a fine idea. Let's do it!"

The next night Connie, in her long flannel nightgown and red and white polka-dot robe, climbed through the hall window, followed by four girls. They hoisted their cots and blankets onto the roof and settled down for the night. The cold air was exhilarating. Connie looked up at the twinkling heavens, which seemed calm and mysterious at the same time, and thought of her mother reading from the Bible, "The heavens declare the glory of God." How could anyone look at that ordered universe and not believe in God?

During her five years at Sweet Briar, Connie did not sleep indoors again, except in stormy weather. Later Miss Benedict joined the fresh air girls. She had a tarpaulin put up in a grove of trees so they could sleep on the ground. She gave Connie an Abercrombie and Fitch sleeping bag that kept her warm, even when the mercury fell to 7 degrees and the sleepers awoke covered with snow. Miss Benedict slept at one end of the windbreak and Connie at the other, with four girls in between. Connie said she was there to ward off the wolves, bears and snakes. But the only animals they ever saw were possums; the Sweet Briar woods were full of them.

Sweet Briar held its first Founders Day in October, 1909, a great occasion, from the stately academic procession in the morning to a ball that ended at 2 A.M. A student named

Mayo Thach had barrels of real Spanish moss sent from Louisiana, and Connie helped the girls turn the refectory into a hanging garden for the dance and then enjoyed a few twirls herself. Unlike Wellesley and Vassar, Sweet Briar — the twentieth-century college — invited men to its dances.

That year the freshmen took a special shine to "Miss Guion" and made her an honorary member of their class. Connie was their companion and chaperone on many adventures, the most memorable one being her first trip of any distance in an automobile. Mr. Martindale drove the only car at Sweet Briar, a Maxwell touring car which caused so much excitement that Miss Benedict had to ask him not to drive past the academic building while classes were in session.

A group of adventurous freshmen chartered Mr. Martindale and the car for a journey to Natural Bridge. Connie and the girls dressed in elaborate "motoring costumes" for the trip — big hats tied on with long chiffon scarves, goggles, gauntlets, and ankle-length coats to keep off the dust. To get to Natural Bridge they had to drive on a narrow dirt road over the mountains. The Maxwell's radiator cap sputtered steam and Mr. Martindale kept jumping out to fill his tea kettle from mountain streams and pour the water into the overheated machine. This added greatly to the adventure and no one minded that the thirty-mile trip took three hours.

It seemed to Connie, after eight long Northern winters, that spring burst forth all at once at Sweet Briar. Suddenly the air felt balmy, the cherry trees behind Carson Hall were white with blossoms, and bright orioles and warblers flew in and out of the magnolia. In the late afternoon Connie and Martha Plaisted would stroll to Monument Hill, passing fragrant peach orchards whose aroma reminded Connie of her childhood. From this hill, where the Fletchers and Williamses

Chemistry teacher at Sweet Briar

were buried, they could see most of the flowering campus. During one of their twilight talks they dreamed up the idea that Sweet Briar ought to have an outdoor play similar to Wellesley's Tree Day or Bryn Mawr's May Day Fête. They took their idea to Miss Benedict, who responded with enthusiasm. They agreed the first production should be *Robin Hood*.

"I can't get over Connie," Virginia McLaws, the art teacher, remarked to Miss Benedict after rehearsals were under way. "She seems so practical and scientific, and now she's an artist, creating a play. It's a delight. You're going to love it."

"I've already seen it," Miss Benedict replied with a wry smile. "Miss Guion has enlisted me as prompter."

May Day was a great event. The queen, announced by a fanfare of trumpets, appeared in a flowing white costume

May Day, 1911   *May Day, 1912*

and flowered crown and she and her court were entertained
by the Maypole dancers. Then followed the first outdoor play,
produced, choreographed and directed by Miss Connie Guion,
with cue lines provided by the president of the college.

During Connie's five years at Sweet Briar, President Mary
Benedict made a great impression on her. Connie especially
admired her fairness and independent spirit. One day she
saw a teacher come out of Miss Benedict's office exploding
with impatience.

"If that woman *ever* makes her mind up about *anything!*"

"You mean you want her to make up *your* mind," said Connie.

"What are you talking about?"

"Didn't she tell you to do as you please?"

"Yes, but I wanted her opinion."

"You can wait till doomsday and Miss Benedict will never
tell you what you ought to do. She wants people to think for
themselves."

Even though Connie was absorbed in teaching, she did not
forget for a minute that medicine was her goal. These were
the years when Dr. Marie Curie thrilled women everywhere

by twice winning the Nobel Prize for her work with radium. Connie told her students, "Madame Curie has shown the world what a woman can do in chemistry. She has discovered a new element, one of the most important discoveries of the century."

Connie was naturally drawn to doctors and she became friendly with Dr. Mary Harley, the college physician. Dr. Harley was lame and lived quite far from the dormitories, so she delegated to Connie many of her nighttime tasks. Miss Guion listened to complaints, gave out pills and advice, and often got up in the middle of the night to aid suffering girls. One morning Martha Plaisted said, "Connie, you look tuckered out."

"I was up all hours using the stomach pump on a fat freshman."

"But you need your sleep. Why didn't you call Dr. Harley?"

"I'm like my mother — I enjoy taking care of the sick. Besides, it's good practice for me."

"Did the stomach pump do the job?"

"In more ways than one. That little glutton won't overstuff herself with sweets again."

There was a social aspect to Connie's life, too. Having a flair for drama, she occasionally gave select supper parties in her shining laboratory. It was exciting for the guests to watch eggs boiling away in the glass containers over Bunsen burners, and to see dark streams of coffee circulating through aerial test tubes into tall beakers.

There were many parties at Sweet Briar, but the birthday party Martha Plaisted's mother gave for Martha turned out to be the most surprising. After a lavish dinner Connie remarked, "It seems awfully quiet. There ought to be some noise and excitement to celebrate an occasion like this."

"It does seem quiet. Too bad none of us can sing," said Mrs. Plaisted.

"Aren't there any firecrackers?" Connie asked.

Martha got up from the table and went into her room, reached into the back of her bureau drawer and pulled out a small, shiny pistol, which she brought into the dining room.

"Martha, where did you get that gun?" cried her mother.

"Now, Mother, don't be alarmed. A beau gave me this because he said it was unsafe for a young woman to live in the wilds of Virginia without protection." She put the pistol in Connie's hands, "I dare you to shoot it, here, in this room, in honor of my birthday."

"Oh, no!" Mrs. Plaisted protested, though her eyes shone with excitement. "Everyone will think there's been a murder."

Connie examined the pistol, turned the cartridge cylinder, clicked the safety catch. "It's loaded?" she asked.

"Sure is."

Connie stood up, closed her left eye, and aimed downward toward the far corner of the room. *Bang!* The reverberations were thunderous. Squealing, the three women rushed to examine the damage. No hole in the wall. No fallen plaster. Nothing.

The cartridge had been blank.

"Well, Connie," said Martha, "you may not be able to shoot, but you sure can stir things up."

"Happy birthday!" grinned Connie.

✳ 18 ✳

How to Succeed by Trying

CONNIE GUION's long love affair with Cornell University began in the summer of 1908 when she was twenty-six years old. She went to Ithaca to study chemistry and physics, in preparation for teaching at Sweet Briar, and became so entranced with her work that she returned for five summers to do research in biochemistry.

It took Connie a while to get used to Ithaca. She thought it was a "junky little town" and the Cornell campus seemed citified after Wellesley and Sweet Briar. But she soon discovered the deep gorges at either end of the campus that were full of rare glacier plants and rocks, reminiscent of Mohonk. On Sundays she and her friends often took picnics to secluded spots like Cascadilla Falls to enjoy the outdoors and search for fossils.

Cornell gave Connie her first brush with coeducation and she enjoyed being in a man's world, despite the fact that the women were really second-class citizens. It seemed to Connie there was no place for women to do anything. She and Miss Louisa Stevenson from Vassar lived in a dreary boardinghouse on Buffalo Street, but it made little difference what her living conditions were, because she studied from 8 A.M. to 6 P.M. six days a week and in the evening tutored five Cornell undergraduates who had failed chemistry. Each boy paid her five dollars an hour, which financed her entire summer. Connie was so immersed in what she was doing she had little idea what was going on elsewhere. Day in and day out she studied, studied, studied.

As often happens when a good student turns into an eager scholar, Connie's zest for learning was ignited by several gifted teachers. Two of them were doctors from Edinburgh, Scotland: Dr. Andrew Hunter and Dr. Sutherland Simpson. The other was a German named Dr. William Orndorff. These men inspired their pupils as much by what they were as by what they said. After class her first day Connie said, "Dr. Orndorff, may I ask you a question?"

"Yes?" The little bald man peered at her over his glasses.

"At Wellesley we studied a textbook called *Organic Chemistry* by W. R. Orndorff. Did you write it?"

"*Ja,* that is mine. Did you enjoy it?"

"I did, Professor Orndorff. I never knew anyone who was a teacher and a scientist and an author all at once."

"You could do it. Come on Sunday to my home and my mother will give you Viennese coffee and coffeecakes and we shall talk. What do you want to do with your life?"

"I'm going to be a doctor, but I plan to teach chemistry a few more years before I study medicine."

"So? Then you should at Cornell work in biochemistry. It will be of value in medicine always."

Under the guidance of Dr. Orndorff and Dr. Hunter, Connie started to do research work on metabolism. Biochemistry was a brand-new science and exciting pioneer work was being done, with Dr. Andrew Hunter one of the leaders in the field. He had two students working on purine metabolism in the blood and he told Connie he wanted her to do her research on animal urine and stools. She chose raccoons, opossums and rats, the mammals most easily obtainable, and became utterly engrossed in the project. When Dr. Hunter saw the caliber of her research, he suggested that she work for a Master's degree and assigned to her, as the topic for her thesis, "Purine Metabolism in Mammals."

Connie threw herself into research wholeheartedly and returned to Sweet Briar in the fall eager to continue the work on her thesis. Sandwiching research in between teaching and her other tasks kept her so busy she had little time to see her friends. Martha Plaisted finally came to see her. "Connie, are you feeling all right?"

"Right as rain. Why?"

"Professor McBride told me he has seen you every morning this week chasing two possums around the academic building. He said he couldn't believe his eyes."

"His eyes must be failing. I don't chase the possums, I hang on to their tails."

"You what?"

"I hold their tails, to keep them from running away. I tried using a leash, but the possums lie down and play dead."

"What are you talking about?"

"My possums. They need lots of exercise."

"Connie, *what* possums?"

"Lord and Lady, the ones old Bias caught for me in the woods."

"You're out of your head," Martha said flatly.

Connie had to laugh at her bewildered expression. "The possums aren't pets — they're for research. I feed them different diets and then collect their urine and study the content of the uric acid. I analyze their blood, too."

"If anybody told me to collect a possum's urine, I wouldn't know how to begin. May I ask how you do it?"

"It's simple. Bias helped me build a cage with a double bottom so the urine runs down to a tin collector underneath. Works like magic."

Connie with her possums

Bias, the white-haired janitor who had once served the Williams family in Sweet Briar House, took great interest in Miss Guion and her possum project. He cleaned the cages and helped care for the animals, talking to them as though they were people. But one morning when Connie came to take them out, he greeted her with a woeful face. "Miss Connie, Lady's disappeared."

"I can't believe it! How could she get out of the cage?"

"Dunno. I've looked every place, but Lady she ain't there. She's bound to be in this cellar somewheres."

Bias and Connie went from room to room in the basement, pawing through crates and old furniture, looking for the lost possum. " 'Pears like she vapo-rated," said Bias.

"Just when my experiment was going smoothly, too."

"Doan you worry, Miss Connie. I'll trap you another possum. I reckon Lady'll make herself known bye and bye."

Every day Connie put food out for the lost Lady, but it

was never touched. Then one morning, when an acrid odor stung her nostrils, she understood what Bias had meant; Lady had died and her carcass was slowly oxidizing. Connie and Bias gave her a proper burial and Connie said, "If I had a tombstone I'd write on it, 'Lady — the Elusive 'Possum — She Gave Her All for Science.'"

Except for the lamented Lady, everything that Connie touched at Sweet Briar seemed to flourish. Her bookshop expanded to include a large variety of items needed by the students and faculty. Finally it had to be moved to a separate building and was linked with the teashop. Her drama group doubled in size and a second dramatic club was formed. A letter Mayo Thach wrote to her parents explains why Connie's classes also doubled: "I don't understand one thing about science, but I signed up for chemistry because I love Miss Guion so much. And guess what, I'm beginning to love chemistry, too." Miss Benedict was pleased with Connie's progress; she raised her salary and gave her an assistant. Alma Booth, a former student, did all of Connie's lab work from then on.

Despite her new position as head of the Department of Chemistry, Connie still looked like one of the girls. She wore ground-gripper shoes and white shirtwaists, and her gored skirts fanned out as she walked briskly across the campus. Except for brushing her curly hair one hundred strokes nightly, she paid little attention to her appearance and made sport of her friends who spent hours wrapping their hair in curl papers. One of them said, "Who are you to tease, Connie Guion? I notice you powder your nose."

"If I didn't," laughed Connie, "I couldn't see over it."

Connie did meet with one failure at Sweet Briar when Dr. Mary Harley asked her to help with a young student who was always having headaches, cramps, sore throats and colds. Connie spent hours trying to capture the girl's interest. Patiently, she took her into the woods to look at hoar frost and explained how it came out of the ground. She rubbed silk and wool together to make static electricity and explained negative and positive poles. She demonstrated how water expanded when it froze and shrank when it thawed. But the girl wanted to dwell only on her own aches and pains. Finally Connie said to Dr. Harley, "I resign from the job — it's hopeless. When that girl is eighty, she'll still be interested only in herself and her imaginary ills."

No problem ever seemed too much for President Benedict and the more Connie worked with her, the more she admired her. A crisis was precipitated when an angry girl cut off one of her roommate's long braids while she was sleeping, but Miss Benedict knew how to calm both the victim and the guilt-ridden culprit. As Signora, Miss Indiana Williams's old servant, said, referring to Miss Benedict's composure, "If things go 'gainst her, or fer her, hit's all one to Miss Benedict."

Often Connie and Miss Benedict enjoyed hiking together across the fields, and one afternoon a ram charged out of the woods directly toward them. Quickly, Miss Benedict ducked behind one oak tree and Connie hid behind another. Then, to Connie's amazement, Miss Benedict walked boldly forth, holding her umbrella before her like a spear. She caught the ram between the eyes and forced him to retreat.

"Good show, Miss Benedict!" cried Connie, coming out from behind the tree. "I declare, you're a whole lot braver than Tom Peet Cross."

"What about Mr. Cross?" Tom Peet Cross, the Celtic professor of literature who dressed in stylish tweeds with leather buttons, added considerable dash to the Sweet Briar campus.

Miss Mary Benedict and Miss Connie Guion of Sweet Briar

"The other day I found him in a clearing down by the lake, stranded on top of a woodpile."

"What do you mean, *stranded?*"

"A billy goat ran him up there and was standing guard at the bottom. Professor Cross was helpless."

"What did you do," teased Miss Benedict, "hide behind a tree?"

"Oh no, when I go hiking alone, I always carry a rubber syringe filled with ammonia water for protection, a trick I learned from my mother. I squirted the goat in the face, and rescued the brave Irishman. He's been avoiding me ever since."

There was little time in Connie's busy life for men. Other teachers at Sweet Briar went out with young men from Lynchburg, but Connie's spare time was spent on chemistry. She didn't do it begrudgingly; she relished it, because she was deeply involved in her work.

At Christmas time Connie returned to Ef's house in Charlotte, the nearest thing she had to a home. Her mother was there and although she was only sixty-three her eyesight was failing, but she was as valiant and uncomplaining as ever. The family spent some time talking over Ef's desire to send Parkie to Northfield and Alice's determination that Jim would go to Exeter, as Dr. Babcock had done. Impossible as these dreams seemed, no one doubted that they would somehow be fulfilled. How Connie would finance four years of medical school was not even discussed. They all knew she would manage it somehow.

Caleb Motz came home from Nashville that Christmas to see his mother and of course he came to call on Connie. Caleb was even gayer and more outgoing than she had remembered him. They went to a dance together and as they circled the floor to the strains of "The Beautiful Blue Danube" he said, "How do you like the new ragtime dances?"

"They're awful — turkey trot, bunny hug, fox trot — sounds more like a barnyard than a ballroom."

"Connie, you're as light as a leaf. I'll bet you've been dancing every night since you left."

"I've been doing research in a laboratory."

"Research on what — frog-spearing?"

Connie looked at Caleb's reddish hair, his smiling gray eyes, and his strong, sensitive face, and thought he was one of the nicest people she had ever known. He whirled her around and around the floor until she gasped, "Caleb, don't you think you should slow down?"

"Would you slow down if your house was on fire?"

"Gracious, how you talk!"

Driving home in the buggy through a light snow, Caleb said, "Connie, may I ask you something?"

"Of course."

"Is there any hope . . . ?"

She looked at him and shook her head. "Not one bit, Caleb. I am in love with my work."

The rest of the way home, Caleb said nothing. At the door he leaned down and kissed her lightly on the forehead. "Good-by, Connie Guion. You're going to make a great doctor." He turned and walked down the path. She never saw him again.

Perhaps because Connie had no real home after the Ninth Street house was sold, she had a strong feeling about gathering the family together whenever possible. She even took one summer off from her work at Cornell to take care of her sisters' children; Kate had just had an operation and Laura had a new baby, and Connie wanted to help them all she could. She and Ef rented a house in Saluda, North Carolina, and collected under one roof Mrs. Guion and her eight grand-children. Running a summer "camp" for her little nieces and nephews was rare sport for Connie. Margaret, Ferebe, and Alice Babcock came from South Carolina, bringing their canary. Parkie McCombs and Jim Vason came from Charlotte, and Laura brought her three sons up from the Haskell farm in Laurens, South Carolina. Ridie, Jo and Alice spent that summer with Don and Mary Wood in Knoxville. Mary Wood was expecting her second baby; her first, a little girl, had lived only two hours after birth.

The Saluda reunion was lively, with lots of Guions, and even some visitors, crowded into a small cottage nestled in the Blue Ridge Mountains. Connie rented a cow and a donkey for the children to ride. She helped them dig and plant the garden and taught them to shoot marbles and spin tops, but even in the midst of the family fun she spent a large part of each day studying.

When the summer ended, Connie's nieces and nephews returned to their homes brimming with the fun of being part of a large family living in the country. In later years, Ferebe Babcock wrote down her recollections of that summer in Saluda:

> *It was in the summer of 1910 that Aunt Connie, the Sweet Briar instructor in chemistry, undertook to gather under one roof in Saluda, N. C., all the Guion grandchildren as of that date. The eight of us came away having learned something. Even baby Louis Haskell was eating with relish, which he was not doing when he arrived. We older ones learned the pleasures of a big family and how to behave away from our homes and parents and, above all, we loved having Aunt Connie to boss us, dressed in the uniform of the day: middy blouse and*

skirt and a ribbon around her hair whether it was in a braid or piled on top of her head. She read aloud to us, took us on mountain picnics, let us "help" her dig out a pair of steps in the red clay bank so that the family could with ease step out of Uncle Alex Haskell's automobile, the first one in the family. No event was more outstanding than her taking us to a fire in the middle of the night when the local grocery store burned up. She gave us each a job and we had to do it well. Alice Babcock, our baby, once found that the regimentation pushed her too far, and in great indignation burst forth to her aunt "Thank goodness you are no kin to my Daddy." Fortunately that has never ceased to amuse Aunt Connie.

Connie returned to Sweet Briar refreshed and eager for work. The college was growing, but Miss Benedict was plagued by the problem of trying to find more girls who could do college work. Going to college was a revolutionary thing for a young woman to do, especially in the South. Miss Benedict would start to talk to parents about college credits and end up discussing whether their daughters should be allowed to ride a horse astride or not. The problem of getting parents to take their daughters' education seriously was pointed up by the girls' tardiness when they returned from vacations; some of them came back two or three weeks late, on the flimsiest excuses.

Sweet Briar's youth was dramatized for Connie and Miss Benedict when they attended three college commencements in three weeks, in the summer of 1911. First, of course, came the Sweet Briar commencement, the second in the history of the college. Five girls — all Virginians — were graduating.

The exercises were held in the "chapel" on the first floor of the academic building, which was actually a large classroom, and the side arms of the desks had to be turned down to make room for the visitors. The ceremony was short and unsophisticated, and, to Connie, very moving.

After college closed, she and Miss Benedict journeyed north together. They went first to Vassar, where Miss Benedict's younger sister Agnes was graduating, then they traveled on to Wellesley for Ridie's graduation and Connie's fifth reunion. The affluence and tradition of Vassar and Wellesley, with their academic processions, concerts, garden parties and daisy chains, was in marked contrast with the simplicity of Sweet Briar.

Ridie's graduation from Wellesley gave Connie a warm sense of fulfillment. She was proud of her little sister, who had made a fine record at college and landed a good job teaching English in a private school in Minneapolis. Ridie and Jo — who had just completed her sophomore year at Wellesley — had also won their "W"s by rowing on the Wellesley crew.

"Only two more years, Con," said Jo, "and I'll be graduating, too, and then you'll be off to medical school."

"Don't rush things, Jo," replied Connie, "I like to keep a Guion chugging along at Wellesley, because I love to come back here."

For Connie, returning to Wellesley was like going home. That June she and Laura Dwight, now an assistant in Wellesley's handsome new library, moved into College Hall and enjoyed a rip-snorting fifth reunion with their classmates. Nobody could match the class of 1906 when it came to spirit. They had the best costumes, the cleverest songs, and the loudest cheers of any class in the alumnae parade. In the fifth reunion year book, each girl gave an account of what she had done since leaving college. Connie's was typically candid and humorous:

Every time I have to face this string of questions —
husband's name, occupation, number of children — I
somehow feel as if I have not done my part by 1906, as
if I were casting a blight on her silvery name when I sign
myself as of old, simple Connie M. Guion — still an
old maid with no addenda.

Soon after I left College senior year I went South and
broke up the house in which I had been kept to date.
Then I began a wanderer's life, landing at Vassar College
in the fall. There I stayed for two years as a scrubwoman
in the Department of Chemistry. The life was so different
from our undergraduate life that I found myself in the
comparative degree all the day. Vassar is splendid and
in some ways surpasses Wellesley. On the whole, how-
ever, I'm always glad I'm Wellesley, for it is, I believe,
more progressive.

But the place that really holds my affections is Sweet
Briar, and you would each join in my chant if you
could just live here. How I pity any of you that don't
know the blues, the violets, and the lavenders of these
mountains! When coupled with work in a new, growing
college, I can't express how fascinating it is. Imagine
working in a place not tainted with precedent but open
to conviction on every point! Our students are surprising
in their sense of responsibility. You should hear how our
student government works and see the rules they enact.
They beat Wellesley and Vassar, too.

In the hopes of meeting some ideal, I went to Cor-
nell in the summers for graduate work, but I found only

*very strenuous married men who were willing to work
me day and night in problems of physics. As a result I
learned quite a store of physics and have been teaching
it for three years. This summer I am going back to study
Spectroscopic Analysis and Crystallography and Calcu-
lus. Sounds awful, but it isn't a bit.*

While she was at her reunion, a fortunate thing happened
to Connie. She had applied to Wellesley for a fellowship to
study medicine, but the request was refused; the college
would grant fellowships to women working for academic
degrees, but not for medical degrees. Dean Pendleton suggested, however, that she go to call on Miss Helen Kimball in Brookline, a philanthropist interested in promoting
medical education for women. Miss Kimball was well along
in years, and the interview was somewhat stilted.

"Dean Pendleton tells me you want to be a doctor, Miss
Guion."

"Yes, Miss Kimball."

"I'm a trustee of the Women's Medical College in Boston,
and nothing means more to me than the crusade for women
in medicine."

"Yes, Miss Kimball."

"Where do you plan to study?"

"I was admitted to Johns Hopkins, but I've switched to
Cornell. I'm working for my Master's there now, and I think
it's a great place."

"Certainly Cornell has been a leader in the training of
women doctors. Dean Pendleton assures me you will do well
there."

"That's kind of her. Wellesley gave me a good foundation."

"It will be a long, hard course, Miss Guion, but I'm sure

you will find it worthwhile from every angle. It even pays
well — eventually."

"I don't care much about money."

"Good. How much do you think you'll need for medical
school?"

"I already have a Cornell scholarship for the tuition, but
I'll need about four hundred dollars a year for rent. I'll be
working for my food, of course."

"Doing what?"

"Tutoring. It pays better than anything else."

Miss Kimball rose from her chair, walked over to Connie
and extended her hand. "Miss Guion, I like the cut of your
jib."

"How's that, Miss Kimball?"

"Ah, we Bostonians forget that all the world doesn't summer at Cape Cod. I like your style, your direct manner. You
will be hearing from me."

Connie returned to Cornell and finally completed her
thesis on "Purine Metabolism in Mammals." The research
had been exacting, but it was nothing compared to writing
the paper. When that was typed it came to a hundred pages.
Connie presented it with considerable pride, but the following week Dr. Orndorff summoned her to his office.

"Miss Guion, I have read your thesis."

"Yes, Professor Orndorff?"

"I am shocked. You have made errors, too many to count."

"I *have?*" Connie was stunned. She had gone over and over
her work. Surely there were no mistakes.

Professor Orndorff rubbed his gray moustache, his eyes
twinkling. "Miss Guion, what, in your opinion, is the possum's nationality?"

"*Nationality?* Sir, I don't know what you're talking about."

"I gather you think he's Irish." He pushed the thick manuscript across the desk. On line after line he had circled in red the word which Connie had spelled "o'possum." Together they had a good laugh at Connie's expense, but afterward she had to go through the thesis page by page, taking out every apostrophe, to repatriate the possum and pacify the meticulous Professor Orndorff. It was only then that he told her she had done excellent work and would be awarded a Master's degree.

Before she left Sweet Briar for good, Connie was determined to have her mother come to see the college. She sent her a railroad ticket and when she saw the familiar thin figure with her black veil and "Vassar" pocketbook, her throat tightened. With great pride she showed her mother around the campus and introduced her to everyone. Mrs. Guion was as peppery as ever and talked continuously. "Wasn't it grand when Taft and Roosevelt started scrapping over the nomination? How I enjoyed seeing them do each other in! Woodrow Wilson is going to save this country. Think of having a Democrat in the White House after all those years of Republican corruption! I never thought I'd live to see the day. Con, I saw old Elsie the other day and she said to me, 'Miss Kate, you don't know how I hate to get old,' and I said, 'Elsie, you've got just two choices. You either get old, or you jump in the river.'"

One of the hardest things Connie Guion ever had to do was to pull up her roots at Sweet Briar. But eventually the day came when she had to tell Miss Benedict that she was leaving to begin her study of medicine. Her sisters were educated; Miss Kimball had come through with the loan; the Master of Arts degree was hers; and she was slated to become a first-year student at Cornell Medical College in the fall. Ahead, the sailing looked clear; at hand, the emotional weather was stormy. How *could* she say good-by to Sweet Briar, her heart's home?

Connie let no one except Miss Benedict know that she was going. She did not want a lot of fuss made over her departure. It would be hard enough to leave as it was. When it was time to leave, Miss Benedict shook her hand sadly. "Of course, I've known for two years you would depart as soon as your sister Jo graduated, but I can't even imagine Sweet Briar without you."

"I've had five wonderful years here, Miss Benedict. I hate to leave Sweet Briar more than I ever hated to leave any place in my life, but I have to get on with my medical training. I've been planning it a long time."

"I understand."

"Miss Louisa Stevenson will do a fine job in my place, I know that."

"Yes."

"Before I go, I want to give you this. I closed my bookshop account." Connie handed the president a check.

Miss Benedict took the check and looked at it. It was made out for the incredible sum of sixteen thousand dollars. She started to speak, then stopped. Her voice choked. "Connie," she said, "Thank you. We'll use this for scholarships."

"Well —" Connie hesitated. "Good-by, Miss Benedict. I'll be coming back to see you when I can." Abruptly, she turned and walked out. She climbed into the horse-drawn stage to ride to the station. As the horses trotted down the red clay road, Connie looked back at the hills and fields and spacious buildings where she had been so happy. A line from Tennyson rose in her mind, "So sad, so strange, the days that are no more."

✳ 19 ✳

Medical School at Last!

ENTERING Cornell Medical College was actually not much of a change for Connie because she had already spent five summers working in Stimson Hall at Ithaca. But putting aside the responsibility of teaching to pursue her life's dream was a new and satisfying experience. On the first day, as she sat listening to Dean Abram Tucker Kerr greet the new students, excitement tingled in her veins. Here she was, at the age of thirty-one, launched at last on her career! The Dean's words echoed her feelings.

"A pretty good doctor is like a pretty good egg," he said, stroking his Van Dyck beard. "Nobody wants a pretty good egg for breakfast. Never forget, my young friends, healing is not just a science, it's an art. *Genus homo*, man, when he is sick, is full of fear, be he rich or poor, and he needs comfort and understanding as much as medical care. Of course, the study of medicine is hard work. You will make some sacrifices; they will not seem like sacrifices, for medicine is a way of life — a way of service."

As a first-year student, Connie lived with the two other women in her class in Sage Hall, a women's dormitory on the Cornell campus. Women were not allowed to go to the Cornell Medical College in New York City until their second year. It was only in recent years that a college degree was required for entrance to medical school; previously, two years of college had been sufficient because the medical school was eager to attract as many students as possible.

Dormitory life in Sage Hall was spiced by a middle-aged woman from Russia who had come to this country to study agriculture. She seemed to Connie like a character out of Dostoevski. At breakfast she would ask everyone to order eggs for her and then she would gulp down six or eight at once. At night, when she went to take a bath, it was her habit to trot down the hall stark naked. Exasperated, Connie went to the housemother and asked, "Can't you do something about that Russian wild woman who runs around naked as a jaybird?"

Fortunately, Connie's modesty did not carry over into anatomy class. A few days later, when she had to dissect her first cadaver, she did it without a qualm. The unclaimed body from the county hospital was wrapped in cloth; only the parts to be dissected were exposed. The cadavers were saturated with carbolic acid, and since all the students, working in pairs, did the dissecting in one room, the gaseous fumes were overpowering. On the first day, one of the men in the class fainted and the poor fellow never heard the end of it.

"I can't work another minute inhaling this carbolic stink," said Connie's classmate Ed Flood.

"Oh, I like it," beamed Connie. "It's strong and clean and smells like the farm. We used to sterilize with carbolic acid when we operated on our sick animals."

"Girl, you've got a strong stomach."

"But weak hands — they're raw and paralyzed from being soaked in carbolic. I can't even manipulate my scalpel, can you?"

Because of her excellent scientific training, Connie could handle physiology, biochemistry, histology and anatomy with ease, but she was disheartened to be confronted with German

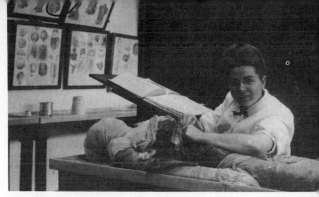

Connie with cadaver

In anatomy class

Connie with brain and skull

again, after the fiasco she had made of it at Wellesley. German was required of all medical students, and she knew she had to gain a reading knowledge of it. Always inventive, she hit upon a novel scheme. She sent away for a German Bible and spent hours reading it and comparing it with her own well-worn Bible. She learned a lot of German that way, and some Bible, too.

In addition to her class work, Connie spent the late afternoons tutoring undergraduates in chemistry, so there was little time left over for fun. Of her life at Cornell Medical College she was to say in later years: "There is no school today in which students work so hard or so long as we did. It was a continuous grind. The work of one day could not be carried over to the next, for every day was full. No one jacked us up. We did the work — or we were dropped. Like Osler, our motto was, 'Look to this day!'"

While Connie was studying at Ithaca, shocking news flashed across the country: *Fire at Wellesley! College Hall destroyed at 4:30 A. M.* Connie's first thought was of her sister Jo, who was doing graduate work in physical education, and of her niece Margaret Babcock, who was a freshman. But after she read that no lives were lost, thanks to strict fire-drill training, memories of College Hall began to flood over her. She closed her eyes and saw the shining columns and marble floors, the white statues and gold-framed pictures, the palms and ferns in the center, the airiness as you looked up four flights of balconies to the sunlit roof. She recalled dear little Mr. Bauer with his flower cart, who used to sell her a fresh rose for her desk each week. Gone, all of it gone, her beloved college home.

Later, a letter came from Jo describing that terrible night.

> *The fire started in the zoology lab, but no one knows what caused it. Miraculously, it took just ten minutes to get everybody out of that enormous building. Then we all stood by, helpless and silent, watching the leaping flames. About five in the morning the whole top caught fire and with a crash the roof collapsed. Four hours after the fire started College Hall was a roofless shell, open to the wind. All of us were dazed, but President Pendleton is equal to anything. We crowded into the chapel, dressed in the most outlandish get-ups, and she led us in prayer, thanking God no one was lost. She said, "We know all things work together for good, to them that love God." Then she announced, "Students may depart for spring vacation as soon as they collect their possessions" — everyone laughed at that — but Miss Pendleton took our breath away when she added quietly, "The spring term will begin on April seventh."*

Wellesley did reopen on schedule, although there was nothing to teach with except the brains of the faculty. Some of the teachers, like Miss Hubbard who taught embryology, had seen years of Ph.D. research go up in flames. Connie received a letter from Miss Caroline Thompson of the biology department, asking her for microscopic slides to use in teaching. She sent all she had from her histology and pathology courses and spent hours making more, happy to have a small part in the job of rebuilding her college.

About Easter time, Connie began searching for a place where she could earn money over the summer. Dean Kerr helped her get a job as a pharmacist in the State Hospital for the Insane in Binghamton, New York, where she could make fifty dollars a month clear, as room and board were free. Since Connie had spent a lot of time visiting Dr. Babcock's asylum, she felt comfortable in a mental hospital. Binghamton had over five thousand patients, and she was busy most of the day filling prescriptions in the pharmacy. She was able to increase her medical knowledge, too, because Dr. Ida Walker, who was in charge of women patients, took an interest in her. She asked Connie to accompany her on her rounds, took her to staff meetings and arranged for her to help with autopsies. To Connie, Dr. Walker was the ideal woman doctor: dedicated, attractive, warm hearted, interested in everything and loved by everybody.

On the afternoon of August 3, 1914, Connie was walking up the steps of the Binghamton hospital when a newspaper lying at the top of the stairs caught her eye. Even before she got to it she could read the huge headlines that made her heart sink. WAR! KAISER HURLS A MILLION GERMANS AT FRANCE. Connie shuddered. War in Europe! War, that horrible, useless slaughter that settles nothing — was loose in the world again. She hoped the United States would never become involved; surely the lessons of the War between the States could not be forgotten.

As usual, the Guions held a gathering of the clan that summer and Connie joined them before returning to medical school. The Guions' will to congregate was equaled only by their mobility and their skill at stretching their stringent budgets. They managed to get around in the most remarkable way, usually about a dozen strong. One summer they took a cottage at Lake Winnipesaukee, New Hampshire; another year they gathered at Chautauqua, New York; and this summer was spent at Corn Hill on Cape Cod, Massachusetts, where they rented a house on the dunes. When Connie arrived from Binghamton, the fun of the summer really began for the younger ones.

"How do they treat you women at medical school?" asked Jo.

"The same as they treat women anywhere else. Nobody cares whether you're a man or a woman. It's how you do your work that counts."

"I can't believe it," said Mrs. Guion, who was interested in the Suffrage movement and very sensitive about women's rights.

"Oh, once in a while I run into a snag, but I've worked out three rules that help."

"Oh, Con, you would," laughed Ridie. "What are they?"

"Rule one: a girl in medical school must never try to be masculine. Rule two: she must never exploit her femininity to get ahead. Rule three: she must never let the men know her good grades."

The family excitement that summer — and there was always some excitement in the Guion family — was generated by Louis and Viv. Louis, at the age of forty, had his first child and Viv, at thirty-five, married Louise Daniel of Durham, North Carolina.

"Your sons are slow starters, Mama," teased Connie.

"They're just like their father," said Mrs. Guion. "They're not interested in speed and greed."

Having completed her first year at Ithaca, in the fall Connie began studying at the Cornell Medical College in New York City. It was located in a slum area on First Avenue between 28th and 29th Streets, where it was difficult to find a decent place to live. Most of the men lived at the YMCA, but there was no local "Y" for women. Connie and Birdina Crosby were lucky enough to rent an apartment in the Phipps Tenement on 31st Street. Some people might not have considered this luck, since it was a fifth-floor walk-up without any living room; there were only three tiny bedrooms, a kitchen and a bath. At Connie's suggestion, Elsie Goddard's sister Harriet, who was working at Best and Company, moved in to occupy the third room. The girls could afford to buy only the most essential pieces of furniture from a second-hand store — beds, bureau, desk and straight chair. They had no curtains, only window shades; no rugs, no lamps and no comfortable chairs. Connie provided the only "extra" by buying boards from a lumberyard and making bookcases to hold her growing collection of books.

Connie had not been at the medical school long when Dr. Stanley Benedict, the brother of President Mary Benedict of Sweet Briar, sent for her. She had met him at Sweet Briar and was eager to know him better because he was one of the outstanding biochemists in the country. He had invented the colorimeter, which allowed doctors to do inexpensive blood chemistry in their own offices, and had worked out the Benedict solution for testing sugar in the urine, a significant step in the diagnosis of diabetes.

"Miss Guion," said Dr. Benedict, "I've been looking at your record. I'm impressed by your extensive background in biochemistry."

"Thank you, Doctor. It's my favorite subject."

"My sister Mary has told me about your boundless energy and capacity for hard work." Dr. Benedict smiled diffidently.

Why, he's as shy as his sister, thought Connie. She liked the look of the tall doctor with the unruly brown hair, bushy eyebrows and thoughtful blue eyes. He was a handsome man, even though his skin was scarred from smallpox.

"Well, I'm no match for Miss Benedict. She's a star."

"Did you know my sister has decided she wants to get her M.D.? She's going to study medicine at Johns Hopkins."

"That is news. Miss Benedict will be a top-notch doctor — but what will Sweet Briar do without her?"

"She's not going to resign. She's going to do both. Now Miss Guion, I have a project for you. I want to promote you from student to researcher. That is, if you're willing."

"What do you mean, Dr. Benedict?"

"You obviously don't need any more class work in bio-chemistry, so I'd like you to assist me in the work I'm doing on blood sugar."

"Oh, I'd like that. What are you working on, Dr. Benedict?"

"I administer different chemicals to dogs and study the effect on their pancreas and metabolism. I know your help would be valuable, especially when it comes to preparing a paper on the research."

From then on, Connie spent the time she would have spent in chemistry class working on Dr. Benedict's project. She thoroughly enjoyed both the work and the professor. Beneath his painful shyness Dr. Benedict was witty and full of fun. He had the incisive mind of an investigator and Connie learned a great deal from her association with him. Connie was fond of all the Benedicts, a unique family. They were as queer as Dick's hatband, brilliant, bashful, independent and aloof. When her work with Dr. Benedict was finished, she wrote up all her experiments and handed them in, assuming that would be the end of it. But when the paper was published, Connie Guion's name came first and his was second. Thanks to Dr. Benedict's generosity, Connie had published her first scientific paper while she was still a student.

That Christmas Ridie came up from Princeton, where she was now teaching at Miss Fine's School, and Jo came down from Wellesley so they could all be together. Although their surroundings were far from festive, the Guion girls did things with a light touch and December 25 was tinged with laughter. They went to church and then had a delicious Christmas dinner in the kitchen before Connie returned to her books. She was trying to learn the name of every bone in the human body for the course in "Gross Anatomy."

"Did you know there are two hundred bones in a human skeleton, not counting six auditory ossicles?" she asked Ridie. "I think it's silly to memorize all those tibiae and fibulae, but if that's what it takes to be a doctor, I'll go along."

When Connie was a little girl Dr. Babcock had told her, "There are three great moments in the life of a medical student — the first time you put on your white coat, the day you get your stethoscope, and the first time a patient calls you Doctor." Connie, crisp and efficient in her white coat, was at the stage where she had a gleaming stethoscope sticking out of the pocket. But disappointment lay ahead. Dr. Lewis Atterbury Conner, the professor of medicine, would not allow his students to use a stethoscope at all. "While you're studying under me," said Dr. Conner, "you will listen to the heart with the naked ear *only*. There is no other safe method. Think of the sounds that come from the friction of the stethoscope on the hair of the chest! Think of the way sound changes as it travels through fifteen inches of rubber tubing to your ear! Too risky! The only answer is to place your ear directly over your patient's heart and *listen.*"

Connie was dazzled by her medical school professors. They were giants in their fields: Dr. Graham Lusk, who was the foremost authority in America in the science of nutrition, had written a textbook that was used all over the country; Dr. Eugene DuBois, who constructed the first machine in New York to measure basal metabolism; Dr. James Ewing, the pathologist, brilliant, scornful, and very lame. He made fun of the kind of teaching that he thought was going on elsewhere and said, "When I get sick I want my family to call a Cornell graduate. At least he'll be able to read a thermometer and know the meaning of a temperature of 106." And Dr. Elise L'Esperance, who pioneered in the clinical search for early signs of cancer and, with her sister, started the Strang Clinic.

The book which Connie used every day in her medical school career was Sir William Osler's *The Practice of Medicine,* a tome of fifteen hundred pages describing every known disease. "Let Osler be your Bible," Dr. Walter Niles told the students. "There is no textbook in existence that can compare with his. It will give you a peg on which to hang the physical examination and history of every patient. Moreover, it's filled with philosophy and is excellent reading." Under Dr. Niles's strict supervision, Connie and her classmates went through Osler page by page, studying each disease in detail. Although they had yet to see most of the diseases described, by the end of the year they had a working knowledge of each one.

One of the aspects of medicine that fascinated Connie from the very beginning was the clinic, the place where the poor came for treatment. Remembering her own experience at the Boston eye clinic, she felt a kinship for these ailing, poverty-stricken human beings who were treated like cattle. No doctor spent more than ten minutes on them; they received only the most cursory care.

Because she was eager to learn, Connie took her lunch with her in a paper bag and worked in a surgical clinic during lunch hour. This clinic too was oversubscribed and understaffed, but Dr. Peter Hoag who ran it did a good job under trying conditions. He welcomed Connie's help and taught her minor surgery. He showed her how to sew up a finger and cut out a sebaceous cyst, and even taught her to bandage by practicing on a table leg. One day when he was helping her open a boil, Connie said, "Once I cured my brother Louis's boil by using a bread poultice."

"Not a bad method," said Dr. Hoag, "but it takes time, and in a clinic, time is what we haven't got."

"Someday," said Connie with a glint in her eye, "I'm going to do *something* about these miserable clinics."

Surprised by the ring of steel in her usually soft voice, Dr. Hoag looked at her and said, "You know, I believe you probably will."

At the end of the long day at medical school Connie would do the marketing and come home and cook the dinner. She hated to waste time in the kitchen, but neither of the other girls knew how to cook anything. As soon as dinner was over she would attack her books again. One night, as she was hauling groceries up the fifth flight of stairs, she heard a cheerful voice call, "Is that you, Connie Guion?" A gay laugh that had a familiar lilt to it, floated down from the floor above.

"Who's there?"

"A spirit from your past. I've come to bring you *another* glass of water."

"Ruth Smith! What are you doing here?"

Ruth ran lightly down the steps. "I came to dinner with my friend Dr. Rucker and she told me you lived below her. I've been waiting for you to come home. What hours you keep!"

The two girls had not seen each other in the thirteen years since Northfield. They sat in the kitchen "parlor" and talked for hours, giggling over old times.

"Tell me what you're doing now, Ruth."

"I teach physical education at the Washington Irving High School, on East 17th Street, and live with Mother in Brooklyn. It's quite a jaunt each day."

"Why don't you move in with us?"

Ruth looked around the cramped apartment. "Where would I sleep, in the bathtub?"

"We'd fit you in somehow. Say, Ruth, can you cook?"

"I love to."

"Then we'll move to your neighborhood. I'd rather travel than cook any day."

The upshot of the evening was that Ruth Smith and Harriet Goddard located a larger place on 22nd Street and all of them moved into it. It was, to the girls, a "tony" apartment with a gilt bird-cage of an elevator that went right up from the middle of the lobby. Their small flat seemed spacious after the Phipps Tenement.

Ruth Smith was friend, chef, and general factotum for Connie. She even kept her up to date on the news. "Say, Con," she laughed, "guess who the *Times* says lead the Suffrage Parade up Fifth Avenue, riding a white horse and wearing a gold crown and a long white cape?"

"Brunhilde?"

"That's close. It was one of your Vassar students — Inez Milholland."

"I have no patience with the suffragettes or the W.C.T.U.,

either one. They're just making spectacles of themselves. You don't get things done by smashing bottles and marching around. Women are going to vote eventually, and men are not going to stop drinking, and all that hullabaloo doesn't amount to a bale of cotton."

"Well, how do you get things done, then?"

"By working as hard as you can, each day. That's how."

During those medical school years, work was Connie's middle name. Most of it she enjoyed, but her third-year course in obstetrics was tedious. In order to pass, each student was required to deliver at least fifteen babies. The class was farmed out to different maternity centers in the city during the summer and Connie was sent to the New York Infirmary for Women and Children. The head of the obstetrical service there was Dr. Caroline Finley, one of the best obstetricians in New York. A striking-looking woman, plump with straight black hair, she had studied in both Germany and France, which in those days was the epitome of status.

Dr. Finley was an excellent teacher and an exacting disciplinarian. On the first day she said, "During the month you are here, you will not be permitted to leave this hospital or mix with anyone outside of maternity. We cannot risk having you bring germs to our mothers and babies. If you want exercise, you may get it on the roof of the hospital."

During her month's incarceration, Connie delivered twenty-five babies. Some of the births were abnormal, but she never had any difficulty because Dr. Finley was always there to see things were done correctly; if it was a forceps delivery she took over entirely. "O.b." held little appeal for Connie, who did not enjoy waiting around for babies to come. "You just sit there and stare at the cervix," she told Ruth Smith later. "If the baby starts coming too fast you put your hand on its head and tell the anesthetist to give the mother a whiff of chloroform to relax her. Then you tell the mother to push again and the durn thing goes on for hours. I wouldn't be an obstetrician for anything in the world. I'm not going to spend my life watching some woman grunt and groan."

"Have you decided what kind of doctor you do want to be?"

"A pediatrician, I suppose."

"Why?"

"Because I like children, and taking care of them seems like a natural thing for a woman to do. Also, it's one of the few fields where a woman can work up a good private practice, and I want to build up a practice of my own somehow. Just because I happened to have been born a woman, I don't see why I should spend my life doing scut work for some doctor whose only advantage over me is that he was born a male. I believe women have a contribution to make to medicine that no man can make."

Doctor Connie

CONNIE GUION spent little time in the classroom in her last two years of medical school. During the first two years she had been building a strong background in physiology, biochemistry and anatomy; she had dealt with cells, bacteria and isolated parts of the body. In the final two years she began to work with patients, studying the diagnosis and treatment of "diseases, disorders and afflictions," and applying what she learned in class to the care of the sick in the wards.

The Cornell Medical College had been built across the street from Bellevue Hospital for the specific purpose of enabling students to get into the wards where they could receive person-to-person training from some of the best physicians in New York City. They spent an equal amount of time studying at The New York Hospital on 16th Street. Because it was a private hospital, it had fewer patients and less variety of disease, but it boasted excellent teachers.

None of the brilliant doctors who taught Connie influenced her more than Dr. Frank Meara, the handsome professor of medicine who was in charge of the Cornell section at Bellevue. It was he who impressed upon her the creed that medicine is not a laboratory science but a healing art that deals with human beings.

Dr. Meara was a man of rare charm, a "black Irishman" with a scintillating wit. A graduate of Yale and the College of

Physicians and Surgeons at Columbia, he was a superb clinician, but he was also a scholar who liked to read Greek and Latin and had a wide knowledge of history and poetry. Connie made ward rounds with him regularly during her Bellevue "clerkship," as the student training was called, and they became great friends.

Before Dr. Meara took his students into the wards, where many of the patients were human derelicts of the most pitiful and even repulsive sort, he would say: "Remember, this is one of God's creatures you're dealing with. Just because he's a pauper in a charity hospital doesn't mean you can disregard his personal privileges."

Connie observed the way Dr. Meara greeted each patient by name, shook his hand and asked how he felt. He took the time to chat, not only to make the sick man more receptive to examination but to gain some insight into his problems. Before leaving, the doctor always said, "If you have any questions, why you let me know tomorrow."

"Dr. Meara," said Connie, "it almost seems like you *waste* time on a patient."

"A doctor must give his patients the feeling he has plenty of time for them, Miss Guion. If he does, they will confide in him and confidence is important in healing."

The personal touch in medicine came naturally to Connie. She had inherited from her mother the trait of being more interested in other people than she was in herself. It was easy for her to form a lasting relationship with anyone, whether he was an illiterate drunkard or a millionaire. She made countless friends on the wards at Bellevue, but none more staunch than John Joseph McLaughlin, an alcoholic heart patient. John was an elderly Irish seaman, handsome, rough and full of devilment, and he adored Connie from the first moment he saw her.

"Praise and begorrah," he would say, "it's a beautiful little woman you are, with your white collar buttoned up your neck and your big eyes dancin' behind them glasses."

"You must have kissed that Blarney Stone more than once, John Joseph McLaughlin," Connie laughed.

She took care of him for several months and one day when Dr. Meara asked him who his best friend was he said, "It's that little slip of a girl that gives me the shots, Doc. She's my best friend."

Dr. Meara lectured his students on the old man's remark. "This is the best report I have had on a student in years. Your patient should always say you're his best friend."

When John J. McLaughlin finally left the hospital, he did not lose touch with his "best friend." Every time he came ashore, he took five or six hundred dollars to Connie and asked her to hold it, while he went out on a binge. She kept strict account of his money, doling it out to him as he called for it.

In Dr. Meara's talks with the students, he was fond of quoting Osler's remark, "The magic word in medicine, the open-sesame that unlatches all doors, is *work*." But for Connie, the clerkship at Bellevue did not seem like work at all. Outside, the black clouds of World War I were beginning to envelop the United States, but inside the huge city hospital life hummed along rapidly, oblivious of the world. Engrossed in medicine, Connie learned to live on little sleep and to take quick catnaps when she was exhausted. Some nights, when she substituted for the interns on the wards, she got no sleep whatsoever. She didn't care; she wished that she, too, might one day earn the right to be an overworked intern at Bellevue.

Although Bellevue was always low in funds, since it was entirely city-supported and riddled with political strife, every ambitious medical student longed to intern there. No hospital anywhere covered so much ground, medically speaking. As a student, Connie encountered diseases that were soon to become practically extinct. There was seldom a time, for example, when cases of typhoid fever couldn't be found in the wards of Bellevue.

It was easy to spot the typhoid cases because the beds would be framed with mosquito netting to keep off the flies. Doctors knew that the fever was caused by a "germ" and transmitted by the three F's: flies, food and fingers. The accepted method of treatment for typhoid was cold baths and starvation. Tubs of ice water were rolled up to the bed of patients burning with high temperature and, in an effort to reduce the fever, they were dunked into the freezing water. Connie winced when she heard them scream. She had a painful memory of the time she and Ben immersed little Alex in a tub of ice when he was burning with fever from typhoid. The typhoid patients at Bellevue were fed a soft diet of only five hundred calories a day, and the combination of starvation and high temperatures wasted their bodies into shadows.

Two of Connie's teachers, Dr. Eugene DuBois and Dr. Warren Coleman, observing the energy expended by typhoid victims, decided to reverse the starvation treatment. They stuffed them with four times the amount of food they would normally eat, including lots of ice cream, whipped cream, and potatoes with butter. These patients responded amazingly and many of them recovered. It was the turning of the tide in the treatment of typhoid, and with the development of an effective vaccine after World War I, typhoid fever became a textbook disease. Connie never forgot the daring and perception of her two teachers.

Unlike most hospitals in 1916, Bellevue allowed both male

and female students to examine every patient. But Dr. Edward Keyes, who taught urology, was more fastidious. When it came time to study the enlargement of the prostate gland, he sent the women of the class to gynecology.

"I don't think your point of view is consistent, Dr. Keyes," objected Connie.

"What do you mean, Miss Guion?"

"If the men can examine women patients, why can't we examine men? I don't see any difference, and I think false modesty is a lot of poppycock."

"Now, now, Miss Guion, that's strong talk."

"Perhaps. But if I ever get a practice of my own, I expect to examine both men and women completely. I don't see why men should find it embarrassing. Didn't they all come out of a woman in the first place?"

As Connie's experience on the wards widened, she learned to handle deathbed cases. She evolved two rules for dealing with the critically ill. The first was to do everything possible to make the patient comfortable. The second was to decide whether he had responsibilities that made it necessary for him to know that the end was near. At Bellevue the patients had few, if any, possessions to dispose of; however, one very sick woman, a mulatto prostitute named Famie, said to Connie, "Doctor, I've got to go home. There's something I have to take care of."

"I'm not a doctor — yet — but I know you're not well enough to get off that bed. Why do you want to go home?"

"My darling dog, Muffin, is going to have puppies. I've got to look out for her."

As she talked with the woman, Connie began to realize those puppies were as much concern to her as if they had been babies. She had no other family.

"If we can get a social worker to take your dog to Speyer Animal Hospital, where the puppies will be taken care of, would you stay here peacefully?"

"Yes, I would."

Connie arranged for the care of the dogs, just as she had promised, though she had some difficulty convincing the social worker that the mission was worthwhile. Each day Famie's condition grew worse. "Miss Guion," she said, "am I going to die?"

"Yes, aren't we all?"

"I don't mean that. I mean am I going to die before those pups are big enough to be taken away from their mother?"

"No, I don't think you are. I think that you will be able to go home."

"Do you think I'm going to get well? I won't have any peace until I provide for those puppies."

"I think if I were in your place I would make arrangements about those pups."

A short time later it became evident that nothing more could be done for Famie at the hospital, and the doctors decided she would be happier if she died in her own surroundings. She was sent home in an ambulance; a friend and a neighborhood nurse agreed to care for her.

One midnight about six weeks later, a friend called Connie and said, "Famie's sick bad and wants to see you." Connie dressed, called a taxi, and explained to the driver the circumstances of the case. The driver agreed to take her to Brooklyn and promised to wait for her.

When they found the building, which was on Sands Street almost beneath the Brooklyn Bridge, it was dark and dilapidated. Inside all was dark except for a dim gas light burning on each landing. Connie called Famie's name several times. The friend appeared at the top of the stairs with a candle and Connie climbed four flights to the apartment. Famie was very ill; her old rheumatic heart had just about given out. All three pups were lying in bed with her, and the mother, a beautiful brown Pomeranian, lay in her arms.

"My time has come," gasped Famie. "I want you to have one of the pups." Connie did all she could to make poor Famie comfortable and when she finally left she wrapped the little black pup in a towel and took it home. It was, for her, a special legacy. She gave him to her mother, who kept him as her beloved pet for thirteen years.

The next term Connie started to study pediatrics under Dr. Joseph Winters. His lectures and case presentations were colorful and interesting, but Connie missed the medical detective work that was an important part of working with adults. She even questioned whether she wanted to be a pediatrician at all.

"I don't think I want to go into pediatrics," she told Ruth Smith.

"Why not?"

"You can't get a case history from a child. Taking care of babies seems to me almost like being a veterinarian."

"Con! What a thing to say!"

"What's wrong with that? Veterinarians accomplish wonders working with 'patients' that can't talk."

"Well, a horse doctor and a baby doctor are quite different."

"Not so different as you think. Any living creature that's sick needs comfort and care, whether he has two legs or four. If I saw a dog wheezing with bronchitis, I'd stop and try to help him. Suffering is suffering, no matter what. The trick is for me to find the place in medicine where I think I can make the best contribution, that's all."

Connie's fourth and last year at medical school gave her a

chance to explore new areas. Her time was divided between surgery and the study of specialties, such as opthalmology, neurology and otology. The specialty courses were not long, but they were excellent and exciting. She particularly enjoyed studying ophthalmology, the science of the eye, under Dr. Robert Reese, and a course in neurology taught by a fiery Irishman named Dr. Foster Kennedy.

Dr. Kennedy was brilliant but erratic. He never came to class on time and his flair for drama made him unpredictable. One of his students, Joe Black, was famous for neglecting his work and then describing the physical examinations he supposedly had made. In presenting a diagnosis to the class Connie said, "This patient did not have a knee jerk."

"Oh, yes, he did," interrupted Joe Black. "I guess I ought to know. I examined him, too."

Dr. Kennedy stepped forward and asked the patient to sit on the side of the bed. Dramatically, he thumped the man's knee with the small rubber hammer. The leg hung limp. "Well, Mr. Black," said Dr. Kennedy with withering sarcasm, "evidently you got this man's very last knee jerk."

The course in otology, the study of the ear, was taught by Dr. Frederick Whiting in the clinic of the medical school. As Connie helped treat the poor who came there with abessed ears, infected tonsils, and mastoids, her interest in clinics was rekindled. The needs of these poor people were so great, and the facilities to care for them were so limited, she felt more strongly than ever the importance of doing something to improve the situation.

Connie's final six months were devoted to surgery, and again the time was divided equally between New York Hospital and Bellevue. The whole drama of the surgical table unfolded before her as she watched skilled surgeons perform their operations. Every Saturday Connie and a few other students made the journey uptown to watch Dr. Irving Haynes do special surgery at the Harlem Hospital. At that time all the patients and nurses there were Negroes, but none of the doctors were. Dr. Haynes's specialty was abdominal surgery, though occasionally they would see him set an arm or leg or reduce a fracture. Afterwards, he took the students around the wards to visit the cases they had seen the week before. This follow-up often brought home to Connie the forlorn aspects of a doctor's life.

"Where is Big Jim who stuck the nail in his finger last week?" she asked.

"He's dead."

"From that simple infection!"

"He died of septicemia four days after he was admitted. There is no such thing as a simple infection, Miss Guion."

To Connie the surgery at Bellevue was more interesting than anywhere else because of the infinite variety of cases found in a city hospital where over a thousand patients were operated on every month. Also, the students were actually allowed to assist in the operations. One of the surgeons who instructed Connie was Dr. John Rogers, a colorful and refreshingly unorthodox doctor. She never forgot seeing him remove a man's thyroid gland under local anesthetic. Dr. Rogers was all dressed and prepared for the operation with his hands wrapped in a sterile towel, and the highly nervous patient was already draped, when suddenly the man turned pale and said, "Aw, Doc, I'm going to vomit."

Dr. Rogers exploded. "Damn you! If you puke on my sterile field, I'll slap you in the face."

The man turned scarlet with anger. "You can't talk to me like that!"

"Well, get off that table and walk out of this hospital."

Shocked, the patient began to simmer down, and when he

was calm Dr. Rogers performed the operation. As soon as he had finished, he looked at the man with the sweetest smile and said, "Sir, I hope you will forgive me for speaking to you so roughly." Then he turned to the students. "Now gentlemen — and lady — do you know why I acted the way I did?"

No one had the nerve to answer. "When anybody gets ready to vomit, the only thing you can do is stimulate some other involuntary nervous center. I had to get this fellow mad enough to take his mind off vomiting." He paused dramatically and looked around. "What did I do wrong in this operation?" Nobody said a word. "A doctor should never, never swear at his patients. That was very sinful of me, but I could not have my operation spoiled by this man's damned queasy stomach."

Dr. Rogers allowed each medical student to do one simple operation; Connie's was an appendectomy. She had seen many operations, but this was the first she was to perform herself and she was excited about it. She went in early in the morning to get scrubbed up, put on a sterile gown, washed her hands in alcohol, and pulled on sterile gloves. Dr. Rogers stood by to direct her. In addition to the anesthetist, there was one student who handed her instruments and another who held the incision open with retractors. The operation took twenty minutes. When it was over, Connie felt a warm glow of satisfaction. "Damned good job," said Dr. Rogers, smiling down at her.

That winter Ridie came to New York to study at Columbia for her Master's degree in English literature. She lived with Connie and studied constantly. Toward the end of the year her usually light step began to drag, and Connie, noting the circles under her eyes and her persistent cough, insisted that she have a thorough physical examination by Dr. James

Alexander Miller at Bellevue. The results were devastating. Ridie, who had never enjoyed robust health, was a victim of tuberculosis.

"There's only one thing to do," said Dr. Miller. "You must go to the Trudeau Sanitarium in Saranac. They do remarkable things up there to arrest T.B. with good food and rest and sunshine and mountain air."

Ridie turned to her sister. "Oh, Con, that would be horribly expensive. How could we ever manage it?"

"We'll figure out a way. We've solved a lot worse problems than that."

In the end they borrowed the money for the sanitarium. Connie could not leave to take Ridie to Saranac because she was preparing for final exams, so Jo came down from Walnut Hill School in Massachusetts, where she was teaching, to go with her. It was a sad day for Connie when she put her ailing little sister on the Adirondack train.

In the spring of 1917 with graduation from medical school looming ahead, a hot contest started among the seniors for internships. As a woman, Connie's opportunities were severely limited. She could go to the New York Infirmary or the New England Hospital in Boston — both of which were staffed by women only — or if she were very lucky she might get an internship at Bellevue. Bellevue had been taking women interns for only two years. This was a revolutionary step; at that time no other hospital in New York City would consider doing such a thing.

The selection of interns at Bellevue was determined by competitive examinations. Connie and a few of the other students could see no point in taking written exams under the same professors who had taught them for four long years. They decided to approach Dr. John Rogers, Dr. Frank Meara and Dr. John Hartwell, the intern committee. As usual, Connie was the spokesman. She found it easy to talk with Dr. Meara because he had known and admired Ef when she was a nurse at St. Luke's.

"We think this system is perfectly silly," she told him.

"Why, Miss Guion?" asked Dr. Meara, obviously enjoying her salty spirit.

"Internships ought to be awarded on the basis of four years' work. No matter how long an exam is, it can't possibly tell you more than you already know about us."

"Don't you trust your ability to write examinations?"

"I do, but I'd rather trust to your wisdom."

After some consideration, the committee decided to hand out internships according to class standing, regardless of the sex of the applicant. Such a thing had never happened before. Connie, who stood number one in the class, got first draw on Bellevue. The rest of the coveted places at Bellevue went to men.

On April 6, 1917, everyone at the medical school was stunned by America's entrance into the war. Germany's repeated attacks on American shipping forced President Woodrow Wilson to go before the Congress and ask for a declaration of war "to make the world safe for democracy." No one at Cornell could guess what the future would hold.

Graduation day arrived at last — and the rain poured down in torrents. The storm outside was matched by the teeming excitement within the girls' apartment as they got ready to go to the exercises. Connie darted about in her cap and gown, while Ruth Smith, Harriet Goddard, and their friend Jean Pattison fussed over hats and gloves. In the midst of the turmoil, the doorbell rang.

"That'll be Parkie," said Connie. "She got permission to come down from Northfield for my graduation." She opened the door, to be dwarfed by a huge gray-haired woman. Connie gasped. "Why, Miss Savage! What a suprise!"

"I *had* to come to see the pride of Northfield get her M.D. I hope you can squeeze me in some place." Miss Savage moved and behind her stood little Parkie McCombs, pink-cheeked and bright-eyed. She ran forward and gave Connie a hug. "Oh, Aunt Con, I'm so proud of you! And think how proud my Papa would have been to have another doctor in the family. I hope I can be one, too."

"Time to go," called Ruth Smith.

"But how will we get there?" wailed Harriet. "I've called every taxi company in town. They're all busy. We can't even go out and look for a cab in this downpour. Con's going to miss her graduation, that's all."

"I'll think of something . . . I've got to," said Connie, a note of desperation creeping into her voice. Here she was thirty-four years old and almost an M.D., stuck with five women on her hands and no way to transport them across town in a rainstorm. Suddenly, light dawned. "I've got it! Mr. Clinchy!"

"The *grocer?*" said Jean Pattison.

"Why not? He's one of my best friends. Every day for three years I've gone in there to buy groceries. I've even borrowed money from him in a pinch. He's got a beautiful delivery wagon and we could all fit in it."

Miss Savage looked pleasantly shocked. "Just about what I expected," she said shaking her head.

Quickly, Connie got Mr. Clinchy on the phone. She explained the emergency as rapidly as her Southern drawl would permit. In less than ten minutes, Mr. Clinchy appeared at the door, all decked out in his Sunday suit, celluloid collar and derby hat. "Your wagon's ready, Miss Guion," he said with a bow. The six laughing women piled into the grocery wagon, Mr. Clinchy flicked his whip, and the horse started off at a brisk trot.

This improbable caravan pulled up to the door of the medical school just as Dean Polk and President Schurman of Cornell were being helped out of a Rolls-Royce by a uniformed chauffeur. As the ladies stepped off the grocery wagon, one by one, they were greeted with laughter from the crowd. But when Connie, the last one, jumped down in her cap and gown, everyone cheered.

"Your career as a doctor seems to be off to a good start, Miss Guion," laughed Dean Polk.

"Thank you, sir. A little luck goes a long way."

Twenty-six men and three women graduated from Cornell Medical College in the class of 1917. President Schurman said, "It gives me great pleasure to announce that the winner of fifty dollars in gold pieces for the highest marks in otology and the winner of the three-hundred-dollar Polk prize for general excellence is the student who stands number one in this class, Connie Myers Guion."

Three hundred dollars! thought Connie. *The Lord must have sent it so I could take care of Ridie!* There flashed in her mind a picture of her valiant young mother lying in the walnut bed on the day Ridie was born. How she wished her mother were there to see her graduate — and Laura — and Dr. Babcock — and all the others who had helped her climb until she reached this peak.

Dean Polk handed Connie her diploma and her prizes and placed on her shoulders the black and green hood of Doctor of Medicine. Then he leaned down and said softly, "Cornell is proud of you, Doctor Guion."

Emergency

✳ ✳

In July, 1917, Doctor Connie Guion entered Bellevue Hospital to begin her internship. A brand new M.D., brimming with energy and enthusiasm, she paused as she walked through the iron gates and looked around. Sprawled about her was a complex of smoky stone buildings stretching along the East River from 26th to 29th Street. For the next two years this big, bustling and sometimes overpowering city hospital was to be her home.

An intern is a graduate physician who lives in a hospital for two years or sometimes more, working in different capacities in preparation for independent practice. During her internship, Connie would be given room and board but no salary. She would have little time off and almost no time to herself. In her day, interns never got married. It was assumed that medicine was their all-absorbing interest and everything else would have to wait until later.

Connie was proud to become a small part of Bellevue, the oldest hospital in America and one of the largest. A city within a city, Bellevue had its own prison, insane asylum, mortuary, fire department, missing persons bureau, crime detection laboratory, and three churches: Catholic, Jewish and Protestant. Since it was entirely city supported, the patients did not have to pay unless they were able, and the doctors who worked there were not paid. It was compensation enough just to be allowed to practice in this famous city hospital. Although there were quite a few women students in the four divisions of Bellevue, there were only three other women doctors in the entire hospital when Connie Guion arrived.

Dr. Meara liked to twit her about the female minority. "Miss Guion, did you know that a wise man once said human beings can be divided into three groups, men, women — and women doctors?"

"Yes, but Dr. Osler said that twenty-five years ago. Times have changed."

Dr. Meara ran his hand over his iron gray hair. "You're pretty well informed about Sir William Osler, young lady."

"He's one of my heroes, Dr. Meara, and I try to live by his theory of the day-tight compartment. Look to this day! That's my battle-cry."

Connie's days at Bellevue were indeed full. She spent six months of her internship in pathology, six months in surgery, and a year in medicine, practicing under the supervision of outstanding doctors. Bellevue, with its well-worn marble steps, tile floors, high ceilings, endless, dimly lit corridors and patched plaster, was a museum of diseases. There were few diseases in Osler's *Practice of Medicine* that Connie did not encounter. She learned to treat scarlet fever, rheumatic fever, meningitis, gonorrhea, syphilis, smallpox, glanders, cancer, erysipelas, tetanus, tuberculosis, and delirium tremens.

Dr. Connie never knew in the morning what the next twelve hours would bring. Each day she had first-hand experience with New York life at its lowest; she took care of the criminal and the violent, the underprivileged and the destitute. In one day her cases would range from an elderly drug addict in a coma to an abandoned waif whose identification said, "no residence, no parents, no friends."

During the six months Connie spent in pathology under the supervision of Dr. Charles Norris and Dr. Douglas Symmers, the largest part of her work was assisting at autopsies and making microscopic examination of the vital organs of patients who had died, to determine the exact cause of death. Dr. Norris and Dr. Symmers urged the interns to do all the autopsies they could, in order to learn about the nature and correct diagnosis of disease. But this was not as simple as it sounds. The intern first had to persuade the nearest of kin of the deceased to sign a permission slip. To convince the families of Bellevue patients to do this was a hard task. Many of them did not speak English, much less understand the mysteries of medicine. But since Connie was by nature a person who inspired confidence, she was very successful in securing the needed permissions.

When Connie moved on to surgery, she got her first taste of ambulance duty. She rode the ambulance day and night, because interns were on call for twenty-four hours at a time. They caught what sleep they could between calls. Bellevue had established the first ambulance service in this country and it was justly proud of its emergency units. No fire or riot or disaster occurred in New York City without Bellevue ambulances' being called into action. In 1917 when Connie arrived, the shiny horse-drawn ambulance had just been replaced by a "bus" with a high-powered engine that could go as fast as thirty miles an hour.

The first time Connie put on the jaunty, dark blue cap, the long blue coat and ankle-length white skirt of the ambulance uniform, she was excited. She clutched her black bag, containing surgical instruments, medications, stomach pumps, and other emergency equipment, and waited. She did not have to wait long; the emergency calls came often. The min-

Connie at Bellevue

ute one came, a gong clanged, the driver sprang into the
front seat, Connie swung herself onto the back, and off they
rattled at top speed. Connie gripped the wooden side bars with
all her might. She did not want to fall off the back of that
ambulance.

They drove at breakneck pace to a tenement on Ninth
Avenue, slowing down to pick up the policeman on the corner. Connie's patient was a poor woman lying on a double
bed screaming, obviously about to give birth. Connie looked
around the grimy room. There were no sheets, no towels,
no pillow cases. She remembered Dr. Caroline Finley's instructions: "No matter what happens, don't ever get nerv-

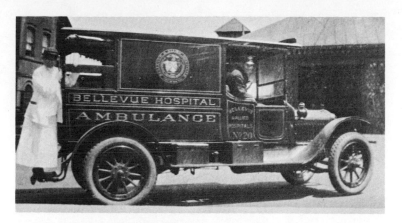

Connie on the ambulance

ous." Eying the miserable husband, she said, "I don't see anything around here to wrap a baby in. Take off your shirt and boil it. We'll have to use that." With the help of the policeman, Connie delivered the baby. It was the first of many such emergencies she encountered.

Sometimes, even in an emergency, people balked at having a woman doctor; they suspected that Connie was really a nurse. But on the whole, the women interns were treated just as the men were. In a day when most women were sheltered from the world, Connie went into prisons and flop houses to care for the sick. If her ambulance brought in a case that was D.O.A. — dead on arrival — or if a mother gave birth to a baby in her ambulance, she was expected to buy beer for all the interns, just as the men had always done.

After a short while, Connie discovered that ambulance duty was often monotonous. Many of the cases were not emergencies at all; they were calls from people who were scared or lonely or unbalanced. Most of the calls came between midnight and five o'clock, and Connie soon realized that as dark came on people's courage disappeared and they began to worry about themselves. She tucked this piece of insight away for future reference. It was to come in handy many times.

After she had grappled with the twenty-four-hour ambulance stint for weeks, snatching what little sleep she could, Connie was on the verge of exhaustion. Finally, she rebelled. Her common sense was offended by the needless waste of human energy. She marched up to Superintendent O'Hanlon and said, "I think it is inhuman to make interns hang on the back of that bus for twenty-four hours at a time."

"Why, Dr. Guion," said the astonished superintendent, "our interns have been doing that for a hundred years."

"Well, Dr. O'Hanlon," replied Connie, her eyes flashing, "the century's up!" Soon afterward, twelve-hour ambulance shifts were introduced at Bellevue, a change that was welcomed by everybody.

By the middle of October the war in Europe was raging and Americans were being shipped overseas as quickly as possible. Ruth Smith and Jo Guion signed up with the YMCA and put on olive green uniforms to go "canteening" in Europe. Many of the doctors and interns joined the armed forces. "It's fortunate Bellevue has some able women doctors," Dr. John Rogers told Connie. "I'm going to appoint you senior intern in the Cornell surgery division, Dr. Guion."

Connie's eyes lit up. "Thank you. I'll try to live up to that vote of confidence."

"Some say women doctors is all swabs," he growled.

"Why, Dr. Rogers," exclaimed Connie, "I wouldn't expect you to talk that way."

"It's not me talking. I'm quoting Billy Bones in *Treasure Island.*" He laughed at his own joke. Actually, he was pleased to have Dr. Guion as an assistant and before long she was performing simple operations like appendectomies and hernias regularly.

One Sunday when Connie was studying in her room at Bellevue she heard a timid knock on the door. She opened it to find a young colored girl. "My grandma sent me. She said you was to come to see her." She handed Connie a piece of paper with "719 W. 130 St." scribbled on it.

Connie was mystified. "Who is your grandmother?"

"Miss Elsie. She says you know her right enough, from North Carolina."

"Elsie! What is she doing in New York?"

"Visitin' my mamma, but she says she's goin' home soon. She don't like New York."

"Tell her I'll be up there as soon as I get time off. I'll be so glad to see her!"

Riding on the subway up to Harlem, Connie thought of the fun she and her brothers and sisters used to have with Elsie at River Bend Plantation. As soon as she saw Elsie, the years slipped away and she felt like a little girl again. They hugged each other tight. "Laws a-mercy, Connie — guess I oughter say Doctor Connie now — you is a sight for sore eyes."

"You, too, Elsie. You don't look one bit different."

"Only thing, my two front teeth don't hit." Elsie threw back her head and laughed and Connie could see that two was the correct number. There were no others. Elsie was meticulously dressed as always, with a white cap that came down to her ears and her white hair sticking out all around it, but suddenly she turned to her daughter and said, "Tood, fetch me my apron. I feel naked without it."

Tood tied the apron around her mother's waist. "Now, that's better. What're you doin' down to that hospital, Connie?"

"I've been riding the ambulance, Elsie, taking care of sick

people all over town. The other day I delivered a baby on the Third Avenue elevated."

"You mean you got to study in school to learn to deliver a little ole baby? Shaw, I been doin' that all my life. Remember the day Ridie was born? How is Ridie? Tell me every smitch of family news."

"Ridie's much better. Thank heaven we caught her T.B. early. The doctors at Saranac say she'll soon recover. Jo has been teaching at Sweet Briar College, where I used to teach, but she's going overseas soon, and Viv is bringing his wife and baby to New York — he's going to do engineering work on the warships."

"How 'bout Miss Alice? I heard she and young Jim moved north."

"Yes, Alice got a job as a housemother at Exeter so Jim can go there to school."

"I declare! You Guions sure do love your schoolin'."

"That's right, Elsie, we do. I suppose you heard about Louis's farm being wiped out by a flood."

"A *flood?*"

"Almost as bad as Noah's. Mama wrote me about it. The dam on the Wateree River broke and washed out everything he had — peach trees, pecan trees, dairy cattle, goats, everything. Even the lake went out. Afterward there was furniture in the trees and bales of cotton strewn all over the place. Everything else was gone."

"Father in heaven," muttered Elsie, "that's the awfulest!"

"Louis and his family escaped and now he's starting all over again. You can count on Louis."

"You can count on all the Guions," said Elsie.

Connie returned to Bellevue with a warm feeling in her heart. "Old friends are the best friends," she wrote her mother. "Seeing old Elsie made me feel good all over."

Little by little, the war drained doctors away from the hospital. Bellevue sent a unit of nurses and doctors overseas — known as Base Hospital Number 1 — to work at the large army hospital in Vichy, France. As more doctors departed, those who remained behind did double duty. Connie moved from surgery to the medical service and had been there for only three weeks when she was promoted to house physician. It was most irregular for an intern to be given such heavy responsibility, but there was no alternative.

As house physician, Connie was responsible for the history, physical examination and treatment of every patient in the three wards of the Cornell service at Bellevue. She had to do a lot of paper work, too, preparing reports and filling out death certificates. In addition, she was given the job of teaching fourth-year medical students. The paper work she loathed; the teaching she relished. Connie was a born teacher and the teaching of medicine was to her a privilege.

Part of Connie's job as house physician was to accompany Dr. Meara on his rounds. One day she heard one of his students, a rather stupid boy, present a case. He did it in a highly dramatic manner, apparently trying to cover up the fact that there was little meat in what he had to say.

Connie whispered to Morton Ryder, one of her interns, "John doesn't realize this patient is

> *Neither a saint*
> *nor a Philip Sidney*
> *but a mortal man*
> *with a mortal kidney.*"

Afterwards, Dr. Meara said to her, "I happened to overhear your remark, Dr. Guion."

"Oh?"

"I not only agree with what you said, I admire your taste in poetry. John Masefield is one of my favorites, too."

As the staff dwindled, Connie frequently came into conflict with Superintendent O'Hanlon. "Dr. Guion," he would say, "I need more doctors in the admitting office."

"I'm sorry, Dr. O'Hanlon, I haven't anybody to send you for the admitting office. I haven't anybody to ride the ambulance or to go to pathology. I've got a lot of sick people here who have to be taken care of. The City of New York could hire somebody to do those jobs, but they can't hire anybody to come in here and work in our wards."

In October of 1918, the situation at Bellevue suddenly became desperate. It had been a dry, sunny autumn and the three wards Dr. Guion was responsible for were half full. On Saturday afternoon three seamen were admitted from a Norwegian freighter. They had high temperatures, but nobody knew what was wrong with them. Connie went to Baltimore that weekend to visit Miss Benedict at Johns Hopkins. When she returned Sunday night, the Norwegians were desperately ill. They were burning with fever, short of breath, and had the bluish color typical of influenza. Two days later they were dead and the great influenza epidemic had begun. It was a nightmare.

Influenza swept through New York City like wildfire. Some hospitals refused to take any cases of the highly contagious disease, and Bellevue was swamped with the cases they turned away. Within a week all the beds in Dr. Guion's wards were filled and she ordered a double row of cots set up in the center aisles. Instead of ninety patients, she now had two hundred and seventy.

There was no known treatment for influenza. Nursing, with lots of aspirin, was all that could be done. Only a few of the victims recovered; some died right after they were admitted to the hospital, others lasted two or three days. Once again, Connie ran into trouble with Superintendent O'Hanlon, who insisted that hospital routine be maintained. "I'm sorry, Doctor," she said firmly. "I can't see any sense in doing tests on a man I know will be dead in twenty-four hours. It is much more important to make his last hours as comfortable as possible."

As things grew worse, Bellevue ran out of beds and cots. With the help of two of her students, Howard Craig and Tim Root, Connie took the doors off their hinges and stretched them between chairs to use as beds.

The shortage of doctors and nurses grew acute as many of them were struck down by the disease. The hospital sent out an appeal for volunteer help and the response was instantaneous. The Red Cross, the League of Women's Voluntary Services and other organizations sent workers to Bellevue. A bevy of girls came down from Vassar and a number of them were assigned to Dr. Guion's service. Although they knew little besides taking temperatures and pulses, Connie was thankful to have them. It required five minutes to take one temperature, so these girls released her skeleton force of nurses for more important duties.

Not everyone was so courageous as the Vassar girls. One of Connie's interns from Texas, who was supposed to go on the wards to get blood cultures, said, "Dr. Guion, would you mind taking bloods for me? I'm scared out of my life to go in there."

Although Connie did not understand this kind of fear, she was sympathetic. She and others took turns bringing blood samples to the young Texan so he could continue his lab work. At the end of a week, he got the flu. Dr. Guion and

Dr. Malcolm Goodridge, her supervisor, put him in a small room off the ward and tried to care for him, but within forty-eight hours he was dead.

While the epidemic raged, Connie seldom had time to go to her room to sleep. If she did, she was immediately called back to the ward. When she was too exhausted to carry on, she stretched out on a lab shelf and shut her eyes; in the mornings, she did take time to shower and put on a fresh uniform. How she kept going, she did not know. It was almost as though she were given extra strength to see her through.

At the height of the crisis, ten members of an Italian family of twelve were admitted with the flu. Only Tony, a boy of fifteen, and his little sister, about two, remained behind in the shabby tenement. Every day Tony came to visit his family. In a short time all ten of them were dead.

Tony took his grief like a man. He came to Connie, his eyes red from crying but his voice steady, and said, "Dr. Guion, what do you think I ought to do now? Do you think I should use up all my money burying my family or do you think I ought to let their bodies go to the potter's field?"

"Well, if you bury one, Tony, you'll have to bury all of them, won't you?"

"That's right — and there's not much money. I've got to look after my little sister, too. I'm not going to let them put her in an orphanage."

"How can you support her, Tony?"

"My father ran a little cigar store on First Avenue. Now I'm going to run it. The neighbors have already said they'll look after Nellita while I'm working."

"Tony, I think it would be better if you let the city bury your family and you keep that money to bring up your little sister. I'll do everything I can to help you."

"Thank you, Doc. You're a real friend."

For the next ten years, Connie kept in close touch with Tony and Nellita. They brought all their problems to her and she helped the little Italians get a good start in life.

The influenza epidemic remained intense for about a month and then, mercifully, the disease began to peter out. It was one of the worst epidemics in the history of New York; over 51,000 people died before it was over. At one time, there were not enough people working in the cemeteries to bury the dead.

By the time the emergency ended, Dr. Connie Guion had many a gray hair, although she was only thirty-six.

✳ 22 ✳

Years of Promise

AT FIVE O'CLOCK on the morning of November 11, 1918, the armistice was signed between the Allies and the Germans, and World War I came to an end. In four years of fighting, ten million people had been killed and twice that many wounded. All over the world, bells rang and people went to church to thank God that the bloodshed was over.

Like everyone else in the city of New York, Dr. Connie Guion rejoiced that the war had ended. She knelt in a prayer of thanksgiving, but she did not join with the celebrants who were tooting whistles and dancing in the street. She remained at Bellevue, working hard to save the life of a little boy named Willie who had spinal meningitis.

Willie had come into the hospital with a throbbing headache, high fever, and contracted neck muscles that pulled his head way back. He was desperately ill. For two nights, Willie's life hung in the balance. Connie scarcely left the little boy's bedside. She was determined to pull him through. Little by little, he grew better and eventually he made a splendid recovery. It was a great day when Willie was able to go home.

About a month after he left, Willie's mother brought him back to see Connie. He clutched a small package in his hand. "Doc," he said, "I went to the store to get you a present. Mom wanted to give you a brooch, but I said, 'I can't see Doc wearing no brooch. I'd rather give her a fork!' "

Connie opened the present and found a small salad fork with an ivory handle. "Willie, from now on this will be my prize possession." Dr. Guion is still using Willie's fork.

Before Connie finished her two years of service as an intern at Bellevue, she applied for an appointment as an assistant resident at Johns Hopkins Hospital. She won the appointment, but after the war ended she began to have doubts about accepting it. She decided to go to Baltimore to discuss her problem with Dr. John Howland, who had given her the position.

"Dr. Howland," she said, "I wonder if it would be better if I didn't take the residency here."

Dr. Howland's expression was a mixture of surprise and relief. "What brings you to that conclusion, Dr. Guion?"

"I understand a lot of pressure is building up to make places in hospitals for the doctors coming out of the army."

"Yes, that's true."

"Well, if a hospital has to make room for the army men, wouldn't the women doctors be the first to go?"

Dr. Howland did not answer her question. He studied her record a minute, then looked up. "You have had an admirable amount of hospital training already, Dr. Guion."

"Yes, sir, I have been lucky."

"If you didn't come to Johns Hopkins, what would you do?"

"I think I could get a job at the Waverley Sanitarium in Columbia, South Carolina. It's a small mental hospital owned by Dr. James Babcock."

"Is he the Dr. Babcock who did pioneer work on pellagra?"

"Yes. He's married to my sister Kate."

"Indeed? I met him some years ago when he lectured at

Hopkins on psychiatry. He was a friend of Sir William Osler's."

"He thinks a lot of Dr. Osler. He quoted him in a letter he wrote me the other day. He reminded me that Osler said: 'The desire to take medicine is perhaps the greatest feature which distinguishes man from animals.' "

Dr. Howland laughed with Connie.

"Dr. Guion, your brother-in-law is a remarkable man. I think you should go down to South Carolina and work with him."

Dr. Babcock was delighted to have Connie join the staff of the private mental hospital he had built outside of Columbia. Connie was happy to be back with Kate and Dr. Babcock and their daughters Margaret, Ferebe, and Alice, and to return to the South where the people and the weather were warm and friendly. She also welcomed the opportunity to learn more psychiatry; she knew it would be helpful in any branch of medicine she pursued.

At first Connie attacked her work at the sanitarium with zest, but she had not been there many months when the strain of working with seriously disturbed patients day in and day out began to tell on her. During the day patients would say to her, "Doctor, I've got rabbits in my stomach" or "Doctor, something is eating my skin off," and by nightfall Connie began to feel that she had the same problems. Much of her work was custodial care; there were few cases of physical disability where she could use the skills she had developed at Bellevue. She longed to return to the practice of medicine. She missed the satisfaction and pleasure of helping people get well.

One day a letter came in the mail from her teacher, Dr. Frank Meara. Its contents took her breath away. "I find," wrote Dr. Meara, "I am in need of someone who is familiar with John Masefield to come into my office as my assistant. Would you consider joining me in my practice, Dr. Guion?"

Connie read the letter over and over. She could not believe it. In 1919 few, if any, doctors would invite a woman to be their assistant. For a well-known physician with a large practice to do such a thing was remarkable. Dr. Meara had a distinguished reputation as a specialist in internal medicine and any young doctor in New York would have jumped at a chance to go into his office. Connie was overjoyed. She lost no time bidding the Babcocks good-by and getting herself back to New York.

When Dr. Meara welcomed Dr. Guion he said, "I suppose you realize that I wanted you to come here specifically because you are a woman."

"No, I must say that hadn't occurred to me."

"There are, however, three conditions which you, as a woman, must agree to if you are to become my assistant."

"I'm so happy to be here, I'll agree to 'most anything."

"You must promise me that you will not smoke, you will not bob your hair, and you will never let your petticoat show."

Connie held up her right hand and said, "I do solemnly swear to live and abide by said conditions. Now may I ask you a question, Dr. Meara?"

"Of course."

"Why did you specifically want a woman doctor?"

"I believe — and the psychiatrists I know agree with me on this — the sicker people are, the more they regress emotionally back into their childhood. In their need for help and sympathy they long, perhaps unconsciously, for their parents, especially Mother. A woman physician has the mother-image on her side."

"That makes a lot of sense to me, Dr. Meara. I have a pretty strong mother-image in my own mind and it stands me in good stead."

Dr. Meara had a well-organized office in the east seventies with one assistant, a secretary, and a laboratory technician. Connie replaced Dr. Malcolm Goodridge as the assistant. Her job was really a postgraduate course in medicine, the kind of apprenticeship that has since disappeared. She worked in the office from 9 A.M. to 1 P.M., taking case histories, supervising laboratory work, and doing preliminary physical examinations.

Every afternoon Connie made rounds with Dr. Meara at Bellevue, and on weekends, when he went home to New Haven, she did the rounds for him. Whenever he went away, Connie delivered his lectures to the Cornell students. He had written out each one meticulously in beautiful English, but she knew he could give the same lectures without glancing at a note.

On her return to New York, Connie found a room in the Brick Church Neighborhood House. Soon after she moved in she had her first caller. She went down to the parlor to see who it was, and there stood her old friend John Joseph McLaughlin.

"Sure and it's Dr. Guion herself. They told me at Bellevue where you was workin' and I traced you to the spot."

"Why, John, I'm happy to see you. Sit right down."

John sat down on the edge of a chair with his seaman's wool cap in his hand. "Oh, Dr. Guion, it's bad news I'm bearin' this day."

"What is it, John?"

"I lost me job on the ship." Then he broke out in a big Irish grin. "But I got another, doin' furnace work in the post office. Will you be after signin' me papers?"

"I'd be glad to, John." Connie took the form and looked at it. Beside the question of age he had left a blank.

"Well, John, how old are you?"

"I don't know how old I am. But I'm not puttin' anything down there and make you sign a lie."

After Connie had signed he said, "I'm about seventy, but I'm not allowed to be over forty-five."

"Where are you going to live now, John?"

"At the 5-10-25-Cent Hotel on Third Avenue."

"The what?"

"The 5-10-25-Cent Hotel. For five cents you get a bed. For ten cents you get a bed and a towel. For fifteen cents you get a bed, a towel and a locker. And for twenty-five cents you get a bed inside a cage with a lock on the door."

"I declare, I never heard of such a bargain!"

After that whenever John J. McLaughlin got sick, he called Dr. Guion and she came and took care of him. He was very clean, but because people would steal his clothes he wore all of them at once. He would put the clean shirt next to his skin and the dirty one over it. When he went to work he would take the dirty shirt off and wash it and hang it on the boiler to dry. He always wore two pairs of socks and wore his extra collars wrapped around his ankles.

John J. McLaughlin never took for granted the help of his "best friend." One cold day he showed up with his hat on the side of his head and a strong smell of whisky on his breath. "Saints in heaven, Dr. Guion, I can't stand the stench of land one more day. I signed aboard a fishing smack and we be leavin' for the Grand Banks in the mornin'. I want to say good-by and tell you what a rare fine lass ye be." He handed her a forty-pound fish wrapped in newspaper and left. She never saw him or heard from him again, so she felt sure he must have died at sea.

Connie found that most of Dr. Meara's practice was consultation work. He was well known as a diagnostician and many doctors called him in on their cases. One day Dr. Arthur Bingham, a prominent internist, called up and said, "Meara, I want you to send your assistant over here to give Mrs. Owen pneumonia serum. She's desperately ill."

"My assistant's pretty busy, but I'll send her as soon as she's free."

"What did you say?"

"I'll have her down there as soon as possible."

"A woman?"

"Yes, a woman."

"I don't want any petticoats mixed up in my practice. Haven't you got a man?"

"I can get you a man, but he won't be as good as this woman. You can have him if you want him."

"Send him over."

Dr. Meara called a man, who went to Mrs. Owen's to give her the injection. She was enormously fat, with arms as big as balloons. The man stuck her arm again and again, but he could not get the needle into her vein. Finally he came back to the office. "I'm sorry, Dr. Meara, I can't get in that fat woman's vein. It's impossible."

Early the next morning the phone rang. It was Dr. Bingham. "Send that damn woman over here! My patient has got to have an injection, and *no one* can get in that vein."

"I don't think she'll go," said Dr. Meara, "because I don't think she liked the way you talked about her. Besides, I'm not going to ask her to go."

"Blast it, Meara, you burn me up. Good-by."

After a couple of hours, Dr. Bingham called again. "Where is that woman?"

"She's busy."

"Let me speak to her."

"Why?"

"Please send her down here, Frank, I need her."

"I'll ask her. She may not come, though."

Connie took a taxi to the Owen house on Park Avenue. When she entered the luxurious bedroom it was dimly lit, but she could see the patient lying in an enormous double bed draped with a dark red canopy. Dr. Bingham was standing in the middle of the room, slouched over with his hands shoved in his pockets. Connie said, "I'm Dr. Guion from Dr. Meara's office." They shook hands and Dr. Bingham looked at her intently.

"You're mighty little. Do you think you can get a needle into her vein?"

"I don't know, but I'll try."

Connie climbed up the steps to the big bed; it was on a kind of stage. Mrs. Owen was lying on three pillows and she was as blue as indigo. Her blubbery arm looked as though somebody had used it for a pin cushion. It had been stuck and stuck. She looked at Connie and asked, "Are you a nurse?"

"No, I am a doctor."

"Do you think you can get into my arm?"

"I believe I can," said Connie, trying to bolster her own confidence as well as the patient's. She put a tourniquet around the arm and felt it. It felt like a well-inflated football. There were no veins anywhere. Connie looked at the two nurses and Dr. Bingham, who were standing by. She prayed, *God better be on the end of this needle.* She took a deep breath and stuck the needle into the flesh. She hit the vein with the first try, and slowly injected the pneumonia serum that the woman so badly needed.

"I'll be damned," said Arthur Bingham.

"Thank the Lord!" gasped Mrs. Owen.

"Will you come back every eight hours and do this, Dr. Guion?" asked Dr. Bingham, with admiration in his voice.

Connie beamed at him. "I'd be glad to, Dr. Bingham."

Before long Connie was doing scut work for Dr. Bingham and they became fast friends. That winter was severe and he had a great many pneumonia patients. Connie spent countless hours going into the homes of pneumonia victims, getting sputum samples, carting them back to the laboratory for typing and then rushing the serum to the patients for injection.

One night Dr. Bingham called Dr. Guion for help on a particularly poignant case. The daughter of his childhood sweetheart had recently married and come down from Vermont to live in New York. She was gravely ill with pneumonia. Dr. Bingham and Dr. Guion worked over her with great care. They gave her blood transfusions and pneumonia serum, but to no avail. She rapidly grew worse and at three o'clock in the morning she died. Her death was one of many that Connie witnessed. Each time she felt more certain that the body was one thing and the spirit was something quite different.

Crushed, Dr. Bingham and Dr. Guion did what they could, and then left. A violent snowstorm was raging outside. The wind whipped the snow into whirlpools of white. They climbed into Dr. Bingham's open car and started to drive down 67th Street. By the time they reached Third Avenue, they could not see a foot ahead. They stopped, and it was fortunate they did. Directly in front of the car were a man and woman they had not seen.

Dr. Bingham put his head down on the wheel, exhausted. "I'm afraid I can't get you home, Dr. Guion. I'd better drop you off at the next station of the elevated."

Connie agreed and he slowly drove her there. The drifts were eight feet high and it took her a long time to climb up the unprotected elevated steps in the driving wind. She bent almost double as the snow stung her face and eyes. It was 5:30 A.M. when she reached the waiting room and dawn was beginning to break. The barren room was freezing and the potbellied stove was little help. Connie asked the ticket agent when the next train was due.

"I don't know when another train will come. Where do you want to go?"

"Twenty-third Street."

He shrugged his shoulders. "I advise you to sit here."

"Maybe I can get a taxi?"

"Not a chance. There's a fancy dress ball in town tonight and any taxis that are running will be there. I advise you to stay put."

Numbly, Connie sat down on the cold bench. She sat in that station until 7:30 when a train came. It was a night to remember.

Although Connie sometimes ran into the apprehension about "hen medics" which prevailed in 1919, occasionally a man who was an advanced thinker would say, "What's wrong with a woman doctor? Why should I be more embarrassed about having her take care of me than my wife is about having a man?" Actually, it was the women who first sought out Dr. Guion. There was an urgent need for topnotch women doctors. Cancer of the breast, for example, went undiagnosed because women would not allow men doctors to examine their breasts. In Dr. Guion they found an expert who could say in no uncertain terms, "This looks bad. You're going to see a surgeon and have a chest X-ray," and the patient would do it.

Many people still maintained God did not intend for

women to be doctors. One weekend when Dr. Meara was out of town, Connie got an emergency call from a patient of his who lived in the Union League Club. She had no way of knowing that this stylish club allowed "no reporters, no Democrats, no dogs, and no women" to enter its doors. She climbed into Dr. Meara's electric car, a handsome black Detroit, and drove to the club. She walked right in, past the astonished doorman, and sailed into the elevator. The elevator operator gasped, "What did you say, lady?"

"Mr. Harry, please."

"I'm sorry, ma'am. This is a man's club. No females above the first floor."

"But I'm a doctor and Mr. Harry is very ill."

"A *doctor?*"

"Yes, a doctor. And I want you to take me up to my patient."

"No women allowed. That's the rule. You better go see the manager."

Dr. Guion hurried into the manager's office. Again, the same argument went back and forth. Finally, the manager picked up the phone and called Mr. Harry's room. When the valet said Mr. Harry needed a doctor quickly, the manager bellowed, "Did you *have* to call the only woman doctor in New York?"

"You had better get me a chaperone and send me up there," said Dr. Guion, "before you have to call an undertaker for Mr. Harry."

Turning pale, the poor man yielded and permitted Connie to go upstairs to her patient. After that, every time she came two bellboys went up with her, one walking before her, the other behind.

After one especially long night by Mr. Harry's bedside,

Dr. Connie left at daybreak. A light drizzle was falling and the deserted streets were silent. She climbed into Dr. Meara's electric and drove down Fifth Avenue. She was accustomed to long days and sleepless nights, but this time fatigue overcame her. In an effort to stay awake, she made a game of trying to drive over as many manhole covers as possible. She had counted seventy when she heard a shrieking siren and a motorcycle cop waved her to the curb.

"What's wrong with you?" he barked. "What do you think you're doing?"

"I don't know what you mean, officer."

"Oh," said the cop in disgust, "a woman. You're drunk."

"I am not. I don't drink."

"What's that bottle of red wine doing on the seat beside you?"

"That's not wine, it's blood."

"*Blood?* And what were you doing weaving all over the street?"

"I was just trying to see how many manholes I could hit."

"You *are* drunk. Stick your head out and let me smell your breath."

Dr. Guion stuck her head out and blew, hard.

"O.K. Where have you been?"

"Spending the night with a man at the Union League Club."

"Holy saints in heaven! You're worse off than I thought. Where are you headed?"

"Home, to 23rd Street."

"Well, go on home, woman, but for God's sake, keep to the curb."

Soon after she went to work for Dr. Meara, Dr. Connie began to teach regularly at Cornell Medical College. She

Dr. Connie Guion in 1940

taught by taking her students on hospital rounds, and she enjoyed trying to fire them with her own enthusiasm for medicine.

She also taught physical diagnosis and general medicine in the Cornell clinic. The clinic was crowded and understaffed. At that time few doctors were willing to spend time in a clinic, which offered only routine work and no prestige whatsoever. The patients paid ten cents to be admitted and they were piled into the waiting room, seldom seeing a doctor for more than a few minutes and never the same doctor twice. Connie was indignant about the deplorable state of outpatient medicine and strove to interest her students in it. She spent part of every afternoon working in the clinic herself, a dedicated service she has continued all her life. Eventually Dr. Guion became the head of the Cornell clinic and later the first woman professor of clinical medicine in America.

Dr. Meara, who took a great interest in Connie's career, insisted that she establish a practice of her own. "You're too good a doctor to be just an assistant," he told her. "You should know by now patients always want the one who is the head, not the assistant. And you should serve on another hospital staff beside Bellevue, where you will be entirely on

Dr. Connie Guion stands before her namesake, the outpatient building of the New York Hospital–Cornell Medical Center. This structure, the first hospital building in the United States to be named after a living woman doctor, houses most of the Center's eighty-nine specialty clinics and the Vincent Astor Medical– Surgical Cardiovascular Clinic.

your own." Following his advice, Connie received an appointment at the New York Infirmary for Women and Children and also at Booth Memorial Hospital.

One day Dr. Meara told her, "Dr. Guion, I have been watching you closely, in your teaching, in the laboratory, in the clinic and in your work with patients. I know you find medicine rewarding, but have you decided what branch of it you want to pursue?"

"Yes, I want to be a family doctor, right here in New York City."

Leaning back in his chair, Dr. Meara closed his eyes and recited: " 'A well-trained, sensible family doctor is one of the most valuable assets of any community, worth today, as in Homer's time, many another man.' " He looked at Connie. "Can you guess whom I am quoting?"

"Sir William Osler?"

"Right! You never let me down. Yes, by all means, you should become a family doctor. You will be a fine one, unless —" his dark eyes twinkled — "you decide to get married and spend your time on your husband and children."

Connie did not smile back at him. She spoke earnestly. "Dr. Meara, many people think the only life for a woman is getting married and having babies. That's true for a lot of women, but not for all of us. In my life as a doctor, every day is filled to the brim with work that is deeply satisfying. It gives me joy."

Dr. Meara looked at her with admiration. "You're a great woman, Connie Guion, and someday you will be known as a great doctor."

Index